Beneath the China Boom

Beneath the China Boom

LABOR, CITIZENSHIP, AND THE MAKING
OF A RURAL LAND MARKET

Julia Chuang

UNIVERSITY OF CALIFORNIA PRESS

University of California Press
Oakland, California

© 2020 by Julia Chuang

Cataloging-in-Publication Data is on file at the Library of Congress.

ISBN 978-0-520-30544-1 (cloth : alk. paper)
ISBN 978-0-520-30545-8 (pbk. : alk. paper)
ISBN 978-0-520-97342-8 (ebook)

Manufactured in the United States of America

28 27 26 25 24 23 22 21 20 19
10 9 8 7 6 5 4 3 2 1

To Ming-Hsia Chuang

Contents

Illustrations

MAPS

Acknowledgments

The decade I spent researching and writing this book was made especially happy by friends, colleagues, and family. They offered company, guidance, and influence; these things made the fieldwork for this book possible. Conversations with them produced a shared lexicon of meaning that transformed the hardships of research and writing into exercises of great pleasure.

As a graduate student at the University of California, Berkeley, I benefited immensely from the support of Michael Burawoy. Through pages of written feedback on countless drafts, meticulous reading of field notes, and well-timed encouragement during moments of flagging faith, he imparted a sense of intellectual life as moral endeavor. John Lie was an especially supportive mentor. Thomas Gold and Cedric DeLeon provided useful advice during the last years of my training.

Many senior scholars invested time in guiding this project along the way. Ho-fung Hung, Martin Whyte, Wendy Wolford, and Cedric DeLeon offered generous comments on an early draft of the manuscript during a book conference funded by the Boston College Institute for the Liberal Arts. Patrick Heller, Sarah Babb, and Julie Schor read the manuscript and offered invaluable comments. Joel Andreas, Michael Kennedy, Peter

Gourevitch, Amy Hanser, Dorothy Solinger, Nitsan Chorev, Ching Kwan Lee, and Ezra Vogel offered support in various ways.

I owe a special thanks to my informants in China, particularly Little Deng and his elder sister Deng Liwen, who extended their trust and opened their homes to a burdensome outsider. They offered up their intimate lives as fodder for a piece of research whose impact will certainly never reach them. My friend, fellow sociologist Qi Xin, helped me maintain relationships with the informants of this study from 2007 to 2012.

A very early iteration of this project took the form of an undergraduate thesis at Harvard College. There, Cameron Macdonald provided careful thesis supervision, and friends such as Victoria Shannon, Eva Shi, and Courtney Bass provided good company and helped shape the person I became. As a graduate student, I learned alongside a cohort of friends who made my time especially enjoyable: Jimmy Tran, Jennifer Choo, Richard Jean So, Malgorzata Kurjanska, Gordon Shen, Christopher Chambers-Ju, Freeden Oeur, Michael Levien, Zach Levenson, Rongbin Han, Naomi Hsu, Jon Norman, Michelle Kuo, Albert Wu, John Yasuda, Jeffrey Weng, Jessica Cobb, Kimberly Kay Hoang, Eli Friedman, Sarah Macdonald, and Gretchen Purser. As a postdoc at Brown University, I found a community among Jonas Nahm, Elena Shih, Hilary Levey Friedman, and Janice Gallagher. Finally, in Boston, conversations with Gowri Vijayakumar, Philip Thai, Yajun Mo, Arunabh Ghosh, Ana Villareal, and Nguyen Le eased the transition into faculty life.

Several people in particular have been fellow travelers, brightening the journey along the way. Lively and ever-evolving conversations with Richard Jean So helped me through the lengthy period of lonely fieldwork. Michelle Kuo and Albert Wu showed me their expansive vision of the function that writing could fulfill in the world. Jonas Nahm provided lightness in the last stretch of the road, and Malgorzata Kurjanska offered a sense of perspective on work and life.

Research and writing were funded by the Wenner-Gren Foundation, the Social Science Research Council, the Bucerius Foundation at the ZEIT-Stiftung, and the Institute for International Studies and Center for Chinese Studies at the University of California at Berkeley. The Watson Institute for International Studies at Brown University provided an intellectual home during the interim years I spent between being a graduate student and a faculty member. Talented undergraduate students in my China's Rise seminar at Brown in fall 2015 helped me clarify my thinking as I wrote the first draft of the book manuscript.

Peter Rosenbaum copyedited the final version of the manuscript, and Jenny Gavacs provided early feedback. Abigail Walters at Boston College helped assemble the reference list.

Finally, over and above the realm of ideas there is familial love. My late mother Ming-Hsia Chuang, to whom this book is dedicated, showed me how openness and vulnerability could sustain relationships; with these she learned how to make a home in an unfamiliar place. My father I-Min Chuang taught by example the twin values of grit and sacrifice. Lively repartee via Skype with Olivia Chuang-Smith and Kelley Chuang eased the loneliness of the years I spent living alone in strange villages. Patricia Cristofaro and Martin Gardiner welcomed me into their home and plied me with delicious meals while I revised the manuscript. Finally, Dan Cristofaro-Gardiner, my partner in all things, brought a happiness and an understanding I hadn't yet known to the last years of the project, and the arrival of our daughter Emily Ming forced the book to fruition.

Index of Characters

The characters are listed in order of prominence in the narrative.

THE LABOR BROKERS

Boss Bo. Lives in Landing Village with his wife, Deng Liwen. Recruits labor in four villages, including Landing and Faming; dispatches village teams to work for subcontractors in numerous coastal cities.

Boss Zeng, cousin of Boss Bo. Lives in Qijiang District; recruits labor alongside Boss Bo.

Boss Zhou. Lives in Chongqing City. Employs Little Deng to recruit labor for him in Landing Village.

Big Gao. Lives and recruits labor solely in Faming Village. Is married to Yue-na's older sister.

Chen Lehai. Lives in Faming Village, where he recruits a small group of migrants to work in Beijing each year. Is married to Wang Ting.

VILLAGERS IN FAMING

Madam Gao, former factory worker, now farmer and housewife. Wife of powerful labor broker Big Gao. Leads an informal loan exchange among the housewives of Faming Village.

Auntie Luo, former factory worker, now housewife. Wife of Luo Guangleng.

Luo Guangleng, former miner, now construction worker. Husband of Auntie Luo.

Chen Zhong, former construction broker. Now works a salaried job as an electrician in Leshan City.

Huang Rong, factory worker. Once engaged to Deng Guang, she choses factory work over farming back in the village.

Little Fatty, construction worker. Married to Sister He. At one time employed by Big Gao, but was later fired for truancy.

Sister He, former factory worker, now housewife. Born in a village in coastal Guangdong Province, only recently relocated to Faming. A young mother and long-suffering wife of Little Fatty.

Shu Li, hotel maid. She and her husband live in a shantytown in Beijing; they want their son to be formally educated.

Luo Jun, migrant worker. Purchased an apartment in a midsized city near his wife's village in order to secure for his daughter a spot in an urban middle school.

Wang Ting, housewife. Married to Chen Lehai.

Wang Fei, daughter of Wang Ting and Chen Lehai. Engaged to be married to an urbanite in Leshan City.

Liu Guang, construction worker. At one time employed by Big Gao in Faming, but later employed by Boss Bo of Landing Village.

VILLAGERS IN LANDING

Wu Guangming, wealthy businesswoman, owner of an auto repair shop in Chongqing City. Resides in a migrant enclave of Chongqing; has relinquished her village land to the state.

Liu Zhaoyin, elderly farmer, housewife. She and her husband care for their granddaughter while their son works as a bank teller in Qijiang County.

Zhou Wenbing, elderly farmer. Is resistant to the wave of land expropriations.

Wu Minjian, former migrant worker turned farmer. Engaged in large-scale contracted rice production.

Wang Deihua, farmer and housewife. Her two daughters have attended college and become government officials in Qijiang County.

Deng Shaoli, employee at the Land Reform Office of the Qijiang County government.

Pen Gang, elected village leader in Landing. Tried to warn the other villagers of the upcoming forced land expropriation.

Secretary Zhang, Party-appointed cadre of New Land Township. Became suddenly wealthy just before the village was torn down.

Luo Xianyu, farmer. Hanged himself after losing his house and land to the government.

Wang Sanbu, farmer and occasional construction worker. Committed suicide after failing to secure work or housing.

Zhou Kai, divorced migrant, remarried to Liu Jingnian, a widow from a neighboring province.

1 China's Rise

In 2007 I was a graduate student with an interest in the Chinese economy. It was only a year before the global financial crisis, but already China's economy was showing signs of shifting away from its traditional export growth base. Profits were continuing to accrue within manufacturing, but the new growth area was construction and real estate, a sure sign of a robust domestic market and an emergent middle class.

That summer I traveled to Beijing, hoping to catch a glimpse of what this construction boom looked like on the ground. There I became acquainted with a gang of construction workers hailing from Sichuan Province, deep in the hinterland. Among them was a rural worker, a thirty-three-year-old man named Little Deng. Little Deng often had difficulty securing pay for his work. When he failed to bring in wages, he would fall back on the efforts of his family in his home village. Deng's wife, Yue-na, lived in a two-story house built with his accumulated wages in Faming Village, two thousand kilometers from Beijing, a thirty-three-hour ride on the slow train.

My examination of China's construction boom soon took me on a sojourn far beyond the influence of coastal cities. Many workers I met in Beijing were like Little Deng: they shuttled back and forth between inland villages and coastal cities. The tactic was what scholars call a "safety-first" practice; it allowed them to retreat back to rural farms during times of unemployment.[1] Migrant laborers around the world live such dual lives. In China, migrants such as Little Deng have become foundational to the country's developmental strategy of labor-intensive export production. They work elsewhere during economic booms and then return home to farm in villages during economic crises. For example, in 2010, just after the reverberations of the global financial crisis had emptied China's factory floors, Little Deng spent a forlorn year in a failed search for work. He left the village with 500 RMB (US$83) and a one-way train ticket to Guangzhou, where a village friend got him a job at an electronics factory. After his first month there production slowed, and Little Deng was fired. He then found work as a woodworker at a Beijing construction site, but within a month a rumor spread that subcontractors had disappeared, leaving workers without wages. At another construction site in southern China, Little Deng worked for several months, only to find that financing for the project had dried up and no laborers would be paid. Finally, Little Deng called his wife, who said with a stiff upper lip, "We have a rice crop and three pigs this year. Worse comes to worst, we can sell two, and butcher one, and that way our son can still eat meat next Lunar New Year holiday." Little Deng started the year with 500 RMB (US$83), visited four cities, and ended with a loss of 1,100 yuan, or US$182. His family weathered the year because Yue-na had opted to stay behind in Faming, raising their son and farming their few plots of village land, which sustained them despite the losses Little Deng incurred in his migration.

For two years (2010–2012) I lived in various villages in Sichuan Province, where I followed migrant workers like Little Deng as they searched for work, socialized with their families, and recorded the daily events of the local community. During this time I learned that rural villages situated deep in the Chinese hinterland perform a central but hidden function in the national economy. This is where the vast labor force retreats when production slows. It is also, however, a changing and uncertain place. The brighter the skylines of Beijing and Shanghai are, the more deteriorated the rural inland becomes, with its crumbling roads and closed schools; the higher the gross domestic product (GDP) growth rate of cities is, the more stagnant are the rural economy and job prospects therein. This book proposes that these phenomena are related—indeed, that the stagnation of the hinterland enables the dynamism of cities.

Yet rural China is also changing. Driven by growing fiscal deficits, rural governments have turned toward land sales for revenue, seizing land from households and diverting it toward urban expansion and contract farming. In addition to being profitable for local governments, such land seizures are also central to an official campaign of controlled urbanization, a central mandate under the regime of President Xi Jinping. Since the State Council's eleventh Five-Year Plan of 2006, urbanization has been touted as a solution to fears that China has become trapped in a low-road, labor-intensive industrialization trajectory. Two processes of urbanization—the territorial expansion of cities and the growth of registered city populations—aid in the pursuit of this remedy. Conversions of rural land, previously collectively owned, to state ownership and urban infrastructure and development allow local governments to lure capital investment, boost industrial production, and unlock potential growth in real estate values. Expansion of the urban population, in turn, boosts domestic consumption, particularly vital in the post-2008 global financial crisis moment, when slowdowns in the global export market left inventories unsold, factories unused, and excess capital with few profitable avenues for investment in manufacturing.

Urbanization creates new frontiers for economic expansion, to wit: former villages become sites for real estate construction, and formerly rural populations become new middle-class bases for domestic consumption. This urbanization occurs at a rapid and accelerating rate. Nationwide rural modernization plans—in particular the "Build a New Socialist Countryside" (BNSC) campaign inaugurated in 2006—cite benchmarks to absorb 250 million rural-born people into cities by the year 2026. From 1992 to 2015 the area of China classified as urban increased from 122,000 to 729,000 square kilometers, a nearly fivefold increase, with an average annual growth rate of 8.1 percent, a rate exceeding the global average by almost 2.5 times.[2]

Yet this breakneck urbanization was implemented in a peculiar fashion. Although urban expansion is regulated by the central state via limits on the amount of rural land eligible for conversion, it is carried out by local governments now largely dependent on land financing for fiscal solvency. Because of this, local governments disproportionately pursue real estate and infrastructural construction, using land parcels as collateral to underwrite large bank loans, which they can use to service old debts, fund public works, or reinvest in new urban development. Moreover, much of this construction is speculative for buyers and developers, meaning that governments access financing and collect fees from land transfers regardless of whether future sales and full-capacity utilization can be achieved. Expectations of future growth substitute for actual growth, as speculation mania fuels rising real estate values from boom to bubble. China's overheating real estate sector not only exceeds the overall limits of housing demand, it also results in the allocation of housing supplies to upper-tier market segments rather than to those in need. Governments that obtain land-collateralized mortgages tend to auction future land to highest-bidder developers to pay off past debts, and the latter tend to build luxury properties at price points prohibitive for the projected 250 million formerly rural residents who will populate China's new middle class.

This runaway urbanization creates yet another kind of disjuncture. As land financing and urban construction become primary revenue bases for local governments, rural localities engage in land seizures that displace large numbers of rural residents from the farming land that otherwise provides a fallback option for people like Little Deng. Thus, such urbanization creates substantial tension in rural communities such as Faming. These villages provide support to rural laborers such as Little Deng, who constitute the majority of China's labor force, and supplement low wages through agrarian activities including farming and selling pigs. But they also house a high-value asset, namely collective land, indispensable to rural governments low on revenues and now empowered to pursue urbanization via central state mandate. Thus, rural land, once a source of security and household support for China's vast labor force, has become a substantial source of profit for local governments.

POSTSOCIALIST LEGACY AND INSTITUTIONAL FOUNDATIONS OF CHINA'S RISE

In the 1990s the Chinese economy began more than a decade of continuous double-digit GDP growth. By 2002 the aggregate size of the economy exceeded eight times its size in 1978, at the start of the postsocialist reforms.[3] This growth period coincided with the rise of global free trade; by 2005 China was receiving 49 percent of the world's foreign direct investment.[4] That same year, the economy produced 4,726 trillion RMB (US$762.3 trillion) in exports to the world. Of this total, 1,012 trillion RMB (US$163.3 trillion) worth of exports was being absorbed by US markets.[5]

China has "exported its way into prosperity," sustaining a low-cost production model for a longer continuous period than most other developing countries.[6] When sending production offshore first began, for example, Mexico was the first to become a hotspot for export processing, and yet Mexico's maquiladora manufacturing industries, which grew as a result of the North American Free Trade Agreement of 1994, were quickly outcompeted in the race for foreign investment by China's special economic zones (SEZs), a dynamic that persisted throughout the 1990s. Moreover, China's status as the factory floor of the world marketplace has continued uninterrupted in the twenty-first century, despite the cooldown in export markets after the 2008 global financial crisis and the emergence of Southeast Asia as a new low-cost production zone. Even in 2013, for example, average Chinese wage levels were still a mere one-eleventh of US wage levels and one-third of Brazil's.[7]

How has China sustained its low-cost production model for so long? The primary condition for this sustained wage suppression is neither the absolute size of China's labor supply nor the ability of its authoritarian government to suppress protest and control labor unions, although these factors do play a role. Instead, the central mechanism enabling long-term wage suppression in China is a postsocialist legacy, specifically an institution of collectivized land and a system wherein rights to welfare and other social benefits are locally administered. Both institutions were originally implemented in the 1950s as a means of assigning rural laborers to agricultural communes. These institutions struck a deal with rural-born citizens: their social rights and entitlements, such as access to schools, health care, pensions, welfare, and social insurance, would be inferior to those enjoyed by the urban born. Moreover, these entitlements would be geographically restricted and only accessible in the place where one's birth or marriage residence was registered in a national household registration system, called the *hukou*. In return, however, the rural born would receive a universal right to lifetime use of a small plot of land, approximately a quarter acre per person, in their village of birth, a source of security in the face of unemployment and other market precarity.[8]

These restrictions are fundamental to China's low-cost production advantage because they have created a workforce whose families are shackled to their village of origin for access to education and by reliance on land. Universal land-use rights in the countryside allow individual laborers to work for employers in cities while leaving their families behind in villages to farm land to defray the cost of food and supplement low wages. Since workers can retreat to farming during periods of unemployment, they can withstand irregular labor contracts and low wages. This has made China's labor force appear self-replenishing, peopled by migrants from impoverished inland regions who cycle in and out of work while an ongoing subsistence farming economy subsidizes wages and absorbs unemployment.

However, there is a price to be paid for this low road of development. As rural China has been transformed into a holding pen for low-cost labor, rural regions have become sites where few industries can flourish and the majority of the workforce is employed elsewhere. Thanks to a postsocialist legacy that has restricted the mobility of rural populations, allowing them to work but not to settle in cities, rural governments are still responsible for providing public services and public goods for a rural workforce. Indeed, as urban economies have surged ahead, with key industries such as manufacturing and construction employing predominantly rural laborers, rural economies have been left behind. Throughout the 1990s central state lending policies favored urban enterprises over rural industries, and a concurrent wave of deepening market reforms quickly forced many collective enterprises in the countryside to privatize, only to be outcompeted and forced into bankruptcy.[9] These policies and reforms led to a rise in rural government deficits, which outstripped those of urban governments as fiscal decentralization reforms offloaded additional fiscal responsibilities onto local governments, responsibilities that rural governments struggled to fulfill as their industrial tax base dwindled.

These fiscal troubles in rural governments were the underside of urban growth, directly related to the export-driven economic boom and its reliance on rural labor. By the early 2000s the central state had taken measures to relieve rural fiscal burdens. In 2004 the State Council released a "Number One Document" stating that China had entered a new era in which "industry should nurture agriculture, and the cities should support the countryside." It was the first time in China's state rhetoric that industry was assigned a role supporting agriculture. In 2006 the phrase "rural-urban integration" was prominently featured in the eleventh Five-Year Plan, which proposed to BNSC, now a top domestic priority. The BNSC campaign had broad goals: to develop production, enrich livelihood, civilize rural habits, tidy up the villages, and democratize management. Significant resources were channeled to the rural sector as household subsidies and earmarked transfers for public goods.

As a fix to the problem of fiscal crisis, however, rural modernization had a hidden twist. It generated revenues for rural governments not because it brought taxable industries back to the countryside, but rather because it allowed governments to expropriate and auction off use rights to rural land. This was an attractive option for county-level governments in areas with large swaths of undeveloped land. For these governments, rural land was an untapped asset that was collectively owned and unable to be bought or sold. Unlike land within the jurisdiction of a municipality or county seat, which is legally owned by the central state and easily monetized through the sale of finite-term land-use rights to developers, rural land is technically owned by townships and village collectives and cannot be contracted out to private developers.[10] Aside from land set aside for environmental protection or infrastructural development, all of China's rural land is carved into small plots and assigned to rural-born residents for housing and small farming. The BNSC, however, allows county-level governments to tap into their land resources by rezoning their jurisdictions, converting collective rural land to state ownership. Once land is state owned, use rights can be sold to private developers for agribusiness development, real estate construction, and township expansion—all uses that are categorized as part of "rural modernization." Moreover, while the BNSC was introduced as a top-down campaign, it is implemented with varying levels of oversight by revenue-seeking local governments, whose interests often align more with those of land developers than with those of local residents.

What does this turn in the direction of Chinese development reveal? The pursuit of rural modernization undermines the institution of collective land that initially made low-cost production possible. In the new terrain of Chinese development, many rural laborers are now bereft of collective land, a socialist legacy that protected them when globalization pushed wages downward. Previously, rural residents were harnessed to a rural economy that provided inferior public goods but compensated them with the guarantee of universal land-use rights. Now, rural people are landless yet harnessed to modernizing townships where public goods are still underfunded. Although the landless are offered the option to convert to urban *hukou* status, they are still required to reside only in townships near their former land, where welfare and social benefits are usually inferior to those in first-tier municipalities. Meanwhile, these landless workers must face the same precarious employment conditions—low wages; irregular employment; and in some industries, wage payment that comes only at the end of each year—that landholding laborers continue to endure. Land dispossession makes land into a commodity, but only at the cost of eroding the conditions that support and maintain China's low-waged labor force.

FROM LABOR-INTENSIVE PRODUCTION TO LAND-CENTERED URBANIZATION: THREE PERSPECTIVES

The central thesis of this book is that the way labor markets have formed in China has created a fiscal crisis that the state must resolve through a shift toward land development and rural modernization. This shift began in the early 2000s and then accelerated following the 2008 global financial crisis, when the central state issued a fiscal stimulus package of 4 trillion RMB (US$586 billion), most of which was used to fund infrastructural construction (a high-speed railway, highways, and expressways). Increased construction generated spillover demand for materials and other inputs. By 2010 China was consuming one-third of the world's steel supply and one-half of the world's concrete supply, and between 2011 and 2013 China used more concrete than the United States used over the entire twentieth century.[11] Somewhere in this urbanization boom, land replaced labor as the highest-value, lowest-cost commodity in the marketplace.

The existing literature offers at least three perspectives on this transformation, each emphasizing a distinct aspect of Chinese political economy. Each perspective captures a mechanism that is necessary but not quite sufficient for understanding the turn to urbanization.

Overzealous Local Experimentation

One explanation for these twists and turns in Chinese reform emerges from the disaggregated character of the authoritarian state, which is centrally coordinated yet assigns a high degree of autonomy to local governments. Local governments have tended to implement their own uncoordinated, runaway plans for capital accumulation. In China's multilevel political system, national governmental bodies, such as ministries and bureaus, have priority over lower-level provincial bodies, which then wield authority over their jurisdictional cities, counties, townships, and villages. Among subprovincial governmental bodies, those belonging to urban regions, namely cities and districts, are assigned higher administrative priority than those assigned to rural regions, namely counties, townships, and villages. Moreover, this hierarchy is nested, meaning that cities contain within their jurisdiction of authority the rural counties, townships, and villages that surround their municipalities and can pass legislation and shape policies that affect the jurisdictions on their periphery.

In this regionally hierarchical administration, local governments are tasked with implementing central state policy yet are given extraordinary leeway to experiment. As Sebastian Heilmann has argued, since Maoist socialism, the central state has presented many policies as "campaigns" and dictated the broad objectives that should guide local-level implementation.[12] Yet these campaigns are often initiated without appropriate legislation and regulation, and localities are empowered to develop policy instruments and set regulations independently. This experimentation works to the advantage of the central state, which can disavow responsibility for policy failures by blaming local governments or conversely encourage and shape further experimentation by elevating successful local experiments as "model sites" for other localities to emulate.[13]

Have overzealous experiments in local capital accumulation created the rural fiscal deficits that prompted runaway urbanization? After all, the policies that supported wage suppression were largely the result of bottom-up experimentation later legitimized by central fiat. The creation of SEZs, spaces of legal exception where capital investment could be lured with enticements such as tax waivers and gratis land deals, gained traction only after some initial success. Land decollectivization, the partitioning of collective land for household use, was widely practiced in northern China before the central state made it national policy in 1981.[14] The risk of this experimentation, however, is that experiments can lead to crises of overproduction before the central state can redirect affairs. For example, in the 1980s collectively owned "town and village enterprises" (TVEs) became major growth engines, largely due to experimentation by local governments, which used them as revenue spigots by expanding the parts of enterprise production where taxes were not required to be remitted to the central state.[15] But in 1994, when central policy makers grew wary of inflationary pressures driven by runaway TVE overproduction, they terminated prorural banking policies, bringing a quick end to the rural collective sector.[16]

However, the current turn from labor-intensive to land-centered development is more than a matter of overproduction; it is a qualitative shift in the way that local governments organize industrial policy. The central state identified an overreliance on export production in the wake of the 2008 global financial crisis, which led policy makers to devote fiscal stimulus funds to investment in domestic construction and infrastructure. Still, the shift toward land-centered development is regionally uneven, with wide variation in regional rates of land development. For example, by 2012 over 50 percent of the nation's annual rural-to-urban land conversions occurred in inland provinces.[17] Moreover, enterprise reliance on labor-intensive production has continued unabated, with manufacturing and construction industries alike continuing to employ rural labor at the same low wages as before. This should indicate regionally specific causes for the turn toward land-centered development alongside labor-intensive development, rather than an across-the-board, centrally organized shift toward land development. While the experimental character of Chinese policy making sheds some light on the urbanization boom, it does not capture its regionally specific causes.

Dispossession as Mode of Development

Another theory that aids in understanding the urbanization boom comes from Marxist geography. Unlike the literature on experimental governance, the Marxist geographical literature focuses predominantly on the economic motives for state intervention. One central tenet in this literature is that states must periodically intervene in markets when rates of profitability decline. A falling rate of profit over time is inevitable, caused by aging equipment and market saturation; during such crises of profitability, idle capital and labor tend to "overaccumulate," meaning that unemployment rises and consumption falls, resulting in a glut of commodities and idle productive capacity. When profits in one location decline, capital owners and investors move, abandoning costly infrastructural structures originally built to lower transaction costs. During such crises, as David Harvey argues, capital investors and enterprises must continually find and create new sites of investment to offset inevitable declines in profitability.[18]

What does this search for new sources of profitability look like? Rosa Luxemburg suggests that the geographical expansion of capitalist development is one form, whether in the form of colonialism, imperialism, or simply global off-shoring and the expansion of consumer markets.[19] Harvey suggests, however, that sites of profitability are sometimes not simply found but are actively made, to wit through state coercion and policies that force down the cost of key factors of production, such as labor, land, or capital.[20] By labeling such processes "capital accumulation by dispossession," he emphasizes the state's role in creating cheap assets for capital to absorb. As Harvey argues, the complicity of state politics with the interests of capital investors is the basis for neoliberal development.

A recent flurry of scholarship has emerged around dispossession as a mode of capital accumulation. Saskia Sassen argues that under finance capitalism, as opposed to manufacturing capitalism, land and other natural resources have become more desirable as assets to state and corporate actors than the people who reside on the land.[21] Michael Levien has made a case for seeing dispossession as a fundamental lens through which phases of capitalist development can be analyzed, characterizing dispossession by the means by which states legitimize it and the resistance that accompanies it.[22] Both scholars agree, for differing reasons, that in the contemporary era, land dispossession is less likely to generate jobs for the displaced and more likely to concentrate resources among the economic elite.

These perspectives shed light on China's ongoing runaway urbanization by suggesting that the expropriation of rural land for urban construction is a political means of injecting land assets into markets at relatively "cheap" prices. For the state, such land is relatively cheaply procured, first through monetary compensation to dispossessed rural residents that is provided at below-market rates, and then via absorption of these residents into the urban welfare state. Local governments in China act as what Levien would call "land brokers," establishing development corporations that compulsorily acquire rural land for speculative real estate development, paying costs of expropriation in order to receive land rents from developers.

What does this perspective on dispossession offer that previous literature does not? The governance literature sees the urbanization boom as a problem of overzealous experimentation, but this writing adds a spatial logic to dispossession and development. For example, rather than viewing rising rates of land expropriation as a result of imperfect political coordination, Harvey would have us view it as a search for profitable frontiers that is inevitably speculative in character. Construction profitability, as he reminds us, relies upon "a certain expansionary pattern of global flows of commodities, capital, and people."[23] In locations where these flows materialize, properties sell, but in those where they do not, properties remain unsold. This unevenness of overproduction gives a fuller explanation of why properties in one urbanizing site sell, while those in another do not.

A shortcoming of this perspective, however, is its inability to account for the diverse causes and conditions of land expropriation. Scholars such as Harvey and Sassen link land expropriation to neoliberal development or financialization, while Levien suggests that dispossession is ever present, its character and consequences changing under different economic regimes. But none save Harvey offers satisfying explanations for why rates of dispossession might suddenly spike. Harvey suggests that dispossession is precipitated by overaccumulated capital: a falling rate of profit that increases unemployment and leaves capital holders without profitable investment outlets. However, in China it was neither overaccumulated capital nor a falling rate of profit that led to the current explosive land development boom. Indeed, before and during the land-centered development boom of the 2000s, the export-oriented manufacturing sectors were still growing. It is true that rising wages in coastal SEZs spurred an inland migration of capital investors, who relocated production facilities in inland urbanizing regions where land rents were lower.[24] But it was no dearth of manufacturing investment opportunities that led capital investors to choose real estate investments over manufacturing.

Instead, the pivot toward real estate investments was state driven. Fiscal reforms created disproportionate pressures on rural governments to raise funds, and rural governments sought out real estate investments, which yielded land transfer fees that could be retained by local governments as extrabudgetary or "nontax" revenues rather than being remitted to the central state. As I argue later, a prior developmental regime of urban-centric manufacturing growth, coinciding with global free trade and successful experimentation with SEZs and other instruments for attracting foreign investment, accelerated the fiscal deficits of rural governments. This prior regime therefore must be analyzed as a possible causal source of the current phenomenon of land dispossession as fiscal recovery.

China's Development without Dispossession

A third debate offers more insight into China's recent turn toward runaway urbanization. Unlike the previous two literatures, it describes not the urban transformation itself but the decades of labor-intensive, manufacturing-led industrial development that preceded it. This focus allows us to isolate the cause of the fiscal deficits that led to the current explosive rise in land expropriations.

If the previous literature described dispossession as a mode of development, another group of scholars have argued that China's development has been successful due to the absence, until now, of widespread dispossession. These scholars have argued that what fueled China's labor-intensive development was the fact that the rural workforce still had access to collective land. This belies the assumption, held by Marx as well as others, that modern capitalism requires a fully wage-dependent labor force, dispossessed of alternative means of subsistence and therefore capable of being pushed to great heights of productivity.[25]

After all, as Giovanni Arrighi argues, a fully wage-dependent laborer is also one who is liable to push back, creating cycles of labor protest that necessitate state concessions, labor protections, and minimum wages. In China, on the other hand, a partially wage-dependent labor force has allowed Chinese development to bypass the emergence of a labor movement. Because workers leave their families in low-cost villages, employers can pay wages calibrated to support the single worker rather than a family wage, and because workers' families farm for subsistence, workers withstand low wages without. Because workers have land-use rights in villages, they tend to return to villages when their employment contracts end, thus reducing their ability to pursue lengthy and protracted labor arbitration cases to collect unpaid back wages.[26] The lack of a national-level labor movement has meant that wages can be suppressed below subsistence level, labor contracts can be informal, and labor laws can remain unenforced.

What made China's political economy particularly conducive to economic growth was the spatial separation of two processes vital to reproduction of a labor force. Michael Burawoy has labeled these the maintenance and renewal of a labor force: one process ensures workers can subsist from day to day, and another ensures that vacancies in the labor force can be filled by new recruits.[27] The spatial separation of both processes means that individual workers live in workplace dormitories in cities, while rural communities bear the costs of cultivating future potential members of the workforce, such as funding for housing, pensions, welfare, education, and health care.

This makes labor cheap for both employers and the urban governments, which can collect industrial tax revenues without building infrastructure for a permanent workforce. But it creates burdens for local governments in migrant-sending sites. As Arrighi foresaw, the exclusion of the low-waged workforce from urban residence and full citizenship rights creates fiscal deficits in rural communities, which house little profitable industrial activity. It also restricts the potential size of the domestic consumer market and generates tensions emanating from increased rural-urban social inequality.[28] These deficits and tensions can erode the capacity of rural communities to ensure the social reproduction of the labor force.

Many scholars underestimated the instability of China's economic growth. Gillian Hart, for example, pronounced China a possible exception to the Marxian developmental trajectory, in which widespread dispossession acts as the precursor to the making of a working class.[29] Based on observations of China's economy in the 1980s, she argued, "A key force propelling [TVEs'] growth is that, unlike their urban counterparts, they do not have to provide housing, health, retirement, and other benefits to workers."[30] Yet these observations failed to take into account that the TVEs did not spatially segregate workforce renewal from maintenance. Enterprises employed local rural residents and could suppress wages, knowing that workers could rely on subsistence farming to defray food costs. Enterprise profits from wage suppression were eventually recirculated back to the rural community through taxation and local government social spending. Of course by the 1990s the rural collective sector faded, and what appeared to be an egalitarian utopia of collective ownership and few capital-labor conflicts mutated into the migrant labor system of today, in which the rural economy subsidizes the fiscal costs of labor reproduction for the urban. Like Hart, Arrighi argued that Chinese development avoided the labor-capital antagonism that Marx wrote so much about, but he also focused inordinately on the rural economy of the 1980s and did not foresee that once industrial production moved to urban centers, rural communities would struggle to support the needs of a workforce employed elsewhere.

Despite their overly sanguine views of Chinese capitalism, what these scholars recognize is the importance of processes of labor reproduction in shaping developmental outcomes. Indeed, while most scholars of China have focused on production and labor relations in urban markets, the rural economy is where labor recruitment occurs for industries such as construction, manufacturing, and mining. It is where future generations of the labor force are raised within households and educated within schools. Rural communities provide a site where laborers can remain embedded within the social institutions that protect them from the corrosive effects of commodification. Keeping in mind Karl Polanyi's argument that labor and land are "fictitious commodities," elements of nature that are fundamental to human sustenance whose full commodification would lead to their destruction, we should understand the institution of collective land in rural China as having provided a place where labor can repair and recover when left unused.[31]

A POLANYIAN VIEW OF CHINA'S DEVELOPMENT

This book extends insights from these three literatures. I argue that China's development is driven by two mechanisms of capital accumulation, one revolving around the commodification of labor and the other around the commodification of land. Since postsocialist reforms began in 1978, the commodification of rural labor has occurred with the support of a rural subsistence economy, which protected laborers from the hazards of wage suppression and exploitation. As Arrighi anticipated, this schema bypassed the labor-capital confrontation that Marx predicted; hence, extreme wage suppression and precarious employment arrangements have continued unabated. Yet over time this arrangement has created fiscal deficits among rural governments, which have funded the renewal of a workforce that is employed elsewhere. These rural governments turned then to land dispossession in order to boost revenues, thus stimulating a round of what Harvey termed "accumulation by dispossession," or economic recovery through the sale of formerly collective land to developers at low costs. What enabled this rapid shift toward land dispossession was the experimental character of the Chinese state, which freed local governments to interpret the rural modernization campaigns of the center as a mandate to expand state capacity by expropriating rural land.

How has a period of wage suppression suddenly led to a period of rapid land expropriation and construction? For decades, a socialist legacy of collective land ownership, combined with a *hukou* system that excluded rural people from urban social rights, had created prime conditions for wage suppression. This wage suppression fueled the growth of industry—first in the rural collective sector during the 1980s and then in the urban private and state sectors in the 1990s. However, local governments began to experience fiscal deficits when a tax-sharing reform in 1994 consolidated tax and fee collection bureaus at the provincial level, thus reducing municipal and county governments' access to tax revenues.[32] Subprovincial governments' share of total fiscal revenues declined through the 1990s and 2000s, from 78 percent in 1993 to 52.1 percent in 2012.[33] This decline was most sharp in rural regions, where rural industries shrank after a wave of privatization that bankrupted many rural-based collective enterprises.[34] Many of these firms eventually failed, partly due to their inability to access state bank credit. Then rural state budgets took another blow in the 2000s after a rising wave of tax revolts, which eventually compelled the abolition in 2006 of all rural household and agricultural taxes.[35]

As local state revenues shrank, social expenditures at the local state level increased. Beginning with a series of fiscal decentralization reforms in 1994, public goods in the countryside were primarily financed by rural governments at the county and township levels. This fiscal burden grew throughout the reform period, due both to large increases in nationwide public expenditures and to the increasing offloading of public financing on localities rather than on the central state. The share of public financing borne by local (subnational) governments, for example, increased from 45 percent in 1981 to 85.1 percent in 2012.[36] Furthermore, after a 2002 tax-for-fee reform, the cost burden of public goods continued to devolve even further down the government hierarchy to rural townships themselves, which became responsible for a fixed contribution to county governments to pay for local public goods programs.[37] By 2015 subnational governments in China accounted for 79 percent of government budgetary expenditures despite only receiving 47 percent of revenues (see figure 1).[38]

Many scholars of China have noted uneven levels of expenditures and revenues among subprovincial governments since the fiscal reforms in 1994, which recentralized taxes to the province level.[39] Since 1994, government bureaus within the Chinese state have been expected to raise their own funds through "nontax revenues," often assessed in the form of fees on enterprises and developers, which unlike taxes, were not required to be remitted upward to Beijing.

This facet of the fiscal state is what allowed subprovincial governments to recover from deficits. In the early 2000s the central state launched a mandate of rural-urban integration that local governments transformed

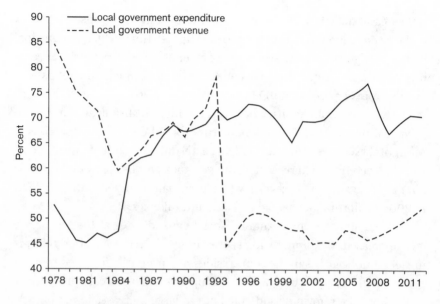

Figure 1. Local governments' share of total state revenues and expenditures, 1978–2011. *Source:* Lu and Sun (2013).

into a funnel for collecting land-related revenues. Several nationwide development programs, most prominently the BNSC in 2006, began to increase capital investment in rural modernization, while also authorizing the legal expropriation of rural land from rural people for modernization purposes. Once rural, collectively owned land was returned to state ownership, local governments could collect fees and taxes from developers, many of which were exempt from remission to the center.

Once in place, this new land-based revenue-generation mechanism became predominant, reinforced by a fiscal stimulus plan of the central government after the 2008 global financial crisis that accelerated land development by channeling capital into construction and infrastructure. Figure 2 presents a timeline of local governments' shift toward a land-centered developmental paradigm. This shift is transforming the geography and political economy of rural regions, simultaneously creating new revenue streams for local government officials and redirecting the pulse of development away from labor-intensive production toward more speculative, rent-intensive forms of real estate development and construction.

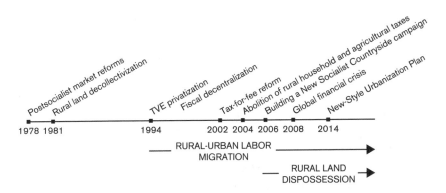

Figure 2. Timeline of labor migration and land dispossession. *Source:* Diagram by author.

Indeed, throughout the 2000s local government revenues in China became increasingly comprised of land value-added taxes on property appreciation, real estate taxes on land rentals, and individual fees for public utilities usage, among others. In 2005 these sources comprised 35 percent of local state revenues nationwide.[40] In inland Sichuan Province, where the events of this book unfold, land-related revenues supplied 66.7 percent of local government budgets in 2007.[41] Indeed, the Beijing Ministry of Land Management, which issues limits on the amount of rural land permitted for conversion to state ownership and urban use by province, began to loosen limits specifically in inland provinces in the mid-2000s. In 2014, amid fears that the BNSC had enabled an unfettered increase in the rate of rural land expropriation, the central state replaced it with a revised campaign, called the New-Style Urbanization Plan, which emphasized the building of townships and the extension of welfare benefits to landless residents.

What are the consequences of this new regime of land development? Since the early 2000s, both rural wage suppression and rural land development have continued simultaneously. Yet land development has undermined the conditions that make rural wage suppression possible. Rural farming communities provide what Polanyi considered protection from the destructive effects of commodification. Because labor markets developed alongside this subsistence farming economy, norms of hiring and employment have developed around the assumption that workers are maintaining households in home villages, to which they repair for holiday and periods of unemployment. Job contracts are generally of short term, with many lasting only eleven months and most beginning in March, after workers return to villages to celebrate the Lunar New Year. Wages and work hours are set with little regard to the central state-set minimum wages, and in some industries, such as construction and mining, wages are only paid post hoc in a lump sum at the end of each year, an arrangement that assumes that workers' families are subsisting by other means until then. Despite a 1995 labor law that mandated the signing of formal labor contracts, surveys reveal that only about 23–30 percent of migrant workers in private enterprises have contracts.[42] Finally, in manufacturing, construction, mining, and service industries, rural labor recruitment continues to be carried out informally, with many employers relying on employees to call on their village-based social networks to identify potential new hires.

Therefore, when rural land is expropriated by the state to raise revenues, the underlying basis of the rural labor market is also removed. Loss of farm land has become the primary reason for a growing wave of rural protests.[43] Many laborers, lacking pensions, had formerly planned to retreat to farming upon retirement. Land loss removes the wage supplement that allows workers to engage in "safety-first" migrations. It removes their ability to defray housing and food costs through farming. And while some workers lose access to collective land, others from neighboring regions retain their access, creating an irregular workforce wherein the landless must compete with the landed in a market where employers continue to engage in wage suppression and short-term job contracts. In addition to losing a farming subsidy, landless laborers also lose access to the place-based social networks where they have sought mutual aid and exchanged information about jobs.

Of course, rural modernization campaigns do not simply dispossess rural residents; they also then incorporate them into the urban welfare state. Dispossessed residents are permitted to apply for urban household registration status. They are asked to relocate to nearby townships, newly built on expropriated land, where they can purchase high-rise apartments and access schools. As urban *hukou* holders, they can apply for health insurance, pension funds, and welfare subsidies under more advantageous terms than they had received as rural citizens. Still, surveys have shown that most dispossessed rural residents prefer their land to urban *hukou*. They cite as objections cuts in government social spending, shortages in subsidized high-rise housing, and the fact that new townships are built to maximize state revenues rather than to accommodate the displaced. Therefore, this land-for-welfare trade is not always an upgrade: It exchanges a land subsidy for a welfare subsidy, with the services delivered susceptible to degradation.

THE UNDERSIDE OF THE ECONOMY

This book is a multisited ethnography that tracks social processes over time: migration and labor recruitment between villages and cities and indeed among villages themselves. This method yields a view of China uncaptured by most studies. Existing research on Chinese development has centered on either the rural economy or the urban economy, rather than linking the two analytically. For example, many scholars have studied urban employment in the service sector and domestic work, in factories and the manufacturing sector, and more recently in the booming construction sector.[44] A focus on workplaces yields a view of markets from the "standpoint of production," revealing industrial variation in the structure of labor market dynamics and the embedding of these markets in the wider urban political economy.[45] Studies of the rural economy have focused on the effects of state governance and urban modernization on rural markets: how migrant remittances have modernized the countryside and how peasant production is situated vis-à-vis the state.[46] Yet because these studies have focused on either the urban economy or the rural economy, they have not linked these disparate phenomena systematically to unveil the structure of capital flows between rural and urban economies, between rural and urban governments, and between rural households and the state.

My study, differently, uses the process of migration seen from a rural standpoint to capture two core phenomena: first, the relationship between rural and urban economies, and second, conditions for the formation of a labor market. For a labor market to develop, laborers must be transported across long distances to employers whose accountability cannot be guaranteed. Laborers must be protected from bodily harm and must be supplied with food and shelter in their places of employment. As Polanyi has suggested, the exchange of labor for a wage is an "act of barter" in which laborers must be "embedded in long-range relations implying trust and confidence."[47] Particularly in China, where rural migrants make up approximately one-third of the national labor force, the act of migration and the organization of labor recruitment are central preconditions to the fact of labor-intensive development.

This book focuses on labor relations in China's national construction industry, a sector that employs a workforce that is 90 percent rural. In 2016, 281.7 million rural migrants were employed in cities, comprising 35 percent of China's total workforce.[48] Twenty percent of this labor force was employed in construction and 31 percent in manufacturing. Growth in the construction sector accelerated throughout the 2000s. During the period during which the GDP growth rate was highest, from 2001 to 2007, the number of construction enterprises in China increased by 35.26 percent. The number of workers employed in construction grew by 48.47 percent.[49] In 2007 alone, Chinese construction's gross value output grew by 22.29 percent from the previous year.[50]

Construction, though less frequently studied than manufacturing, reveals undercurrents of the economy less visible in other industries. Construction utilizes both labor and land in a peculiar way that makes abundantly visible the dual dynamics of China's development: its tendency to produce rural underdevelopment and its resolution of underdevelopment through urban expansion. This is because construction relies equally on low-cost labor and rising land values for profitability. The two are related. Land values lend the largest margin of profits but fluctuate widely. As a result, construction enterprises must coordinate production to enable sudden speed-ups during price peaks. They also face potential losses if properties do not sell. The volatility of land values, therefore, is the reason that labor relations in construction are so precarious. Enterprises buffer themselves from short-term losses by subcontracting labor recruitment to intermediaries, subcontractors who hire brokers to recruit labor. These subcontractors absorb the immediate costs of labor recruitment. Then, enterprises pay them for labor delivery only at the *end* of each fiscal year, after property revenues materialize, and subcontractors then disburse wages to brokers and workers. Once-a-year wage payment is widespread across construction, particularly in first-tier cities, where land values fluctuate most widely. It amounts to a credit that labor brokers provide to enterprises by charging them for labor after it has already been utilized. This is particularly important because construction enterprises have severely limited access to formal credit sources, either via foreign investment or through state-backed financing.[51]

The employment of rural labor makes this delayed wage payment possible. Its legislation into legality coincided with the expansion of labor demand for urban and infrastructural construction. Since the 1950s, construction enterprises have sporadically utilized rural labor, particularly during periods of intensified production, whether on or off the books, but in 1983 the State Council issued a formal decree for construction enterprises—which were largely state owned at the time—to recruit labor outside of the then-current formal state recruitment system.[52] At first enterprises turned to rural labor bases (laowu jidi) and labor service markets (laowu shichang).[53] The following year the State Council sanctioned the "separation of management from field operations," a deregulation that separated construction enterprises from suppliers of labor.[54] Soon labor service contractors emerged, private companies that functioned solely to coordinate variable costs of materials and labor. In 1984 the central state released a document entitled "Tentative Provisions for Construction Industry and Capital Investment Administration System Reform."[55] Enterprises managed procurement, government codes and regulations, and construction contracts, but subcontractors carried out field operations.[56] Materials contractors, for example, delivered steel, concrete, and lumber to construction enterprises but would only collect payment at the end of each year. Labor contractors did the same and delivered labor first, then collected payments for wages and recruitment services later.[57]

In construction, however, delayed wage payment practices persist for an additional reason. Construction in China is debt fueled. Since 1984 the central government has legally blocked construction enterprises from accessing state-backed banking credit, one of several measures taken to prevent a speculative building boom. As a result, about half of all construction projects in China lack adequate funding at the time of budget approval.[58] When construction projects are initiated by urban property developers, these property developers can access financing through private equity and foreign investment to cover the costs of securing land-use contracts. However, they then outsource labor and materials costs to construction enterprises, which must carry out production without access to state-backed credit. These enterprises therefore carry out materials and labor procurement via subcontracting relations that allow them to delay labor costs until the end of each year, when they receive payments from property developers. Aside from a selective core of state-owned enterprises that operate with authorization from the national-level Ministry of Construction and receive funding from the Chinese Construction Bank for large-scale infrastructural projects, most construction enterprises bypass bottlenecks or shortages in bank funding by building first and paying for it later.

Only by extracting labor from the countryside could cities engage in debt-fueled construction. Before central state authorization of subcontracting in 1983, the construction workforce was majority urban; since then, it has become majority rural (see figure 3). Today the national construction workforce is 90 percent rural.[59] This workforce is composed of men like Little Deng: subcontracted laborers, recruited by middlemen, who collect wages just once a year and leave their families in villages to farm for survival in the meantime. Because of this, the expansion of the construction industry has knit together urban and rural economies in an ever-tighter relationship of interdependence. The more rural workers are employed in construction rather than manufacturing, the more they force members of their households to wait for the better part of each year for remittances to materialize—if they materialize at all. Frequently these remittances never do arrive. Workers are paid by village brokers, who are themselves paid by informal subcontractors, with whom they share limited bases of trust and reciprocity. Incidents of wage nonpayment and wage arrears are widespread in construction. In 2009, for example, the *Beijing Evening Paper* reported a deadly confrontation between a fifty-one-year-old construction broker and his subcontractor over unpaid wages totaling 980 RMB (US $66) owed to each of seven workers from the broker's home village.[60] Such confrontations reveal migrant workers' small margins of survival and their consequent need to leave behind household members to farm village land as a safety net.

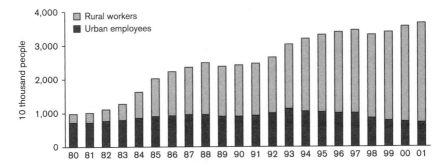

Figure 3. Rural and urban workers in China's construction industry, 1980–2001.
Source: Qian and Hui (2004).

The construction labor market links together urban growth and the rural economy in a tight relationship. We know from government statistics, journalistic descriptions, and firsthand experience the drivers and outcomes of construction growth in China's cities. Reports of the merging of Beijing with its neighboring city of Tianjin and the entire surrounding province of Hebei into a megacity, Jingjinji, larger than the area of Japan and housing 130 million residents, have spread through Western media.[61] In recent years researchers have begun to investigate the unique labor and employment relations within construction and to characterize the extreme and unique precarity of construction work in cities.[62] Yet the majority of urbanization in China, measured in terms of territorial land reclassified from rural collective ownership to state ownership and urban jurisdiction, occurs from the bottom up—that is, through the transformation of villages into townships and townships into counties.[63] This book turns away from the glimmering facades of newly built cities toward what we do not know, namely how the rural economy has fared in the meantime.

METHODOLOGY OF THE STUDY

If the construction industry is a prime site for observing the mechanism through which rural labor and land have come to supply China's comparative advantage, then we must understand how labor and land are transformed into commodities. *Beneath the China Boom* goes to the countryside for this view.

This book unfolds through a multisited ethnography, based on over two years of fieldwork undertaken during various periods between 2007 and 2011. To capture a snapshot of the long chain linking urban construction to its roots in rural labor recruitment and labor expropriation, I conducted ethnographic research in three sites. In 2007 I spent three months observing two labor brokers in Beijing. Named Boss Bo and Boss Zeng, they were rural entrepreneurs who recruited workers from two villages in Sichuan Province: Faming Village and Landing Village. I visited their worksite dormitory daily. On some days I accompanied the brokers as they made their rounds to other construction sites throughout the city, to which they had dispatched other villagers. I conducted interviews with other labor brokers and with labor and materials subcontractors at construction sites in Beijing. This initial research allowed me to see the intense production pressures the enterprises faced in the pursuit of speculative real estate profits.

But the core of this book comes from the research that followed. It was not enough to observe labor relations in Beijing's construction industry, especially after it became clear to me that subcontracting was a mechanism through which construction enterprises offloaded financial risk and labor costs onto rural communities. In 2010 I began following laborers to the two villages where the brokers recruited labor. First I lived in Faming Village, located in the rural county of Qianwei County, within the jurisdiction of Leshan City in southern Sichuan Province. There I rented a room in Little Deng's household for ten months. Then I traveled to Landing Village, located in the now urban district of Qijiang, within the jurisdiction of Chongqing City. (See map 1.) For ten months I rented a room in Boss Bo's household. In each village I became embedded in the everyday life of one to two "sections" of the village—such sections largely corresponding to the production brigades that had been formed under socialism.

I understand the brokerage of both labor and land to enterprises as a process of commodification, making each available for sale on a market. This definition is centered around Karl Polanyi's premise that labor and land, as fictitious commodities, provide a subsistence function as well as a market function.[64] In Chinese villages, one can observe land and labor's dual function as both source of subsistence and commodity for exchange.

Map 1. Faming and Landing Villages, China. Map by author.

To observe transformations in this dual function, I documented how the political economy of the countryside has been organized to facilitate the transformation of labor and land from sources of human subsistence into commodities for market exchange. This organization is important because it leads to systemic consequences for both forms of commodification.

The politics of the countryside shape the flows of rural-to-urban labor migration. After all, labor markets do not simply appear as a response to supply and demand, and migration does not automatically exist when wages are higher in one place than another. Indeed, migration is initiated by people: In construction, migration begins when village brokers cultivate relationships with subcontractors, who rely on them for the delivery of village labor every year.

What did I see in these two villages that illuminated the dual dynamics underlying the Chinese economy? The two villages—Faming and

Landing—regularly send laborers to work construction in coastal cities such as Beijing. This is because they are linked in a larger brokerage network for construction labor; since the 1980s, Bosses Bo and Zeng have established social networks linking villagers to informal construction subcontractors in cities. Yet the two sites developed in very different ways. In Faming Village, the *hukou* system continues to attach rural people to rural residence and to guarantee secure land rights. These conditions allow the emergence of a thriving household farming economy that supports labor migration. A subsistence-oriented farming economy becomes the basis for the informal brokerage of rural labor to urban employers. In Landing Village, five hundred kilometers away and just within the border of the Chongqing Municipality, a wave of land expropriations has uprooted the farming economy that supports labor migration. In Landing, rural people are "upgraded" from rural to urban *hukou* registration and dispossessed of land rights. They are then thrust into a race to secure housing and livelihood in new townships. As land expropriation dismantles the rural subsistence economy that supports China's low-cost labor force, brokers from Landing begin to divert their previously local labor recruitment toward Faming.

While I lived in the two villages, I observed these different trajectories of development. I observed in particular their antecedents. In Faming, I saw the workings of a more recent development of labor migration. Proximity to a waterway and a dense network of townships had led to a proliferation of coal mining in the region. These mines were active throughout the 1980s, producing a local employment option that prevented large-scale labor migration until privatization throughout the 1990s. Landing Village, on the other hand, sits just within the border of the Chongqing Municipality, a self-governing district directly under central government administration. Proximity to a large municipality was not a boon to the village, however. A jagged set of rocky cliffs separated the village from both the city and the Yangtze waterway, and this prevented the village from developing industry throughout the 1980s. Therefore, labor migration began far earlier. Bosses Bo and Zeng left the village out of necessity.

These factors are significant because they have led to different fiscal situations in the two villages. In both villages, ongoing labor migration has created and reinforced a rural economy that serves the needs of urban employers. Both villages have become sites of unprofitable subsistence farming, while still providing crucial social services—schools, health clinics, roads—to support children and the elderly. Yet only one of the villages—Landing— has developed deep deficits, which have resulted in the selling of village land for private development. This outcome is due to Landing Village's prolonged maintenance of out-migration. In some Landing households, three consecutive family generations had worked construction in cities. Their migrations continually sucked labor out of the local economy yet did not result in a substantial productive economy of entrepreneurship among returned migrants. In Faming Village, by contrast, substantial out-migration began later and had not yet resulted in an asymmetry of rural-urban relations as severe as in Landing. In addition, Landing Village also underwent large-scale land expropriations due to its proximity to Chongqing, a municipality that was at the epicenter of preliminary *hukou* reforms and urbanization during the late 2000s. In 2010 Chongqing government announced that peasants who give up their rural *hukou* can enjoy the same social benefits as urban residents.[65] In the years between 2010 and 2016, three million rural residents on the outskirts of Chongqing gave up their rural land plots, as the city more than doubled its urban land area.

My activities in the villages varied slightly. In both, I lived with villagers in their rural households. I paid rent to the household where I resided, and I lived with key informants whom I knew well. It was Little Deng who hosted my stay in Faming, and in Landing it was his brother-in-law, Boss Bo. In both sites, my residence was registered with the local Public Security Bureau. In both sites, I identified myself as an American student interested in studying village life. In both sites, labor brokers vouched for me with local village leaders. It was largely due to their informal sponsorship that I was able to conduct fieldwork in both villages without inviting the suspicion of higher-level government officials.

In Faming, I attended village banquets and accompanied village women as they went to market and tended to their crops. In the mornings I helped village women feed their pigs and chickens. I learned that country life had a monotony that could be pleasant or dull, depending on how long one had endured it. One form of respite from the monotony came in the form of village gossip, which was ever present and occasionally vicious. I learned much from listening to village gossip. Many rumors circulated about young women who had left to work in factories and returned pregnant, or who had married outside men and then neglected to support their farming parents. Other rumors spread about men who had become rich through exploiting other villagers, or who had engaged in extramarital affairs while away from home. These controversies reflected the uneasy relationship between agrarian life and industrialization: labor migration disrupted the agrarian life course, yet households desperately relied on it for survival.

As I drew near the end of my residence in the village, I wanted to get a sense of how this village economy compared to others nearby. I lived for several weeks in two neighboring villages, where rates of out-migration were slightly lower. I also spent time with young Faming migrants who eschewed construction jobs for lower paying but less onerous factory and service sector jobs. To get a sense of the policies that shaped villagers' lives, I interviewed village officials about *hukou*, land, and welfare policies as they were locally implemented. And finally, I interviewed county officials to get a sense of the county's fiscal health.

In Landing, I lived in the household of a family awaiting eviction. I documented how village land is earmarked for sale, how household land rights are terminated, and how families are relocated to townships. My analysis shows how the process of land expropriation undermines the wage supplement that farming once provided and how a new urbanizing class structure replaces the old agrarian structure. My residence was fortuitously timed, as I was able to record the events of land expropriation in real time. I also conducted additional fieldwork to ascertain the representativeness of these local policies. To compare land expropriation procedures in Landing to those carried out elsewhere, I accompanied a coastal capital investor to Yilong County, Sichuan, where he was planning on relocating a Shenzhen electronics processing plant. In Yilong, I sat in on three days of county-level government meetings, at which potential investors negotiated with local government officials over land-use contracts. There, I inquired into land expropriation policies and found procedures that varied from what I had found in Landing, in terms of land compensation payments, *hukou* incorporation rules, and county-level land-use plans.

Much of the data I present in the chapters to come resulted from conversations conducted during idle moments, while tending a fire or preparing a meal with villagers. These conversations were conducted in Mandarin Chinese on my part and Sichuan dialect on their part and later transcribed in fieldnotes, written every evening in English. Formal interviews with local officials were conducted in Mandarin Chinese, recorded, and transcribed in English. Where I use run-in and block quotations, I reproduce exact transcriptions. A more detailed account of the ethnographic methods employed here is provided in the appendix.

Finally, a note on the argumentative strategy of the book. This study of two villages aims to illuminate a developmental dynamic generalizable to China's entire economy. Yet my argument is not that these two villages represent typical or statistically modal states of rural economic development. Instead, I have selected these villages for their reliance on construction jobs for livelihood and their linkage in a common network of construction labor recruitment. In construction, due to the industry-wide practice of delayed wage payment, farming provides a necessary subsidy to households and thus enables labor delivery and economic growth across an entire sector. In other industries, such as manufacturing, wage arrears are commonplace, but delays in wage payment are neither as long nor as institutionally normalized as they are in construction. A study of villages in which manufacturing jobs were a primary source of livelihood thus would not fully capture the mechanisms through which the rural economy enables labor delivery for urban development. This book therefore pursues a strategy of theoretically driven case selection, wherein Faming and Landing Villages are deliberately examined for their embedding within a dynamic of rural-urban interdependence. There, social and economic life reveals underlying developmental processes less visible elsewhere yet nevertheless latent across the entire economy.

OVERVIEW OF THE BOOK

How can we explain China's transformation from a state of postsocialist malaise into the second largest economy in the world within a single generation? What follows in this book attempts an ethnographic immersion in the undercurrent of China's economic success, namely its plundering of the rural countryside for labor and land to fuel ever-expanding production.

Through a winding story that follows the journeys of Little Deng and his neighbors and kin in both Faming and Landing, it tells of both economic growth and its aftermath. The bulk of the book unravels this narrative in chronological fashion.

Chapter 2 introduces the two villages, Faming and Landing, where distinct mechanisms of capital accumulation are visible. In Faming Village, a riverine community far from any municipality, a legacy of rural industrialization has left behind strong norms of agrarian solidarity. Landing Village, however, is a mountainous village where a lack of rural industrialization forced laborers to seek work in cities from the start of the reform era. This chapter narrates the different trajectories of each village, throughout the reform era, to show why each site developed distinct mechanisms of development.

Chapter 3 examines everyday life in Faming Village, where migration creates and necessitates two parallel economies: one in which households allocate resources to send migrants to cities and withstand wage arrears and another in which members of an entrepreneurial class then broker migrants to employers. This entrepreneurial class draws capital upward out of villages and toward the vertical brokerage networks that subsidize urban industries' labor costs. Meanwhile, families of laborers get stuck alternating between subsistence farming and migration. Due to demographic dynamics that require migrants to support the elderly farming generation, they pass on few resources to their children.

Chapter 4 examines the dualism between rural and urban economies, as it relates to labor migration. It shows how despite *hukou* reforms that have opened new pathways to de jure urban citizenship for rural migrants, most labor migrants in Faming maintain households in the village or in nearby townships and county seats, where they enjoy wider access to social services. In addition, this chapter shows how the absence of a universal pension system until the late 2000s has made an aging generation reliant on migrants for support, thus prolonging migrants' obligations to kin left behind in villages.

Chapter 5 examines how local governments have expanded their extractive capacity by implementing rural modernization campaigns. In Landing, long-term labor migration has drained the village of population and capital, and the county has implemented a New Socialist Countryside campaign to open new capital flows. The central source of profits in this new development strategy lies in the expropriation of rural land from rural households and its sale to private developers. This is accompanied by an in situ urbanization of village residents. Though they are given the option of upgrading to urban *hukou* status and relocating to a New Land Township, a nearby designated evictee rehabilitation site, housing is undersupplied, and the new policies have created a competitive atmosphere full of uncertainty and misinformation.

Chapter 6 then elucidates the consequences of this forced urbanization. Just as the model of labor migration had indelibly shaped the social structure of rural communities, the new model of urban development in Landing created new lines of stratification. Entrepreneurial villagers such as Boss Bo participated in the modernization by investing in real estate or participating in the new service-based economy forming around new urban construction. Yet those who had adapted well to the previous ways of life—migrant labor and subsistence farming—were perversely left behind. Without land, few workers could withstand the end-of-year wage payment prevalent in construction. At the same time their employers, brokers such as Boss Bo, tended to divert their labor recruitment activities to places such as Faming, where subsistence farming continued to subsidize wages. As the previous economy of labor migration broke down, some tried to cling to land plots in other villages, thus continuing a wage subsidy through farming. Others continued to work construction but took on debts to survive as they awaited wages. Reliance on kin support became a last-resort lifeline. In Landing Village, three elderly farmers resorted to suicide when their debts mounted and they could not secure housing.

What is the likely future trajectory of Chinese development? Chapter 7 links the stories this book has told—all-rural livelihoods, glimpses of the economy from the view at the very bottom of society—to larger trends in the economy. China's rural-urban divide has subsidized labor-intensive production. It has also locked the country into an export-oriented pattern by limiting domestic consumer markets to cities while leaving the countryside behind. Today, the central state is attempting to dissolve these limits by subsidizing infrastructure and modernization in rural regions. Urban development is creeping into the countryside, elevating some and leaving others behind. Two distinct mechanisms of capital accumulation—one still coursing through farming villages able to support themselves through the flow of labor into cities and another transforming these same villages into places of official commerce, where land values have soared and agriculture has become mechanized—continue to facilitate the movement of capital between rural and urban societies.

Yet new crises emerge. First, a rising wave of protests related to land loss has swept the countryside. Second, as urbanizing villages disrupt long-established labor recruitment channels, brokers reach further into the hinterland for labor recruitment, and these new channels are precarious, as brokers recruit laborers from faraway villages where they have few social connections to generate trust-based relationships. Finally, even as land development defuses the rural fiscal crisis generated by labor migration, it creates new tendencies toward overproduction. Local governments expropriate rural land beyond the limits of state regulation, threatening food security; real estate markets overheat beyond demand, showing signs of impending bust. This book reveals boom-and-bust patterns of the Chinese economy, created by mechanisms of capital accumulation that outrun the political reforms governing them.

2 A Tale of Two Villages

After three decades of market reform, Faming and Landing Villages, two communities in Sichuan Province and the Chongqing Prefecture, respectively, have evolved distinct political economic arrangements. Divergent trajectories of rural industrialization have shaped patterns of employment and labor migration. Histories of migration, over time, have shaped kinship structures and agrarian practices in each community.

FAMING VILLAGE

Faming Village, for example, was a fount of rural industrialization throughout the 1980s, and though these rural industries have since withered, kinship structures and social norms strengthened by that period have become the basis for the survival of migrant households. On the other hand, Landing Village, located on a mountainous ridge on the periphery of Chongqing Municipality, had roads too steep to transport goods in and out on a large scale; as a result, villagers ventured out of the village to find work early on. Early out-migrations diluted the intimacy of extended kin ties. Yet the same conditions and mountainous land that blocked trade in the 1980s then became an advantage in the 2000s, when real estate developers from nearby Chongqing found the site an ideal location for tourism.

To the extent that Chinese development can be characterized by the interaction between rural and urban economies, this chapter argues that these villages are ideal sites for observing mechanisms of capital accumulation. It illustrates three periods of Chinese reform—first a period of rural industrialization in the 1980s, then a period of rural decline and increasing rates of rural-urban migration in the 1990s, and finally a period of land redevelopment in the 2000s—and narrates these three periods of reform from the vantage point of each village. The events illustrated in this chapter are largely reconstructed from interviews with local government officials and older residents of both villages and supplemented with archival data taken from local gazetteers of both localities.

The 1980s: Flourishing Faming Village

Faming Village is a farming community located deep in the heartland of Sichuan Province, one of China's two primary labor-sending regions. Its parent county, Qianwei County, is a rural periphery of the small metropolitan area of Leshan City (see map 2). Qianwei consists of a county seat along the Minjiang River, a minor tributary of the famous Yangtze River, and surrounding villages.

Qianwei County is home to a cluster of farming villages huddled along the Minjiang River, which supports convenient transport for goods and equipment in and out. Since the 1980s, bamboo forests on Faming's mountaintops have provided the basis for a booming forestry industry. Rich deposits of coal supported early mining efforts, and coal mining attracted investment in a local cement industry. Though today these industries have largely disappeared, relics of earlier decades of rural prosperity remain. An unused mini railway links abandoned mines to the county township. Now the mini railway sits unused, providing amusement to the occasional tourist.

The evolution of Faming Village, located fifteen kilometers from the center of the Qianwei County seat, reflects the twists and turns of the rural economy, from the prosperous 1980s to the current era. Coal production

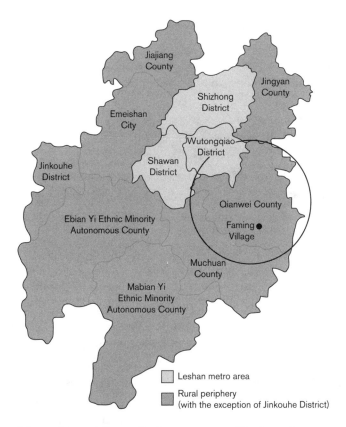

Map 2. Qianwei County, Leshan metro area. Map by author.

and forestry in the 1980s supported local employment, allowing rural laborers to work off farms without leaving the village. The TVEs that were so central to the rural industrialization ongoing across China were especially robust in Faming.[1] In 1989, local employment in Qianwei County was high, and nearly 84 percent of the county's working-age population was employed locally.[2] Some of the mines were state owned, for example the still-standing Jiayang Mining Corporation, which runs today at less than half capacity. Most were collective enterprises managed by the Qianwei County government.

Scholars have argued that local rural employment had beneficial effects for households, and based on interviews describing Faming's mining history and employment data taken from local government gazetteers, these arguments might well apply to Faming. TVEs were economically successful and were managed by local governments, which drew the majority of their revenues from the TVEs' coffers. Employment at TVEs conferred social goods and other benefits administered by local governments, which financed public goods through TVE profits. Thus, as Arrighi has noted, collective enterprise ownership created a redistributive cycle, wherein laborers received relatively full welfare benefits despite low wages.[3] One might link this redistributive dynamic to the findings of other scholars such as Martin K. Whyte, who has shown that disparity between rural and urban household incomes remained low in the 1980s, far lower than the disparities seen in the 1990s.[4]

Mining incomes varied widely. Most villagers related to me earnings in the 1980s that were the equivalent of 1,000 RMB per month in 2010, but experienced miners, they said, could earn up to 2,500 RMB—still not as much as a villager earns working construction in cities today. The bosses in the mines were the real earners. Many foremen earned the equivalent in today's currency of 4,000 or 5,000 RMB a month.[5] The only drawback to mining, villagers explained, was physical risk. Two villagers had been crushed to death in the mines in that decade. One was employed in the Jiayang state-owned mine, and his relatives received a windfall death compensation payment from the mine. The other was employed in a collectively owned mine, which was losing revenues by the early 1990s and could only provide a small compensatory payment.

Bamboo production generated a smaller segment of village income and was organized as a household-based cash crop, as it still is today. Every season, middlemen contracted by local furniture factories appeared in Faming Village with trucks and pricing schemes for the year's bamboo crop. Villagers clamored for access to the work of bamboo cultivation, a safer alternative to the mines. Yet there were barriers to entry into the bamboo business. Not all land in Faming, for example, was suitable for bamboo cultivation. During the 1981 land decollectivization period, village leaders had divided village land into one- or two-mu (0.165-acre) plots, with each household receiving as many plots as it had household members. Yet these plots were categorized according to altitude and moisture levels, and only the high lands were suitable for bamboo growth.

Not unexpectedly, many of the villagers who became bamboo growers in the 1980s were local elites, those who had been elevated to leadership positions during the socialist period. One villager, Elder Che, now a seventy-year-old farmer, had been appointed kitchen cook of the commune during the 1950s, when villagers were assigned grain tickets for subsistence. Elder Che's children told stories of their father's heroism during that period, claiming that during the disastrous Great Leap Forward (1958–1962) and the ensuing period of starvation, Elder Che regularly fasted, saving his own grain tickets to give them to those in greater need. Other villagers disputed these stories. One claimed that Elder Che smuggled food to those in advantageous positions and watched people die around him without lifting a finger. "Their family did not lose or suffer anything, not like other families," the villager said. Regardless of which version of what occurred is correct, Elder Che had friends in high places. When decollectivization came, his household was assigned high land, and he became a leading bamboo grower.

1990s: Rural Decline

As a source of local employment, the mines gradually waned throughout the 1990s. Coal production reached its peak in 1987. Nationwide, collectively owned enterprises were losing money due to declining efficiencies, urban-centric banking policies, and rising competition from foreign-funded enterprises. Urban domestic markets grew, and global free trade policies opened export markets, but TVEs were increasingly outcompeted by foreign enterprises—not surprisingly, as they suffered from poor transportation infrastructure, poor quality control, and an inability to scale up to meet rising demand. Yasheng Huang has documented gradual changes in the State Council's stance toward rural finance. Rural, private, fixed-asset investments fell sharply in the 1990s. Furthermore, the relative portion of these investments financed by state banks declined as well; in 1987, nearly 6 percent of fixed-asset investments were bank funded, and by the mid-1990s this portion had declined to 3 or 4 percent.[6] Rural credit cooperatives were stamped out, other forms of underground financing were criminalized, and state banks were instructed to capitalize state-owned enterprises in cities.[7]

Central state officials began advocating policies designed to slowly phase out the rural collective sector. As Ho-Fung Hung argues, several key policy moves contributed to the gradual decline of the TVEs. First, as early as 1993, Vice Premier Zhu Rongji began making public pronouncements about the need to dampen TVE production and divert resources to the more efficient export sector.[8] Next, after a gradual move to liberalize grain prices throughout the 1990s, Zhu Rongji called for the repression of grain prices to protect the urban livelihoods sector.[9] Finally, fears of TVE over-production, a source of inflationary pressure, led many provincial officials to sell off collective assets to foreign enterprises.[10]

As a result of these policies, rural off-farm employment opportunities grew sparse. A study undertaken in Jiangsu Province between 1988 and 1992 showed a 24 percent decrease in average per capita income, a 40 percent drop in the number of rural residents employed in factories, and a 40 percent drop in total days worked on nonfarm activities. Real rural wage levels in construction and manufacturing stayed constant during the period.[11]

These changes came to Faming gradually. After the closing of the mines, villagers began to fall back on a subsistence and cash crop farming economy that had developed since the 1981 passage of the Household Responsibility System, a reform concurrent with land decollectivization that greatly reduced the grain production quotas operational under social-ism and allowed households to sell or retain surplus grain production. Villagers laid off from coal mines, or suffering diminished bamboo yields, could return to farming during times of need. Older villagers who were retired but had no pensions and few welfare subsidies to speak of could maintain a baseline level of subsistence.

Economy of Migration

The Faming Village that is visible now has changed from the mining community it once was, and labor migration and construction work have since become primary sources of livelihoods. Construction came to Faming Village rather coincidentally when, in 1992, a nearby coal pro-cessing factory was still in operation, and migrants from nearby regions often came in search of work. One migrant came from a village five hundred kilometers away, Landing Village. This migrant, a man named Boss Bo, was a recruiter for construction subcontractors in Beijing. He took the first group of Faming villagers to work construction in Beijing that year.

As migrant labor gradually became a viable source of livelihood, households continued engaging in farming, both for subsistence and for cash crops. These farming practices that began after the inception of the Household Responsibility System became far more important than they had been in the 1980s. With its flat land suited for rice and vegetable cultivation, Faming Village began to produce small cash crops for local township markets. Government policies gradually eased other burdens on farmers, primarily by abolishing household and agricultural taxes and various fees in 2004 and then later by offering subsidies on agricultural equipment and fertilizers. In Faming Village, these subsidies were used to support the raising and selling of pigs, a side activity to accompany bamboo cultivation, small-scale vegetable sales in nearby township markets, and construction work. Small cash cropping, bamboo cultivation, and pig farming were reliable supplements to migrant labor.

Visible signs of the symbiosis between these small-scale agrarian activities and migrant labor were abundant in Faming. The village landscape was dotted with large new houses, two stories high, brightly tiled and built of concrete and brick. Migrant households saved remittance income, tore down the mud-and-mortar houses they had inhabited during the 1980s and 1990s, and built these gleaming houses. They were tailored to the various functions of the household; nearly all had large pig stalls attached, and nearly all were built with a separate attachment for elderly generations, who farmed their entire lives. The village was also largely inhabited by women, children, and the elderly, who engaged in these agrarian activities and in child rearing while men worked construction in cities.

This particular configuration of economic activities was specific to Faming Village and was a product of the geography of the village. For example, while Faming's land was relatively high, suitable for bamboo growth, another region just to its north was on riverine low lands, where a riverine village called Shuang-ba was located. In Shuang-ba, the 1980s had not brought much by way of industry, and there was nothing in the earth to mine. Yet the soil itself was fertile. Throughout the 1990s, vege-table cultivation became so productive that during the early 2000s the county became a state-appointed designated vegetable production base, where county-appointed "dragonhead companies" signed contracts with farmers for annual quotas of crops and provided them with technology, seeds, and fertilizer subsidies.[12] In Shuang-ba the average self-reported monthly household income from an informal survey of eighty households was over 5,000 RMB, while in Faming an informal survey of eighty households showed an average monthly income of only 3,000–4,000 RMB.[13]

Among eighty surveyed households, only 10 percent were engaged in regular labor migration for their livelihoods. In most households, men were present along with their wives, entire families together. Yet as Qianwei County officials noted during interviews, the prosperity of Shuang-ba Village was anomalous; no other village within the county had developed contracts with dragonhead companies.[14] Faming had a more difficult tra-jectory than Shuang-ba; the 1980s had brought the mines, after which the 1990s became a decade of decline. By the time Boss Bo arrived, most vil-lagers were willing to seek work in cities.

In Faming the new economy of migration extended rather than over-turned the extant social structure of the 1970s and 1980s. Like most vil-lages, Faming is divided into several sections, directly corresponding to the commune production brigades demarcated under socialism. Today, each section has an elected or self-appointed leader, and in Faming most of these section leaders themselves or their parents had been brigade lead-ers in the 1970s. In Faming I became embedded in the everyday life of Section 8. Approximately thirty-two households resided year-round in Section 8 during my research. Four lineage groups were predominant in Section 8: one was led by a pair of brothers surnamed Gao, another was surnamed Luo, another Che, and another Chen.[15] Many members of these lineage groups migrated together, especially those groups in which one or two members had become labor brokers.

Many of the lineage groups that had become powerful during the socialist period remained so, their social capital transposed onto a new village economy. Two brothers of the Gao lineage had also converted an advantageous social position in the 1970s and 1980s into valuable social capital in the current village economy. Their father, a brigade leader in the 1970s, had organized an herbal medicinal root business with several other men in surrounding regions during the 1980s. The accumulated profits from this medicinal root business were later given to the Gao brothers, who eventually used the funds to become labor brokers for nearby construction subcontractors during the 2000s.

Authority in the new migration economy was as highly valued as political connection—in some cases, possibly even more highly valued.[16] The Gao brothers, for example, were widely recognized as the most powerful men in Section 8, for reasons that will become clear in chapter 3. Even the elected village leader, Leader Cha, who resided in Section 2, deferred to the Gao brothers. Leader Cha himself was a man of not-insubstantial stature. His father had been an urban resident of the nearby county seat before he married a villager. As a result of inherited status, he had also received much high land and then further leveraged his office to develop close connections with county-level bamboo middlemen. Thanks to the bamboo business, Leader Cha's family resides in a three-story tiled house in a section of the village nearest to the high lands. The home is well-furnished; in addition to a refrigerator (3,000 RMB), other highlights in his home include a large-screen television (2,500 RMB) and a solar-powered water heater for showers (3,000 RMB).

Yet despite his comfortable lifestyle, the structure of Leader Cha's livelihood is not that different from those of the rest of the villagers. During dry seasons when the bamboo yield is thin, his wife works at a factory in the Qianwei County seat. No one in Faming is unaffected by the seasonal fluctuations of informal jobs and thus the need to diversify livelihood strategies. In the larger scheme of things, Leader Cha's livelihood pales in comparison to that of the Gao brothers. Brokering migrant labor, after all, affords a more expandable source of income; more villagers recruited means more earnings. Leader Cha's deference was visible. At a birthday party held in his honor at a restaurant in the nearby township, at which local luminaries including the township Communist Party secretary, the township mayor, the vice village leader, and a township schoolteacher were present, Leader Cha's last toast was to Big Gao, a friend from childhood, a villager to whom so many villagers owed their livelihoods.

LANDING VILLAGE

The 1980s: Arid Land and Moribund Industries in Landing

Five hundred kilometers to the east of Faming Village lies Landing Village, home of Boss Bo. Landing Village presents a striking counterpoint to Faming in several respects. First, whereas Faming Village emerged from the end of socialist commune production with robust industrial and agricultural sectors, Landing Village had scant industry, few local jobs to speak of, and arid land. An initial premise of this book is the argument that Faming's farming economy provided protection for the poor, but that this protection later became an impediment, obviating the "do or die" desperation that pushed early Landing villagers into risky entrepreneurial investments.

Landing Village is located on mountainous land, with steep and winding roads leading up to the village center. Until the end of my fieldwork in 2011, the village lay on the rural outskirts of Chongqing Prefecture, a peripheral rural village in the southern part of Qijiang County, itself under the jurisdiction of Chongqing. (See map 3.) Though Chongqing is a municipality, in 1997 it was elevated to the administrative status of a province. Therefore, Landing ranks at the same administrative level in the rural-urban political hierarchy as Faming, namely a village on the periphery of a county on the margin of a municipality, both equally deprioritized in the hierarchy of urban governance.

The Qijiang County seat is nestled in a valley on flatland between two mountains, its numerous skyscraper apartment complexes gleaming in the sunlight. It lies along the Qijiang River, another minor tributary of the Yangtze River, and from a short distance the county seat looks as if it is surrounded by stretches of farmland, forest, and hills as far as the eye can see.

In the 1980s the agrarian life of Landing Village was unprofitable. Many elderly villagers recalled making two-day trips by foot to the market center in Chongqing to sell vegetable products. Even then, cash cropping was not profitable. Most of the land in Landing is classified as high and middle lands, dry and arid, suited for varied small crops such as peanuts, yams, and corn. Yet unlike Faming's land, Landing's mountaintops are too dry for bamboo growth and remain forest covered. Much of this high land, in fact, has been marked by the central state for

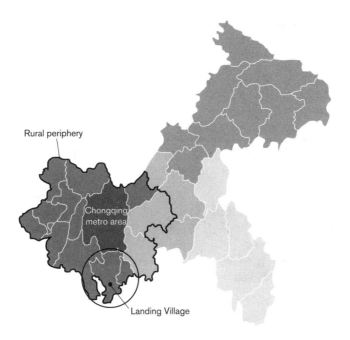

Map 3. Qijiang County, Chongqing metro area.
Map by author.

forest protection and cannot be cultivated by households. No equivalent to Faming's bamboo industry was possible in Landing. Instead, rice and wheat cultivation, combined with small vegetable farming, became purely subsistence-oriented activities. This farming economy was nevertheless important to households, particularly because village men soon began to undertake high-risk labor migrations to cities in search of construction work. Even a small wheat, rice, and vegetable crop became a source of survival for households during the early years of migration, when wages were low and arrears frequent.

Local off-farm jobs were few and far between. The absence of subsurface minerals and coal discouraged mine development, and although food processing plants became abundant in the rural periphery around Chongqing City, most of these were located near the county centers rather than the townships and villages. A salt mine located slightly to the south of Landing Village was in operation, yet its workforce was recruited at the county level, via subcontractors appointed by county government officials. Few villagers in Landing recalled knowing anybody who had secured a full-time job in either the food processing plants or the salt mine. Instead, villagers began to seek work in the construction industry, and here, proximity to Chongqing conferred its own benefits.

Boss Bo, for example, was one of the first men in Landing Village to seek work outside of the region. When I met him in 2010, Boss Bo was a forty-six-year-old man with a lined face who frequently dressed in a fur-lined leather jacket. He had begun working construction in 1983, when he was nineteen years old. At a young age, he had learned that the world owed nothing to men like him. He had to suffer to earn, and this suffering became a rubric for knowing the world:

> In my own village . . . many of us were working starting in 1980 and 1981. We could eat a lot of bitterness, we were willing to suffer to live. . . . Not like people in Faming. . . . [T]hey are not willing to do whatever it takes like we are.

Boss Bo's first job paid him the equivalent in today's currency of 600 RMB per month; he worked as an apprentice to a man he met on the platform of a train station in Chongqing. It was a risky gambit, and he was frequently cheated by subcontractors who docked his pay or by other migrants who stole from him and cheated him, then disappeared. He described hard lessons learned on the road. Cash stored in one's socks while sleeping on the floor of a train station, for example, could be stolen by pickpockets, who stealthily wandered the stations, grasping for feet in the dark.

Throughout the 1980s Boss Bo and an older cousin, now known as Boss Zeng, worked construction job after construction job. They built a solid social network stocked specifically with subcontractors they met at each job. The two saved their wages each year. When Boss Bo was twenty-seven, they asked his kin relatives for loans, so that he and Boss Zeng could begin bringing one or two other men from Landing Village to work every year. All of the men resided in makeshift dormitories and took meals in cafeterias, typically provided by construction subcontractors; costs of room and board would later be deducted from their year-end wages.

By the late 1980s Bo and Zeng had transitioned from simply bringing villagers with them to seek work in cities to brokering their labor formally.

The two were bringing ten or twenty men with them every year. They were earning the equivalent in today's currency of 2,400 RMB monthly, and they were also paid brokerage fees by subcontractors, who now relied on them to staff an entire team of specialized workers: carpenters one year, concrete pourers another. During each Spring Festival, typically in the month of February, Boss Bo and Boss Zeng returned to Landing Village and began making plans via cell phone calls and day trips to Qijiang County seat, where they met with local subcontractors and other brokers. They called upon village men to offer them spots on their construction team and negotiate rates. They purchased train tickets for each of their recruited workers and covered their living expenses for the year.

In 1992 Boss Bo planned to take a break from construction work and, on a tip from a man he met on a train, he decided to take his team of Landing laborers to Qianwei County, where jobs were available at a coal processing plant. On this trip to Qianwei, he and members of his team met several villagers from Faming. It was on this trip that members of the two villages became mutually acquainted.

Entrepreneurship in the 1990s

In the 1990s labor migration had become the primary source of livelihood for residents of both Faming and Landing. Yet the character and trajectories of these migrations varied. Unlike Famingers, who had invested their earnings from migration in renovated houses in the village, Landingers focused their investments outside of the village. They invested their earnings in properties and small businesses in nearby townships or in petty commodity activities in the periphery neighborhoods of Chongqing Municipality. One reason for this was Landing's proximity to Chongqing. Entrepreneurs operating on the margins of the city often came to the Qijiang County seat and hired villagers for small tasks and hard labor jobs. Another consideration was pure necessity. In Landing there was no use investing in a rural economy that was so moribund, devoid of opportunities.

In Faming Village the 1990s brought a diversification of economic activities. Households transitioned away from mining jobs gradually and toward migration, first engaging in bamboo cultivation and selling vegetable wares at market, then raising pigs and farming for subsistence alongside the migration economy. However, in Landing Village cash cropping was particularly unprofitable. Some village women sold pickled vegetables for a pittance (15 RMB per half kilogram), and some men fermented rice wine for township markets. Farming remained strictly oriented toward subsistence. Therefore, migration was more of an all-or-nothing affair. Labor brokers took substantial risks to scale up their recruitment activities quickly. As Boss Bo recollected, the prospect of falling back and working as a common laborer was so unappealing that he suffered financial losses in many years in order to continue brokering labor.

Though agricultural production remained minimal, the migration economy flourished. By the 1990s not just Bo and Zeng, but a number of other Landing villagers, had become full-fledged labor brokers. Entrepreneurs like these brokers bridged a rural-urban gap, and their economic activities increased the level of rural-urban integration in the surrounding counties of Chongqing.[17] This was because, in contrast to Faming villagers, who reinvested remittance earnings in rural life, building houses and expanding pig cultivation, investments that provided psychological security but conferred few future returns, Landing villagers had no choice but to reinvest their earnings in apartments and small businesses in nearby townships and the Qijiang County seat. Moreover, the wealthiest villagers in Landing were more cash rich than the wealthiest in Faming, owing to a pyramidal structure of labor recruitment in which labor brokers profit both from suppressing migrants' wages and from expanding recruitment activities.[18]

The rise of the entrepreneurs splintered many kin networks, as some individuals accumulated enough wealth to relocate from the village to nearby townships, and others continued to alternate between labor migration and stagnant subsistence farming. In Section 2 of Landing, where I resided, three major lineage groups predominated. One was surnamed Deng, another Wu, and another Wang. All three kin groups became increasingly geographically dispersed in the 1990s, as entrepreneurial members of each decamped from the village to relocate in townships. As a result of the exodus of Landing's entrepreneurial elite to townships and the county seat, by 2011, in the section of Landing where I lived, only fourteen of thirty households had at least one member residing in the village full time.

As many kin groups spread themselves across the rural-urban border, class divisions and resentments also arose. The Deng-Bo clan, for example, was divided into two camps. On one side of the family was a forty-eight-year-old woman named Deng Liwen, wife of Boss Bo. Her siblings-in-law, the Bos, have all become relatively wealthy. One of Boss Bo's siblings relocated as far away as coastal Zheijiang Province, where his son has opened a noodle shop. The entire family works and lives in the noodle shop and also maintains an apartment in the township near Landing, to which they will one day retire.

But Deng Liwen's three brothers are common laborers, mostly employed by Boss Bo, with households that remain engaged in subsistence farming and reside in Landing Village. One exception is Deng Liwen's uncle, Deng Cisong, whose children have attended college and secured formal jobs in the post office and other government offices in the Qijiang County seat. The differences between the families engender bitterness. Deng Cisong's wife, for example, considers the other side of the family, whose members all depend on migrant labor in the construction trades, crass and low class: "[They don't] know how to handle money. . . . They only do hard labor because they are uneducated. . . . They don't know how to use their heads to make money." On the other hand, Deng Liwen and her brothers minimize the accomplishments of Deng Cisong's upwardly mobile children. "They all moved to the city, but they don't earn very much," Deng Liwen commented once. "They earn less than what we earn working construction. But they still look down on us because they think we are country people." At the same time, she bears no resentment toward the more wealthy Bo kin who employ them, regarding the Bos as hard-working, no-frills strivers.

Urbanization and Fiscal Recovery, 2000s Onward

The other major difference between Landing and Faming, aside from Landing's more extensive migration history and its greater class inequality, is the rapidly expanding character of the nearby Chongqing Municipality. In 2007 Chongqing and the Sichuan capital city of Chengdu were appointed as pilot areas for Comprehensive Reforms in Coordinating Urban and Rural Development. Many rural counties within their jurisdictions began to undertake reforms in *hukou* and land policies, both designed to convert rural land to urban use and thus enable counties to meet new targets for agricultural, commercial, and industrial production.[19]

In Chongqing, these changes occurred under the regime of Bo Xilai, a later disgraced Communist Party secretary of Chongqing and Politburo member who pioneered a developmental model known as the "Chongqing model," emphasizing rural modernization and the reform of the *hukou* system beginning in 2010. In August 2010 the city established a 400 bil- lion RMB initiative that aimed at converting ten million rural people into urban citizens by 2020, thus raising the portion of nonagricultural popu- lation from 29 percent to 60 percent.[20] Eligibility for *hukou* transfer in the Chongqing region is more relaxed than in other regions, extending to those who have permanent residence in either their own house or a rented domicile, those who have worked in the city for a certain number of years, and those who have paid taxes above a certain level.[21] *Hukou* reforms, as Zhan Shaohua notes, are implemented in regionally varying ways and often conform to the interests of various stakeholders: agribusinesses, real estate developers, and urban welfare officials.[22] Other scholars have argued that in Chongqing, the rapid opening up of urban *hukou* member- ship to rural populations was linked to local government interest in con- solidating land for real estate development.[23]

These *hukou* reforms created a culture of urban aspiration in Landing. Villagers, young and old alike, were bombarded with physical reminders of the appeal of urban middle-class life. As part of an urban beautification push led by Bo Xilai, tall ginko trees were planted along roadways across Chongqing City. In Qijiang, large billboards proclaimed the virtues of the county's middle-class residential offerings—"Verdant Qijiang! Safe Qijiang! Healthy Qijiang!"—and displayed middle-class families engaged in various leisure activities, such as bicycling and window shopping. In addition, this urban beautification movement coincided with a visible downsizing of the rural townships surrounding the county seat. In prepa- ration for land reforms, public services in two townships near Landing were downsized and consolidated. One of two middle schools was shut down, one of two primary schools was boarded up, one of two police sta- tions was disassembled, and the number of elected and government administrators was halved.

One bus, departing twice a day, carries residents from these diminishing townships to the Qijiang County seat. Its daily passenger load reflects the recent and rapid transformation of the village. On a typical day, the bus carries a range of rural people. Occasionally the bus carries village entrepreneurs from the land they still retain to their small businesses in the county seat, where they now reside. More often, elderly villagers ride the bus. Some are on their way to visit adult children who reside in city apartments; others are heading to the county government bearing shakily handwritten letters requesting an increase in their monthly land subsidy, stamped with red watermarks by village leaders. A small proportion of bus passengers, though, are part of the fading subsistence economy: women carrying large baskets on their backs to carry the tools and foodstuffs they will purchase in the county.

WHAT THE VILLAGES REVEAL TODAY

The postsocialist developmental trajectories of Faming and Landing Villages reveal a larger picture of the Chinese economy. In the 1980s, rural collective industries became the epicenter of the economy. The majority of local government revenues came from "nontax revenues," largely fees extracted from TVEs. Faming Village bears a legacy of that history of rural industrialization. From the 2000s onward, however, land became a central source of economic growth and government revenues. The majority of governmental extrabudgetary revenue is now extracted through land development. The eventual demolition of Landing Village, its reconstruction as a New Land Township, and the transformation of Qijiang County into Qijiang District reveal the process of this urbanization.

During my research I visited several other villages in surrounding regions of Sichuan, where I found that some were like Faming, in that they functioned as holding sites for China's immense labor force, places where migrant workers' families subsist and future workers are recruited. Other villages resembled Landing, subject to rural-urban land conversions as local governments generate capital by converting collectively owned land to state ownership and urban redevelopment. Furthermore, as I continued my research, I learned that these two kinds of villages, ones that sent laborers to cities and one that converted land for urban development, are two sides of the same coin. They represent two channels of capital accumulation providing labor and land, primary factors of production, to Chinese enterprises. Moreover, they are interrelated, as the political economy of Faming is the result of *hukou* and rural land policies that have cordoned off the countryside as a nonmarketized segment of the economy serving to prop up the dynamism of urban markets. The political economy of Landing, however, is created by reforms enabling marketization to penetrate the rural economy, this time in the form of urbanization.

These structural differences have created distinct local cultures and lifestyle norms in both villages. Whereas Faming is populated by women farming year-round to underwrite men's risky labor migrations, Landing's resident population is confined to the elderly and those households that have been unsuccessful in entrepreneurship. In Faming, the wealthiest families maintain spacious, newly renovated houses, where they cultivate small crops, raise children, and plan for retirement. Migrants in Faming are expected to return, and those who do not are considered unaccountable and are excluded from labor recruitment. In Landing, on the other hand, the wealthiest families of labor brokers and entrepreneurs are conspicuously absent from village life. Everyday conversations are dominated by rumors about the affairs of these entrepreneurs: where they live, how much they earn, how they make their livelihoods. In Landing, the less villagers know of a migrant's whereabouts, the more likely it seems to them that he has become a success.

In addition, villagers in each site hold perceptions of the other that reflect these differences. The two villages were linked by a social network initiated when Boss Bo first took a group of Landing migrants to seek work in the Faming coal processing plant in 1992. Among these migrants was a man named Little Deng, a younger brother of Boss Bo's wife, Deng Liwen. Little Deng eventually met and married a woman in Faming, Yue-na.

When Little Deng proposed marriage to Yue-na, he assumed the two would set up house in Landing Village, per patrilocal rural norms of marital residence near the husband's natal home. Yet Yue-na objected. Yue-na's mother, she told him, had three daughters and no sons, and she wished the two might live on Yue-na's household plot instead.[24] He agreed after a period of negotiation.

Little Deng's initial reluctance was based on his perception of the county of Qijiang as an urbanizing place, where jobs and a higher standard of living would eventually arrive. "You will see, Qijiang County seat is much bigger than Qianwei County seat," he told me after he first offered to take me to his natal home in Landing Village:

> I keep telling Yue-na that our Qijiang is much more developed than Qianwei, but she doesn't agree with me. We have people who buy apartments in cities. We have skyscrapers there, twenty stories high. We have a bridge over the Qijiang River.

On the other hand, where Little Deng saw a city on the rise, Yue-na looked at Landing Village and saw a depopulated, desolate landscape:

> There is nobody there to talk to. The village is empty. Nothing like here where we are always going house to house socializing. The houses are all stone houses, they look like they are made of dirt. Nothing like our houses here, we use bricks and tile, not just stone.

The two views are equally apt. Compared to Qianwei, Qijiang is an urbanizing site, one reflecting coming changes in the political economy. Even long before demolition began, Landing Village was already gradually emptying out, farmers in its agrarian economy being left behind. The wife of a labor migrant in Faming would understandably be discouraged by the prospect of living in an urbanizing region where she might be one of those left behind.

CONCLUSION

This chapter has demonstrated the differences between two villages, Faming and Landing. It has narrated the historical trajectories of each village since the early 1980s, reconstructing events based on interviews with villagers and local government officials and on archival sources (gazetteers from each county). In Faming, a period of rural industrialization in the 1980s, combined with a marginal cash cropping economy, protected many households from the last-resort necessity of labor migration. When households did begin to rely on labor migration for income in the 1990s, they created a labor recruitment structure that had its origins in the commune production structure of the 1970s. A decade of agrarian life in the 1980s created a sense of continuity in the social life of the village and preserved existing power dynamics among lineage groups. This helped to create a thick sense of trust and reciprocity, which facilitated the organization of local labor brokerage.

In comparison to Faming, Landing Village had a more difficult transition, marred by desperation and risk taking. A dearth of rural industries and local off-farm jobs, combined with arid land and an unfriendly topography, pushed villagers into cities to seek work from the early 1980s onward. As migrants searched for work elsewhere, those who became labor brokers eventually accumulated the capital necessary to sponsor their kin in petty entrepreneurial activities. Even before the onset of urbanization reforms and land expropriation, the village itself was a fruitless place to settle, and so the upwardly mobile segment of the population invested its earnings in apartments and small businesses in nearby townships and cities, a process described in chapter 5. By the time urbanization reforms arrived in the late 2000s, many villagers had already decamped for nearby urban areas.

Continuity characterizes Faming's transition from rural industrialization to rural-urban labor migration. The wealthy households of Faming Village maintain expansive, newly renovated homes on village housing plots. Labor recruitment networks developed along lineage lines still retain much of the power dynamics of the 1970s and 1980s. On the other hand, disruption marks Landing's transition from rural-urban labor migration to urbanization. Labor brokers and the entrepreneurial elite of Landing Village reinvest their earnings in nearby township and county economies. They receive higher returns on investment than the households of common laborers, which struggle without a robust agrarian economy to maintain their economic standing. These differences lay the groundwork for mechanisms through which commodification of labor and land transform village relations.

3　Into the World of Chinese Labor

The Gao family of Faming Village are the owners of a newly built, three-story house, the largest house in the village. The house was built in 2010, and its construction was made possible by the prominent role of the Gao family in village society. Many villagers were indebted both to Big Gao, a labor broker who provided employment for many able-bodied local men, and his wife Madam Gao, who coordinated an informal lending network within the village. They had contributed, through Madam Gao's lending network, the 150,000 RMB in pooled loans that funded housing construction.

Big Gao and his brother, Little Gao, had spent the 1980s running a small medicinal herbal business, selling herbal concoctions in the township and later in county markets. By the 1990s the two brothers had reinvested earnings from this business into a career in labor brokerage. The brothers began bringing Faming villagers—only small groups of ten at first—to Xi'an City in the north and Chongqing City to the east to fill slots in construction contracts that other labor brokers were unable to fill. By the 2000s the Gao brothers had become the primary source of employment for the many Faming men who were still able-bodied but no longer able to find jobs in the nearby mines.

As brokers, the Gao brothers spent many years in arrears or just breaking even. They were responsible for covering transportation costs for other villagers whom they took to fill contracts. They also provided upfront cash as living allowances for their recruits in the cities where they worked—around 100 RMB ($17) for each man every ten days. Room and board were covered at construction sites by subcontractors, who had installed makeshift dormitories to house workers, ten or twenty to a room. The costs of housing and food, provided in construction-wide cafeterias, were later deducted from workers' pay. Wage payments, with costs of room and board deducted, came only once a year—in January, after a full year of work and just before migrants all boarded trains to return to their villages to celebrate the Spring Festival (or the Lunar New Year) in February. Because the upfront costs of labor delivery were substantial, the Gao brothers were among the few villagers with sufficient starting capital to maintain a regular brokerage network.

While Big Gao is away from the village working, Madam Gao lives in the village, where she cultivates the land and participates in a mutual aid network with the wives of her husband's recruits. As this chapter shows, their respective social networks fulfill two symbiotic functions necessary for labor reproduction: one of women maintaining the agrarian safety net that enables labor migration, and the other of men negotiating with village brokers over the terms of migrant labor. This chapter outlines the pathway toward this particular configuration of labor migration in Faming—that is, the disappearance of alternative off-farm employment options in the 1990s, followed by the arrival of an outsider named Boss Bo, who would launch the first venture outside of the village in search of construction work. It asks why migration produced a traditionally gendered rural social structure in Faming, relegating women to domestic and agricultural work while sending men away to work as migrants, and contrasts Faming Village with a neighboring village where migration rates are low and agricultural work is undertaken by men and women alike.

A NEW ECONOMY OF MIGRATION

In Faming Village, only two of the coal mines active during the 1980s remained operational by 2010. One of the two, Jinshu Mine, paid its miners

1,000 RMB a month and even offered an employer-sponsored pension. But because Jinshu hired its miners on a temporary and contingent basis and only during seasons of intensified production, few men worked for the twenty continuous years required for pension qualification.[1] I met very few Faming villagers who worked in the mines, and those who did worked there in years when they could not secure jobs in construction. Construction was a higher-paying option than mining. In 2010 the average construction wage for a mid-range laborer—excluding wage levels of brokers and subcontractors—was 2,200 RMB monthly, more than twice the average mine wage. For that reason, when the mines shut down and labor migration became necessary, construction seemed at first a relatively more attractive option.

Construction jobs were introduced to Faming villagers by a chance encounter with a labor broker from another village. As mentioned previously, in 1992 an outsider named Boss Bo came to the village to recruit men to work construction with him in Beijing. Some, Boss Bo said, would work as ironworkers and others as concrete workers or rebar workers. Training for such specialties was not intensive, and Boss Bo assured the men that they could learn on the job for a year and then produce at full capacity the following year. Higher-paying specialty positions—pipefitters, masons, carpenters, electricians—were reserved for migrants with substantial prior experience. Once the Faming men had more years of experience, they too could train for these specialties.

The men soon discovered the terms of employment were different than what they had expected. When they arrived in Beijing, they went to the appointed location and found the appointed subcontractor, who tasked them with pouring concrete for a building foundation. They slept in tents erected near the worksite. One Faminger recalled the year as a series of bitter realizations:

VILLAGER: On March 18th, we arrived in Beijing, and on March 19th we went immediately to work. After the first month or so of work, the other workers went to Boss Bo, and they told him they wanted their wages for the month so they could send them home to their families. Their families needed the money, or were expecting the money.

JC: What did Boss Bo do?

VILLAGER: Boss Bo told them, this is how we do it in Beijing, this is how every employer does it, you get your wages at the end of the year, with your living expenses deducted from them. For now, if you want more money, you have to take it out of the wages at the end of the year. We thought Boss Bo was cheating us.

JC: And?

VILLAGER: And we quickly found out from other workers that this was actually the way things were done.

After they realized that wages were paid annually in arrears, some villagers balked, particularly those who were older and did not have the capability of maintaining a full crop at home. Many of them chose instead to seek construction jobs that were lower paying but located closer to home, in nearby townships and counties, where subcontractors paid workers on more frequent terms.

Still, construction became a dominant source of employment because it was higher paying than other options outside of the village. Factories in faraway coastal cities, for example, also hire villagers at wage levels that are higher than those available in nearby inland cities. These factories are preferred sites of employment for the youthful, who seek adventure in cities after spending their childhoods in the relative monotony of the countryside. But factories tend to impose an age cap on hiring, firing workers once they reach their thirties. Other jobs can be found in the growing service sector in neighboring townships and counties, where villagers can work as janitors, hair dressers, shop clerks, waiters, and cooks. But inland jobs do not pay as generously as construction jobs in coastal cities. One thirty-year-old Faming Village man, for example, worked in a furniture factory in Chengdu City, the capital of Sichuan, about a four-hour bus commute from Faming. His monthly wage there was 1,200 RMB, and he rented a bed in a worker's dormitory, which reduced his monthly wage by 300 RMB. When he began working construction in Chengdu, the same inland city, he began earning 2,000 RMB per month, with promotions and pay raises expected. Now he works construction in Beijing, where he earns 3,000 RMB per month, before food and dormitory expenses are deducted at the end of the year.

This is an economic strategy shared by many villagers in Faming. It is the result of a failure of local development. Leader Cha, for example, views the privatization of the local mines as the primary problem plaguing Faming's economy and necessitating the outpouring of local labor to cities. Once the mines closed, Leader Cha told me, the county government attempted to support households by offering fertilizer and equipment subsidies to farmers. But in terms of generating local jobs, the county government could do little. "There used to be many factories nearby, in Leshan City," Leader Cha noted, "but industrial development is more complicated and higher level than agricultural development. We can give subsidies to farmers to boost agricultural growth. But for industries, well those subsidies are given out at a much higher level."

So when migrant labor became a viable option for villagers, village leaders welcomed it. Leader Cha was aware of the work that Boss Bo did to bring villagers into construction work. When in later years two Faming brothers known as the Gao brothers also became local labor brokers, Leader Cha thanked them himself. He never became a migrant, but he recognized that without local labor brokers, he would have to handle many more grievances from villagers. In many ways these labor brokers exercised more influence in villagers' lives than Leader Cha, whose primary work was to handle land disputes and family grievances and encourage villagers to purchase pensions through a nationwide rural pension scheme established in 2009. The elder Gao brother, after all, had built for his family a house far more grandiose than Cha's. Leader Cha left the business of employment to labor brokers. "People get jobs on their own, and they introduce their relatives and friends to bosses in the city. . . . [T]hey have their own ways."

Villagers also found ways to coordinate these construction jobs with their families' needs. In particular, construction jobs work well—better than factory jobs, in fact—for families with children to care for. One villager, Auntie Luo, a thirty-eight-year-old woman I met the day I arrived in Faming Village, worked in a coastal factory until she married, then stayed in the village to farm while her husband worked construction. Auntie Luo was tall and heavyset, and was well-liked for her blunt wit. Since her days as a factory girl, Auntie Luo had dipped in and out of sporadic illness. She had poor face color, the villagers said, but the more likely culprit was hepatitis. But the real reason Auntie Luo no longer worked in the factories was not health related. When Auntie Luo worked in the factories, she was single and could not seem to save up her wages. "I never saved a mao to send back home," she told me. "I couldn't; every month I'd make 1,000 yuan and all of it would go to food and other living costs in the city." Then she came home to the village. But things there were the same. All farming was subsistence oriented, due to the small size of the plots. "In the village, we break our backs to grow enough rice to eat for the year, but we have not a mao to show for it."

Things changed after Auntie Luo married. Her husband, Luo Guangleng, usually worked in construction but sometimes in nearby coal mines that had not yet closed down. She quit her factory job and kept house in the village, farming her land, raising her son, and caring for her aging parents-in-law. While she stayed behind, Luo Guangleng usually worked construction, and with his higher wages he could cover his food and housing costs in the city and still have money left over when he returned home. It minimized costs to have only one household member—the higher-earning member—actively incurring living costs in cities.

Auntie Luo had aging parents-in-law; she also had a bachelor uncle, and these elders lived with her own nuclear family. Her son was twelve years old. She cooked for her elders and looked after her son; she farmed all of their land plots diligently, and considered that labor just as central to the household livelihood as her husband's work. The day we met, she had just been hospitalized for her hepatitis. However, she had left the hospital prematurely, against her doctor's wishes. The doctor had cautioned her: "Where do you think you are going? Toward an early death?" Auntie Luo's eyes flashed as she recounted the story. "I told him, 'I am a peasant! I am worried about the harvest!'" The crop kept the entire household fed while they all awaited Luo Guangleng's return. He returned home each year with money left over. In this way, the introduction of construction work to Faming Village created split-household strategies that involved leaving one member of the household tied to farming while the other worked in the city.

HISTORICAL EVOLUTION OF MIGRATION

What are the original policies, prior to the current transformation, that created the split-household arrangements in Faming? These household

arrangements were the result of larger institutional shifts that transformed the countryside into a holding pen for surplus and redundant
labor. One change was the reforms that pushed rural labor out of the
countryside, namely a 1994 privatization wave that targeted rural collective industries, slowly bankrupting most of them while leaving many
larger state enterprises, mainly located in cities, untouched.[2] A shift in
bank lending policies halted loans to small rural businesses, resulting in a
gradual disappearance of rural jobs.[3] Rural people were forced to seek
work in cities. These reforms bankrupted the Faming mines and hindered
the spread of an indigenous entrepreneurial sector in Faming that might
otherwise have replaced them.

Another change was the reforms that allowed Auntie Luo and Luo
Guangleng to seek work in cities and permitted employers to employ
them. These were gradual market reforms after 1978, which loosened the
institutional structure of the previous socialist system, designed originally
from 1950 to 1958 to establish a "unified allocation" of rural labor to agricultural production and urban labor to industrial production in cities.

For this to happen, the population had to be pinned down, in terms of
both mobility and occupation. To this end, in 1952 the socialist state had
established a nationwide *hukou* register, which recorded China's population according to their residential (rural or urban) and occupational
(agricultural or nonagricultural) status. This created four categories of
citizenship: urban nonagricultural (urban workers), urban agricultural
(suburban peasants), rural nonagricultural (workers in state or collective
enterprises in rural areas), and rural agricultural (rural peasants).[4] Most
rural residents were registered at birth to the agricultural occupation,
which restricted them to employment on communes. Urban residents,
meanwhile, were assigned to work units in industry.[5] This division of
labor placed rural agriculture in the service of urban industries. Communes
produced grain quotas that were distributed to urban workers as part of
the socialist dream in cities. Urbanites enjoyed full employment with full
benefits in urban industries, including grain ration coupons for each
household member.

The loosening of this system after 1978 had the effect of diverting rural
labor from communes to urban industry.[6] It did so without emptying out the
countryside. This was accomplished through a historically unprecedented

egalitarian wave of land reform. The first step of this reform was the dismantling of the commune, and the second was the decollectivization of former
commune land, breaking it up into small plots and allowing households to
cultivate crops for subsistence.[7]

From 1952 to 1982, all land in China was state owned. After 1982, rural
land—defined as all land not located within the jurisdiction of municipal
governments—became collectively owned. This gave village collectives the
right to allocate land as they saw fit. In most regions this involved distrib-
uting use rights to small plots of land to all residents registered at birth or
by marriage in the local *hukou* register.[8] These plots averaged 1.7 mu (.16
acre) per member.[9] They ensured a baseline subsistence level for all rural
people. This was particularly true after the 1979 implementation of a
household responsibility system, a policy accompanying land decollectivization that allowed each household to retain any crops left over after the
mandatory sale of a specified quota to the state. This coincided with a
sudden spurt in agricultural productivity, which it is estimated made
between 100 million and 156 million farmers, or between 35 and 55 percent of the rural population, free to seek off-farm employment.[10]

In Faming in 2010 land plots were a central concern of most families.
Though some, particularly families of younger migrants, left their village
land fallow, even these migrants lent their desirable land plots to kin and
neighbors in exchange for a small portion of the rice crop. All villagers
enjoyed the psychological security of knowing that they still had land in
the village. They considered their land-as-security attitude superior to any
alternative. For example, when Little Deng's wife Yue-na once mentioned
Shuang-ba Village to the north, she expressed skepticism. There, villagers
had ceded their right to use land for their own subsistence needs, and all
farming was dictated by county-level agribusinesses that determined
which crops households were to plant and which fertilizers they were to
use. Yue-na was wary of the risks involved in making farming market oriented: "They seem to make money [for now], but who knows what they
do if there is flooding or a drought."

When privatization hit Faming Village, universalized land rights
allowed villagers to make the livelihood calculation that Yue-na, Auntie
Luo, and Luo Guangleng made. Today, the occupational (agricultural or
nonagricultural) category of *hukou* registration is all but defunct. But the

residential restrictions remain in place insofar as rural people are still largely barred, by *hukou* policy, from registering for long-term residence in cities. Without urban residential registration, they cannot access housing subsidies or mortgages at reasonable rates.[11] This is why Auntie Luo and Luo Guangleng could not both simultaneously work in a nearby city. So they relied on the land for security.

The dynamics of the construction industry amplify and reinforce the uneven relationship between the rural and urban economies. Faming Village, for example, had a relatively more egalitarian rural social structure during its mining period than in its construction period. During the 1980s rural-urban household-level and fiscal inequality in China remained low.[12] This was attributable to many factors, among them the availability of rural employment as well as the ownership structure of collective TVEs, which shared a portion of profits with laborers via wage increases, social benefits, and grain bonuses.[13] Rural households could dispatch several members to work in rural enterprises without leaving the village. This arrangement was directly encouraged by central state officials, who exhorted rural people to "leave the land but not the village" (*li tu bu li xiang*).[14] It was also the arrangement that Arrighi first identified as a form of capital accumulation without dispossession. It brought rural labor into the industrial workforce without severing its dependence on land for subsistence and did so without initiating a one-way drainage of labor out of the countryside.

In the 1990s, as labor left the countryside, both average income and household income inequality levels grew. Average household incomes in the county where Faming is located rose nearly twofold throughout the 1990s, from 9,427 RMB in 1993 to 18,200 RMB annually in 2000.[15] Yet the gap between the richest quartile and the poorest quartile of households widened. By 2010 the wealthiest households in Faming Village were building on village land three-story houses whose costs of materials and labor totaled 150,000 RMB. One family purchased a high-rise apartment in a nearby county seat worth over 500,000 RMB.

Why did household-level inequality grow in Faming throughout reform? There are complex reasons for this. Income inequality had grown between two rural classes: households that engaged in wage-labor and subsistence farming and households that engaged in the entrepreneurial brokerage of labor. The classes engaged in realms of economic activity that were separate but intertwined; one could not exist without the other. But they were symbiotically linked, in that entrepreneurial brokers recruited laborers who could rely on the subsistence-based farming economy to supplement their low and irregular wages.

A FEMINIZED AGRICULTURAL ECONOMY

How are households arranged so that subsistence-based farming supports labor migration? In Faming the social structure that supported migration was distinctly gendered. This is because construction, a male-dominated industry, was the main source of livelihood, and the villagers doing the waiting in Faming were predominantly women. In 2010 in Faming Village, of the approximately thirty-two households that comprised Section 8, twenty-two households were inhabited year-round by women while men worked in urban construction. They were engaged in "safety-first" family farming, cultivating a crop that could sustain the household in case year-end wages did not materialize. On a larger level, many scholars have recently documented a trend of feminization of subsistence agriculture coinciding with the rise of labor migration.[16] Many factors likely account for this phenomenon on a nationwide level, but in Faming it was the predominance of construction work as a source of livelihood that compelled many women to stay on village land.

Of course the spread of construction work to Faming Village was path dependent. The first excursion of Famingers into construction work was a chance phenomenon, initiated by the arrival of Boss Bo in 1992. But in the following years construction workers began to organize their household affairs in ways to support future years of migration. After the first generation of migration into construction work, Faming villagers had built a web of gendered expectations, reciprocal mutual aid, and hierarchical authority structures that helped them coordinate present and future generations of migrant labor.

These gendered expectations enforced a strict division of labor: men migrated, women farmed. In migrant households, the work of women—farm chores, pig cultivation, child care—is considered one side of a gendered bargain, a necessary condition enabling men to work without worry and eventually remit wages. Yue-na herself describes the division of labor in her household in spatial terms: Little Deng earns wages in cities, while she manages the harvest in the village:

> He does his part in the city, and I do my part here in the country. In the end I rarely ask him about his work in the city, and the most he wants to know about farm work is to ask how many chicks hatched in the roost, how many baby pigs we have this year. He was never any help to me at harvest anyway. I trust him in the city and he trusts me here at home.

Although many younger women, and those with vocational training or who had continued past a middle school education, tended to prefer city life, the norm among women whose husbands worked in construction was to valorize farmwork. For example, Madam Gao was known for her diligent work on the farm, and she was widely respected for it. One younger woman commented of Madam Gao, "When her husband is away, she is always working in the fields. . . . Even though they are the richest household in the village, Madam Gao . . . still raises pigs, and does farm work, and plants a crop."

In the daily life of village residents, the activities of men such as Big Gao were not immediately apparent. His business was dependent on the influence of Madam Gao. He relied on her to ensure that each of his workers had a dutiful wife farming his land. This way, during years when he was periodically unable to pay wages on time, his workers' families could still maintain a baseline level of subsistence at home. Big Gao needed Madam Gao to police the wayward wives of his newer migrants, and she exercised the moral authority to do so thanks to him. Villagers deferred to the Gaos because their household was the wealthiest in the village. When the time came for migrants' families to collect small loans for house construction, many families were likely to turn to Madam Gao—particularly those villagers who were or had in the past been employed by Big Gao. Madam Gao would then visit close members of her husband's network, calling upon each household for a small contribution. She herself was likely to contribute as well. It was in her family's interest to contribute, as any migrant indebted to her husband could be counted on to remain in his employ over the long term.

This ideal of women's agrarian domesticity was important particularly for young women, among whom leaving for cities was a rite of passage.

Nearly all young women in Faming left the village to work in factories in coastal cities, most after they finished middle school. Some chose to work in hotels and salons in more local counties and cities. It was not an automatic decision for a young woman to return to work on the farm. But such a decision was in the interest of the larger household, which could not forgo the security that farming provided.

In Faming, when young women became engaged it was customary that they make plans to return to the village eventually. Yue-na, for example, had worked in a furniture factory in Chengdu for two years after she married, but once her son came, she returned home. She, like many village women, was critical of younger women who were tempted to do otherwise. When a twenty-five-year-old village girl named Huang Rong returned to her job in a factory in Guangzhou after she became engaged to a village man, for example, Yue-na expressed her displeasure. "While her fiancé is out working, she wanders everywhere," she commented; here, "everywhere" implies the possibility of promiscuity. Yue-na believed that it was proper for an engaged woman to stop seeking employment upon marriage, as she herself had after she became engaged to Little Deng.

The expectation that women in Faming will "retire" from migration when they marry is overwhelmingly reinforced not by men but rather by other women. Auntie Luo was particularly opinionated on the issue. When Huang Rong attended a village banquet with permed hair and a stylish dress, Auntie Luo offered a caustic remark: "She looks like a city girl!" It was not meant as a compliment. "There is nothing we can do about young people like that," Auntie Luo explained later. "This is how young people are nowadays. Even if you teach them right from wrong in childhood, they go to the city and they take on city airs." Many village women viewed the labor migrations of young women such as Huang Rong as youthful diversions that should be temporary.

AN ENTREPRENEURIAL BROKERAGE ECONOMY

While a feminized subsistence farming economy supports the needs of migrants, migrant men operate within a high-risk world of migration. The economy of migration, moreover, is formed around a vertical chain of

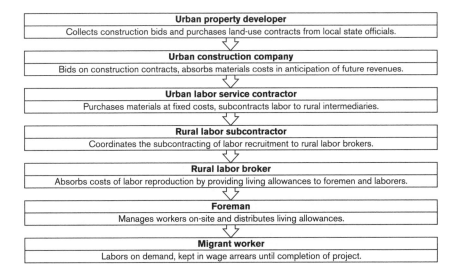

Figure 4. Construction subcontracting system. *Source:* Pun and Huilin (2010).

subcontracting, designed to delay labor costs for employers while shifting the risks of wage arrears downward onto villagers. Yet the higher migrants ascend in the hierarchy of subcontracting, the more rewards they can reap. This possibility of promotion, moreover, keeps migrants working for subcontractors whom they rarely meet and for brokers whose ranks they wish to join.

Labor subcontracting in construction in its current form emerged throughout the 1990s (see figure 4). During that decade, urban enterprises ramped up the pace and scope of construction and eventually began to bypass the municipal labor service contractors that had conventionally fulfilled their labor recruitment needs. Today, most contracts with rural county-level labor subcontractors are located closer to villages than the municipal service agencies.[17] These rural subcontractors have direct access to village brokers—entrepreneurial men who can be relied on to recruit and manage small teams of workers.

Labor brokerage was a pricey and risky venture. On occasion, subcontractors delayed wage payment even beyond the end of the year of labor, sometimes claiming insolvency themselves and then promising to pay the previous year's wages during the following year. In these situations, brokers not wishing to alienate their labor supply had to pay wages to needy work-ers upfront and then seek reimbursement later. For these reasons, Boss Bo was able to begin brokering labor in Faming only after he had saved wages from nearly a decade of migrant labor himself. The Gao brothers drew on earnings from their family's herb business to cover brokerage costs.

These brokers placed substantial capital at risk to maintain recruit-ment. In his first year brokering labor, Boss Bo's cousin Zeng recruited a team of fifteen villagers and netted annual earnings of 15,000 RMB, only marginally more than his average laborer. But once a broker began jug-gling multiple construction teams at multiple construction sites in cities, he could significantly increase his earnings. By 2010 Boss Zeng was earn-ing nearly 50,000 RMB per year. He had purchased a ten-year-old Volkswagen Jetta that he used to drive between his various construction sites in Beijing. He had also rented a one-room apartment on the outskirts of Beijing, which he used during the construction year.

Compare this with the annual pay of a novice worker. In 2010 a new laborer in Faming was paid a 1,800 RMB monthly wage and was employed for ten months. After deductions for living allowances, food, and travel costs, he received only 12,000 RMB for ten months of work. A more experi-enced worker might earn more than twice that, up to 30,000 RMB per year.

At present, promotions from laborer to broker status are rare but highly coveted. Many laborers with aspirations toward brokerage tend to stay employed by a single broker throughout their careers in hopes of increas-ing their social access to that broker's subcontractors in cities. A typical broker recruits laborers to fill multiple sites. At each, he appoints a fore-man to manage workers in his absence, while he cultivates new relation-ships with subcontractors and moves between his sites to defuse problems. The worker who becomes a foreman, moreover, gains direct access to the subcontractor at his respective site, usually hoping that this subcontractor might come to rely upon him to broker the labor himself in the future. For example, Boss Bo's brother-in-law was Little Deng, Yue-na's husband. He began as a carpenter, but after ten years of working construction he had been promoted to the position of foreman. It was his responsibility to manage productivity and prevent attrition among the Faming villagers who worked for Boss Bo. In 2009 he earned, by his count, 35,000 RMB after all deductions.

Such promotions could be difficult to arrange, however, due to the upfront costs that even foremen faced upon promotion. For example, in 2007, the first year that Little Deng was appointed by his brother-in-law Boss Bo to become a foreman, Little Deng was charged with providing daily on-site management for one of Boss Bo's labor brigades at a Beijing worksite, but he had trouble supporting his workers in Beijing. Little Deng received an appeal from one Faming laborer, citing a family emergency, for a personal loan of 700 RMB. The laborer, under immediate financial duress, asked Little Deng to advance him the cash under the condition that Deng would later deduct the sum from the laborer's year-end wages. Boss Bo had already left the worksite, and the matter was left to Little Deng for resolution.

Primary among the qualifications for labor brokerage is the ability to underwrite temporary debt obligations, as this capacity is essential to worker satisfaction. Little Deng did not know this at the time. When the Faming supplicant asked Little Deng for the loan, he did so knowing that Boss Bo had recently disbursed to Little Deng the team's living allowances for the month. Bo was said to have left Little Deng an envelope containing 4,000 RMB to distribute to the fifteen-man team in small sums, 100 RMB per laborer every ten days. The team watched as Little Deng contemplated the loan request. Many of the men had expected Deng, their protector in Boss Bo's absence, to deduct the sum from Boss Bo's monthly disbursement, then borrow money through his personal network to make up the living allowance fund later in the month. But Little Deng, wary of the ever-present possibility of wage arrears, was reluctant to take on the personal debt.

As Deng refused the supplicant, he unknowingly incited a low rumble of worry among the Faming workers. When Boss Bo heard of the incident, he returned to the worksite, paid the loan to the supplicant, then demoted Little Deng and replaced him with another worker. To Boss Bo, the situation was indicative of Little Deng's ineptitude for brokerage and his unsuitability for further promotion within the labor recruitment system. According to Boss Bo,

> If it is me, if a worker comes to me and says, "I have a family emergency, I need 700 RMB right now." Then I give it right to him right away. How does Little Deng approach this same situation? He is afraid that this project will not pay out. . . . He is thinking like a worker, not thinking like a foreman. . . .

The laborers too will sense that Little Deng is afraid of the investment risk. . . . [They will] worry that they will not get their wages. . . . He looks selfish in their eyes; he looks like he is only really worried about his own pocketbook. So they will think, well, if he is worried about getting paid too, then what are we doing here?

As Boss Bo explains, informal moneylending provides a signal of a broker's capacity to provide for and pay his laborers. In this light, Little Deng's refusal to put himself 700 RMB in debt was a failure of management. It disrupted the tranquility of a team of expectant migrants, creating suspicions of financial insecurity. After that year, Boss Bo no longer employed Little Deng as a foreman.

VILLAGE TIES AND LABOR DISCIPLINING

How are the two realms of economic activity in Faming Village—subsistence farming and labor brokerage—mutually reinforcing? As previously stated, households use subsistence farming to hedge risks of wage arrears. But brokers also call upon the village economy for support in their own activities. They do so because labor recruitment is a tenuous task, rife with inherent tensions.

Labor subcontracting creates a central tension. Brokers must discipline their workers and manage their productivity, and workers must find brokers who are trustworthy and will pay wages and living stipends on time. These interests often put villagers at cross-purposes. Labor brokerage asks a lot of brokers. It requires them to keep workers in arrears until the end of each year while still maintaining the latter's consent to long-term employment. It requires them to keep labor turnover down, minimizing the costs of on-the-job training and preventing shortages in their labor deliveries to subcontractors every year. Conversely, the same arrangement hampers workers' ability to switch employers freely, since new brokers— particularly those who are neither local nor from the same origin village— often leave workers unpaid if they can move on to a new labor source in subsequent years.

In Faming Village there are three primary labor brokers. The elder Gao brother, Big Gao, is the village's biggest broker. He recruits up to forty

Faming men each year to work for subcontractor Little Liu, an old middle school classmate who holds multiple contracts with construction enterprises in Xi'an City and Beijing. His younger brother, Little Gao, runs a slightly smaller migrant network.

Another Faming man, Chen Lehai, is a relatively unseasoned broker. He has worked for over ten years as a cement layer and foreman and every year makes arrangements with a county labor contractor to bring about twenty Faming men to construction sites in Tianjin. He returns there after the Chinese New Year with the same men he comes home with each year.

It behooved migrants to stay loyal to these local brokers. When laborers occasionally switched brokers, they often encountered trouble. First, they could have trouble getting paid. It was true, as the Gao brothers took every opportunity to point out, that nonlocal brokers could abscond with their wages with impunity. "They don't treat you like family like we do," he often intoned to new recruits. "Outsiders will not invest in your future." One Faming laborer, Liu Guang, spent 2010 working for a broker from the county seat whom he had met on the train during a previous migration. But when the time had come to distribute wages, the broker had taken Liu Guang aside to explain that his share of wages had been reduced to half of what he had been expecting, due to his lagging productivity during the second half of the year. Neither the broker nor anyone else had informed Liu Guang of any such productivity issues prior to that moment, and he suspected his broker had pocketed the other half of his wages. But Liu Guang had no allies on that work team to support his claims.

Still, trust was not a sufficient basis for migrants' loyalty to brokers. Brokers such as Big Gao also took more paternalistic measures to ensure a regular migrant base. To this end, they enlisted their wives, back at home, to keep an eye on the wives of their recruited laborers. Big Gao, for example, entrusted Madam Gao to distribute mutual aid and personal loans among the wives of his many recruits back in Faming Village. One of the primary expenses that migrant households faced was housing renovation, and migrant households engaged in a network of informal lending to cover the costs of these renovations. Madam Gao coordinated this network and kept a small notebook in which she recorded debts. The houses were typically two-story houses, brightly tiled over sturdy concrete walls. The most ostentatious of these houses was owned by Big Gao and Madam Gao themselves, built with 150,000 RMB of saved earnings. The most modest house in Faming cost 40,000 RMB to build. Not many Faming households had accumulated sufficient savings to cover the full cost of their houses. They could take out bank loans for housing from the rural cooperative banks that serve many rural residents, but these loans came with high interest payments. Instead, most villagers turned to Madam Gao's network for help. The average family borrowed sums of 10,000 RMB from multiple parties, then paid back the money over time. Madam Gao's role within this lending scheme was helpful to Big Gao. It also created a conduit through which they could keep workers happy—by extending to their families loans for building houses, as well as mutual aid during harvest time.

One incident in particular highlights the efficacy of this system. In 2010 Big Gao had one worker in Faming who harbored grievances with management. He was Little Fatty, twenty-four years old, and he worked on Big Gao's team along with his father, a fifty-six-year-old man admittedly past his physical prime. That year Big Gao had sent the Faming team to Xi'an City, where they worked for a subcontractor friend of his. It was then that Little Fatty began noticing changes in his status within the Gao network:

> When we got to Xi'an, I noticed the subcontractor looked at my father differently from the rest of the workers. Several weeks later he fired my father. Said his work wasn't up to standard.

Little Fatty's objection to his father's treatment, however, had more to do with owed back pay. Though it was accepted as an informal norm that fired workers rarely received back wages, Little Fatty protested that his father was let go for reasons unrelated to performance. No subcontractor, he reasoned, should be allowed to use up an old man's labor for free, then fire him later to cut costs:

> Maybe I was being foolish but I kept on bringing it up. . . . At the end of the year, when it was time to pay up, only the other men got paid. The subcontractor told me he would put the money in my Postal Savings Bank account, but when I got home I checked and it wasn't there.

Little Fatty held Big Gao accountable for the firing. If the subcontractor would not pay his father the back wages, he reasoned, then Big Gao should have paid the wages. It was Big Gao, after all, who had delivered what the subcontractor considered a subpar workforce. He should pay the penalty for poor selection of recruits. When Big Gao disagreed, Little Fatty left the construction site to look for work elsewhere. Big Gao was now short two men. He needed to get Little Fatty back, as Fatty was well trained and had been useful to him in the past; it would be costly and bothersome to replace him with a novice recruit.

Wives were useful in such situations. To compel his return, Big Gao sent Madam Gao to influence Little Fatty's young wife, a twenty-one-year-old woman named Sister Hu. The couple had met while working in a factory in Shenzhen. Sister Hu was young, just eighteen when she met Little Fatty, and she moved to Faming to marry him from her home village in wealthy Guangdong Province. Some village women pitied her. There was a rumor that Sister Hu was "tricked" into marrying Little Fatty, who had wooed her with apocryphal stories about a supposedly wealthy factory-owning father back in Sichuan. Whether or not this was true, Sister Hu did speak often of her dissatisfaction with life in Faming. Life was less difficult in her natal village, and she had not fully acclimated to the gendered expectations of female agricultural labor in Faming:

> In Guangdong, nobody works as hard as people in Sichuan do. In Guangdong, we wake up late, around 9 or 10 a.m., eat breakfast, and then go to the market . . . [and] in the evening we all bathe and then put on pajamas and socialize, play *mahjiang*. Nobody does much farm work. We don't need to; we don't live off the crops like they do here. . . . It's all labor here. It was very hard for me to get used to.

This dissatisfaction with the life that Fatty had given her made Sister Hu a prime target; she was highly susceptible to outside influence.

Madam Gao was aware of the difficulties her husband was having managing Little Fatty. She also knew that Little Fatty might make a better worker if he were better domesticated and accountable to the remittance needs of his family. To this end, Madam Gao thought that she might influence Sister Hu to make demands of her husband. Gradually, throughout the summer, she insinuated herself into Sister Hu's trust. When Sister Hu's three-year-old son needed new clothes for the fall, Madam Gao collected old clothes from other village mothers to give to the young mother.

Eventually Sister Hu opened up, admitting to Madam Gao, "Sometimes, because my husband doesn't come home with money, I have nothing to eat, and I have to ask my husband's grandmother for rice and vegetables." When she heard this, Madam Gao offered Sister Hu a loan of 3,000 RMB. "This is a small gift so you can buy meat for your son," Madam Gao said when she presented Sister Hu with the cash, carefully placing clean bills on the crumbling hearth during a private visit to her household.

On a drafty winter evening when Sister Hu's three-year-old son was howling incessantly, Madam Gao suggested it was the cold that was to blame. "Sichuan winters are cold and dry. If you bathe him once a week he won't be as cold. I have my son take a bath once a day in the wintertime, to keep him warm." Sister Hu, who lived with Little Fatty's grandparents in their unrenovated, dirt-floored, one-room farmhouse, protested, "But my house is drafty in the wintertime, he'll catch cold." Madam Gao promptly changed gears, turning the conversation into a gentle inquiry into the financial state of Sister Hu's household. In the end, Madam Gao shared with the younger woman a common tactic for pressuring husbands into increasing remittances:

> You may not know this, but in this village, a man can build a one-story house with about 40,000 RMB, maybe even 30,000 RMB in saved wages. You can tell your husband that he must build you a house next year or you will leave him. Women can do that these days. You tell him to look at his son. Your son will start going to school in two years! And you still have no house to live in, you have to live in the old house with your husband's grandparents.

Though Big Gao had never explicitly suggested these tactics, Madam Gao knew that if Little Fatty worked hard and sent money home, her husband's problem would be solved just as Sister Hu's would. To this end, upon learning that Sister Hu had no cell phone and thus no way to contact Little Fatty, Madam Gao bought one for her and suggested she track down her hapless husband.

Other village women, too, had also taken note of Sister Hu's unhappiness in Faming. Their concern was motivated by sympathy. For example, Yue-na took care to invite Sister Hu to her family banquets, and she took on the project of teaching Sister Hu to knit a sweater for her son. "Her husband is not sending her money," she often commented upon returning from these social visits. "I would not be surprised if she took her son and returned to her mother's household in Guangdong." But other women also concluded, from Sister Hu's worries and Little Fatty's wayward tendencies, that the family's misfortunes originated from Little Fatty's disloyalty to Big Gao. Yue-na, for example, derided Little Fatty's choice of employers. "One year," she mused, "he even worked for a man he had only just met on a train. No wonder he has trouble getting paid."

The lesson that other migrants took from the incident was that perhaps it was better to stay with the Gao brothers despite whatever grievances they had. By winter 2010 the villagers had all the more reason to believe this. By then Sister Hu had made enough phone calls to her husband to compel his return to Faming. It turned out that Little Fatty had been only a five-hour train ride away the entire summer and fall. After leaving Big Gao's Beijing worksite, Little Fatty had secured a position on a middle school classmate's work team in a nearby city. Yet after several months there, he had argued with management over long work hours and quit. Upon quitting, he was told that his wages would be given to his classmate at the end of the year; this classmate would later deliver the pay to Little Fatty back in Faming. In the meantime, Little Fatty took a train to Emeishan, a tourist town to the north of Faming Village, and sought work there. Unsuccessful in his search for work, Little Fatty eventually returned to Faming Village, where he used his father's cell phone to make repeated calls to the middle school classmate who would purportedly return with his wages. The phone calls were never returned. Big Gao had been right, many villagers mused. Perhaps it was better to stay with Big Gao, despite whatever grievances one might have. Working for outsiders posed many more risks than working for even an exploitative native broker.

RECRUITMENT POLITICS

There were two reasons that villagers trusted local brokers such as Big Gao over others. One was that the variable labor demands of construction often created production bottlenecks, during which brokers often dismissed redundant workers, but which were quickly followed by speed-ups once the bottleneck disappeared. During such speed-ups, subcontractors were often at a loss for labor and turned to local villages to seek workers to carry out unfinished work before the end of the fiscal year. Little Fatty himself was once the victim of such a scheme. At the end of Little Fatty's own lost year, after he returned to Sister Hu empty-handed, he made one last play for pay. It was late December, and after calling upon his friends and acquaintances in the nearby township, many of whom had already returned home from a year's worth of work in anticipation of the February Lunar New Year, he heard about a short-term job opportunity. A labor contractor from faraway Hebei Province in the nearby county seat was hiring Faming villagers for construction on a bridge in Sichuan. The construction site was state funded; thus, the contractor assured Little Fatty that the wage rate was high: 260 RMB per day, more than twice what Little Gao's recruits earned in Beijing. The only complication was that the worker would get paid half of the wages at the time of service, with the other half in the following year, on the condition that he returned to work on the bridge the next year during Lunar New Year.

Little Fatty was not aware, as more veteran migrants were, that the job was meant to replace a worker previously dismissed. When the others heard of the same offer, they were skeptical. Yue-na explained:

> [Little Fatty] is going to get cheated by an outsider. Those kinds of construction sites are very black; they work you to death the first year, give you a little money, then work you to death the next year, then they disappear. Anyway all the labor contractors are outsiders, not from Sichuan. So, when they disappear you have no way of tracking them down.

Auntie Luo was present as well, and she continued Yue-na's line of thought:

> Why wouldn't this Hebei labor contractor bring men from Hebei? Why does he need to recruit Sichuan men instead? Most contractors will bring men from their own villages if the wages are going to be that good. Also, why are they only hiring men at the end of the year, these last two months before Spring Festival? All the other bridge workers have left to go home, and they have gotten paid. My guess is that the most black-hearted of the labor contractors have already paid their men for the work, but they still want to squeeze in a little more labor so they can finish the bridge on time. So they put the word out that they will pay these high wages to local men, and then they can get free surplus labor at the end of the year. Then next year, same

thing, they finish the project, and then the labor contractor disappears without paying the Sichuan men.

It is true that outside brokers are impossible to track down, and they may abscond in the middle of the night just before wages are due. Little Fatty, for his part, worked the job and was never paid even the half wages he was promised.

The second reason that Faming villagers worked for men such as Big Gao, even under paternalistic conditions, is more complex. Villagers widely believed that Big Gao and his brother did in fact treat Faming workers with greater respect than outside brokers did. But there was another reason for this apart from trust and reciprocity, namely that Big Gao and his brother Little Gao were not large-scale brokers. They operated on a single-village business model; they supplied multiple subcontractors with labor drawn solely from Faming Village. This was why it was important for Big Gao to compel Little Fatty's return to his employ, as he could not easily replace him with another migrant.

The feature of brokerage that was incrementally exploitative for migrants was not unfamiliarity, but expanded recruitment. For example, Boss Bo, the outsider from Landing who was the first to bring villagers into construction work, was not a native of the village. But he did attempt to establish long-term working relationships with Faming villagers. He had trust-based relationships with many villagers. His wife's brother was Little Deng, who had relocated from Landing Village to Faming when he married Yue-na. Little Deng was originally one of Boss Bo's many workers, and when he married into Faming Village, he created a conduit for Boss Bo to access more Faming migrants.

Boss Bo built Faming into his expanded migration network after an early migration, when he brought his Landing migrant brigade to Faming. At that time he brokered labor solely from Landing. During a period of unemployment, he and his recruits traveled to Faming, where they had heard that a coal processing plant was hiring workers. Thereafter, Boss Bo kept returning to Faming because he recognized the village as a potential long-term recruitment site, a place where he could build a long-term migrant network. Faming was a new site of migration, and the place then had no other local brokers who could traffic villagers to construction subcontractors in cities. The market was open, because there were as yet no other entrants.

Because Boss Bo was a multisited broker, he approached labor recruitment in a rather cavalier fashion. By 2010 Boss Bo, along with his cousin Boss Zeng, was regularly recruiting laborers from five discrete villages in Sichuan and Chongqing. Famingers found that Boss Bo was usually more concerned with making sure subcontractors continued to seek his services than with keeping villagers happy. Bo, unlike Big Gao, did not need to assuage discontented migrants to keep them in his labor supply, as he could easily replace a problem migrant with another migrant from another village. This led to more coercive, less paternalistic, employment practices. In 2007, for example, Boss Bo employed a team of Faming migrants yet did not pay any of them for the year's work. Instead, he promised wage payment at the beginning of the following year, provided they returned to the same construction site after the Lunar New Year. One villager recalled the incident:

> Boss Bo . . . did not allow us to leave the worksite even after work, and he [withheld] our weekly living allowances for certain rule violations. . . . [W] e never learned what they were. When the year was over and it came time to get paid, he told us there was a problem with the financing, and he would have the money for us when we came to work for him again next year.

It is a common practice to withhold wages to ensure a labor force for successive years. It is widely implemented by many brokers like Boss Bo, and it is the reason for exceptionally high rates of wage arrears and nonpayment in construction.[18] It is a relatively risk-free practice for a broker with an expansive migrant network. Indeed, if a couple of Faming villagers left Boss Bo's employ, he could simply call his contacts in Landing Village to acquire replacements. Such a managerial tactic would have been disastrous for Big Gao, however. He might have kept his twenty migrants in his employ for an additional year, but he undoubtedly would have lost the trust of the majority in successive years, and he would have had no place else to turn for recruitment.

Most Faming migrants saw large-scale brokers such as Boss Bo as risky employers. Local brokers such as Big Gao, of course, saw him as a threat to their livelihood. They themselves operated on a more local scale. Big

Gao regularly delivered labor only for his colleague Little Liu, a county-level subcontractor he had known for years. He wanted to establish working relationships with additional subcontractors who had construction contracts in more distant cities, but to do so he had to make ready a deployable labor force at home—and so it behooved him to maintain a reputation as the sole reliable source of employment in the village.

Many friends and associates of the Gao brothers also kept their distance from Little Deng, who regularly worked for his brother-in-law Boss Bo. They believed he occasionally poached villagers away from the Gaos by recruiting laborers to join him working for Boss Bo. Madam Gao, for one, provided some offhand commentary when she heard about Little Deng's bad year in 2010, during his forlorn and failed search for work. She was often an inscrutable woman and usually did not make even the slightest twitch when Little Deng's name came up in conversation. But when another villager first told her about Little Deng's return to Faming with no remittances in hand, she responded with a knowing glint in her eye:

> Little Deng is a clever man but it seems like nobody is clever enough to make it as a lone agent working for outsiders. You see, outsiders do not necessarily have the same values as us. Some of them see us as cheap labor. It is best to rely on locals and kin.

LABORERS AND BROKERS: TWO SEPARATE CLASSES

Two economic realms thus coexist in Faming Village: one a subsistence farming economy, the other a network of labor brokerage. They have developed symbiotically; brokerage in its current form, with delayed wage payments and local recruitment, has remained stable thanks to the confinement of women to a form of agriculture that defrays costs of food that would otherwise accrue during periods of arrears.

This arrangement has led to an across-the-board increase in the living standards of migrant households. As Sister Hu knew well, remittances built better lives. Madam Gao's house boasted three stories and four bedrooms. She had a refrigerator, a flat-screen TV, and a spinning clothes dryer. However, the improvements in lifestyle that migration brought did not lift all households equally. Notably, the lives of laborers did not improve as rapidly as those of brokers and their families. This was because brokerage in construction allowed brokers to recruit labor under conditions that offloaded all risks of wage nonpayment onto laborers.

If laboring households cannot easily accumulate savings, is there a way for them to close the gap that separates them from entrepreneurial households? One might consider the possibility that brokerage capital eventually trickles down, creating an indigenous economy in Faming Village that is autonomous from subsistence farming. Such an arrangement would over time equalize the bifurcated class structure between laboring households and entrepreneurial households.

Scholars have documented such trickle-down effects for other localities in rural China. For example, in her study of three rural counties in Jiangxi Province, located near China's more developed eastern coast, Rachel Murphy argues that return-migrants have created an indigenous economy by bringing back resources and know-how to establish shops, food stands, and small-scale commodity trade in their home villages.[19] This economy is undoubtedly shaped by the character of migrant networks in coastal regions, where migrants can work in nearby cities where they face fewer risks of wage arrears. There, closer rural-urban proximity also creates denser social connections and infrastructural spillover from cities: roads, local marketing structures, mutual aid, and information networks. In addition, the migrants in her study work in service and manufacturing, sectors in which labor recruitment, and therefore migration, does not require or create an intermediary class of rural brokers.

I also found trickle-down effects in research that I conducted outside of Faming Village. Directly to the north of Faming Village, in Shuang-ba County, the gendered household division of labor wherein men migrate and women farm is absent. Villagers indeed migrate for work, but they do not engage in the safety-first, split-household strategies that Famingers practice. This is because Shuang-ba's migrants do not seek work in construction. In contrast to Faming Village, Shuang-ba's local economy is thriving. Income from market-oriented farming provides villagers with a comfortable living. These earnings then trickle down, allowing young people to invest profitably in productive businesses. One young man purchased a truck for hauling vegetables and became a delivery man for local food vendors. Others open noodle shops or sell wholesale clothes in small stalls in the weekly township market. More than one villager is engaged in motorcycle repair, serving the many residents living in migrant enclaves on the margins of cities. Some of these productive entrepreneurial ventures are even long distance: Another villager, Fan Bing, used his family's farming earnings to open a snack and general goods store in Shenzhen, a coastal SEZ in south China:

> The first year we went out to Shenzhen, it was just my wife and I. My son went to work in a factory elsewhere. My wife and I rented a small place in Shenzhen, several hundred a month, and we bought snacks and noodles from a wholesaler, then sold them for a profit on a street near some factories. In several months we made over 10,000 RMB.

Notably, all of these ventures create capital exchanges that are autonomous from the farming economy. Fan Bing's general goods store, for example, became so successful that he shut down the watermelon farm that had generated the starting capital for the entire venture. He lent his land to a cousin to farm and collected no rent from it.

These counterfactuals reveal the particularity of Faming. In Faming, very little capital trickles down from labor brokerage activities into the local village economy. Rather than bringing wages and human capital, such as job skills and social connections, into village economies, construction creates an entrepreneurial class whose sole business is the transaction of human labor. In Faming, it leaves intact the feminized subsistence farming economy that exists solely so that households can withstand the wage arrears that make construction profitable for urban enterprises.

There are several reasons for this phenomenon. The first is infrastructural. In inland regions, particularly remote regions such as Sichuan, cities are distant from villages, and infrastructure such as highways and aquifers is built to service urban populations, to the exclusion of villagers. During my period of research, for example, a highway was being built that ran through Faming in order to link Sichuan's capital, Chengdu, to its north, with Leshan, a city directly to its south. There is no exit allowing drivers from the highway to access Faming or its neighboring villages, and the toll is prohibitive even for entrepreneurial villagers with vehicular access. At the time of my research, too, an aquifer was under construction at the village border that was intended to serve the growing middle-class residents of Qianwei, the nearest county seat. Villagers, in the meantime, drank from small wells dug in their own jurisdictional land. Faming Village is not infrastructurally linked to local marketing structures, hindering the growth of indigenous industries.

The second condition that creates Faming's bifurcated class structure is the character of the construction industry. Construction subcontracting necessitates a class of intermediaries who broker migrant labor under conditions so precarious that they must expand their brokerage network to profit. As geographer Doreen Massey writes, mobility is always differentiated— some "initiate flows and movement, others don't; some are more on the receiving-end of it than others"—and in Faming, those who initiate flows then channel their hard-won gains upward rather than downward, toward building social connections and making investments in cities rather than in the rural economy.[20]

Active labor brokers such as Big Gao continually channel their resources toward building social connections with urban subcontractors to expand their brokerage networks. Aside from home renovations, few migrants reinvest earnings in productive entrepreneurial activities within the village. This is a characteristic of migration particular to Faming Village and is due to its poor infrastructural access to cities and the employment of the majority of its population in construction, an industry in which profitability requires one group of migrants to recruit another group under exploitative conditions.

CONCLUSION

In rural China, migration represents an adaptation to the failure of local development. As access to local jobs declines, villagers seek out jobs in cities. In Faming, a chance event in the 1990s integrated the villagers quickly into an inter-village network of subcontractors and brokers in the construction industry. Construction soon proved an expedient solution. It was high paying enough that potential earnings outweighed the risk of wage arrears, a practice far more prevalent in construction than in other industries such as manufacturing or mining.

Construction jobs may have come to Faming in contingent fashion, but once there, they became incorporated in a livelihood strategy that interlocked conveniently with the dynamics of subsistence farming. In Faming, men sought construction jobs through local brokers, and women farmed land to defray subsistence costs. This split strategy reinforced a dual class structure; men such as Boss Bo cut deals with subcontractors in cities, and back in the village, women such as Auntie Luo sustained the farms that allowed families to survive until migrants returned home. These roles are interdependent. Boss Bo cannot deliver village labor to cities unless village laborers have the security of farmland for subsistence. A traditionally gendered division of labor helps turn villages into agrarian communities where mutual aid relationships form a bedrock for labor recruitment.

What is the importance of the fact that everyday life in regions such as Faming revolves around the tensions of labor brokerage? As this chapter has shown, the economy of migration facilitates a cycle of rural underdevelopment. Migrant remittances are disproportionately distributed to brokers, who use saved capital to expand their brokerage networks. Laborers, meanwhile, dissipate their meager earnings on housing and pensions, costs they bear in the absence of state support. Both capital flows serve to subsidize labor costs that the construction industry and the state would otherwise bear. The organization of the village economy has adapted to support a delayed wage payment scheme in construction that supports enterprises otherwise lacking access to state bank lending.

4 Rural/Urban Dualism

Wang Ting, a forty-four-year-old woman, is married to Chen Lehai, a labor broker in Faming Village. It was Lunar New Year, and she was in a particularly upbeat mood; the year had been particularly auspicious. Her daughter Wang Fei, age twenty-four, had recently become engaged to a coworker, a young fellow in Leshan City. He was of urban extraction, and he had plans to purchase a high-rise apartment in the nearby county seat. The two met when they worked together in a real estate agency in Leshan City, where he was her manager.

On a wintry day in January 2011, Wang Ting packed up pickled vegetables and meats in preparation for a trip to the city. When a motorcycle driver arrived to take her from her farmhouse in the hills to the nearby township bus station, he raised his eyebrows. "Leaving again? So soon? Where to now, the township or the county seat?" Wang Ting interpreted a demarcation of status in the driver's query and answered: "Chengdu City, actually. My daughter is marrying a young fellow in Leshan City; I am visiting her parents-in-law. They own property near Chengdu and he is planning on buying an apartment in the county seat when they marry." Wang Ting was eager to make known an urban affiliation that was hard won.

The marriage of their daughter would be a crowning event toward which Wang Ting and her husband had been working their entire lives. Chen Lehai regularly recruited twenty workers from Faming to work in carpentry with him in Tianjin City, just south of Beijing. For many years, after their daughter grew older, Wang Ting accompanied him there to find work in nearby factories. Their household had been low on income ever since they had taken out bank loans to cover the tuition for their daughter while she was attending a vocational school in Leshan City. They were still paying off these loans. They were also paying premiums on a social pension plan that they hoped would support them in old age, after Chen Lehai retired from the brokerage business. The couple planned to keep their rural *hukou* tied to their village land.

This chapter explores the obstacles that migrants face in becoming urban. Most migration scholars would expect, on the aggregate, a long-term trajectory similar to Wang Fei's: a second generation tending more toward resettlement in cities. But not all migrants can detach themselves from the subsistence farming economy that supports industries such as construction, and even fewer can meet the high costs of living in townships and cities. Low rural wages and rising urban consumption costs are produced by a single program of capital accumulation that is difficult to alter. In cities, employers seek out and underpay rural laborers, and rural laborers then maintain practices of subsistence farming to support this low pay. Village households with no other job options then continue to send migrants to seek these low wages from urban employers.

On a macroeconomic level, urban enterprises collect profits that accrue from the utilization of low-waged labor, and these profits circulate predominantly within the urban economy. Enterprises remit taxes to urban governments, funding social programs that service urban households. Urban consumption costs rise as capital is injected into cities. In the countryside, social programs are underfunded by local governments lacking a substantial industrial tax base of their own. With inadequate rural welfare programs to rely on, migrants channel the majority of their resources toward supporting elders and children back in rural homes. People such as Wang Ting and Chen Lehai have little left over to support their own relocation to cities.

SOCIAL MOBILITY VERSUS LABOR REPRODUCTION

A primary assumption in migration studies is that ongoing migration flows lead eventually to intergenerational upward mobility and a scale-up in quality of the labor force to more highly trained, educated migrants. Migration scholars such as Douglas Massey have explained this mechanism. Over time, origin communities such as Faming accumulate resources for migration. Migrants solidify information networks and social connections and accumulate human and economic capital that they pass on to younger generations.[1] Indeed, recent studies of the newest generations of China's rural migrants show that they are more likely to have more discretionary income, more likely to be graduates of vocational schools, and less likely to express interest in returning to farming.[2] Finally, *hukou* reforms have opened for some migrants a pathway to citizenship. In specific regions, rural residents who meet specific requirements, such as property ownership, particular job skills, a university degree, or a history of stable, formal employment, are able to apply for urban *hukou* status and gain access to more substantive rights. Scholars of migration would expect these factors to lead to a shift toward permanent rural-urban settlement rather than circulatory migration.

Many studies of rural-urban migrants in China have tended to focus on attributes of households and individuals and on how these shape decision making in a changing economic environment but have neglected the dynamics of labor recruitment and labor reproduction, which shape how resources are shared and distributed within origin communities.[3] In Faming Village, for example, the structure of wage payment in the construction industry creates real obstacles to urban relocation. Because the speculative character of the construction industry requires enterprises to undertake projects even before they secure financing, employers delay wage payment. Most migrant households thus adopt a gendered division of labor, wherein men work construction and women engage in subsistence farming.

Due to this gendered division of labor, many women in Faming migrate only during their youth, then return home when they marry. The trend has been observed in many rural contexts across China. Murphy cites a survey that reports 36 percent of rural migrants from the inland provinces of Jiangxi, Anhui, Hubei, and Sichuan having returned to their registered place of origin.[4] One survey finds that more than 28 percent of migrants from rural Sichuan and Anhui have returned after working in urban areas for an average of 2.9 years.[5]

Women in Faming speak of this casually. "We have a saying here," Auntie Luo tells me. "There are three big things in life for a villager. First, to find a wife. Second, to build a house. Third, to support one's parents." After a pause, Auntie Luo adds an addendum to the adage. "And all three require migrant labor." Auntie Luo had enjoyed her years working in a factory, where she had discretionary wages for entertainment and shopping. But her parents-in-law and uncle-in-law are still living in her household. "I would much rather be in the city again," she admitted to me. "I ask myself, why am I here? It's because of the three big things. Wife, house, parents. I've done the first two, now it is my parents that keep me at home." Auntie Luo often mused that if it were not for the number of aging dependents in her household, she and her husband might like to migrate to the city together rather than live apart for the majority of every year. She thought that at least this would be an option in later years after her parents-in-law passed and her son joined the workforce himself.

This pattern, wherein women eventually cease migrating and relegate themselves to the farm, is not simply a demographic cycle. It is part of the invisible work that goes into the production of a labor force. Recall Burawoy's argument (see chapter 1) that just as workers (such as Luo Guangleng) must be actively made available for employment, so too must a workforce be actively renewed through multiple generations. Both processes require invisible work, whether through the efforts of women like Auntie Luo or through larger social institutions such as the schools that educate future workers such as her son. Migration does not simply emerge as a response to persistent wage gaps between regions; instead, migrants were first freed from farmwork by the household responsibility system, then were selected, recruited, and delivered to employers by brokers. Moreover, construction selects migrants for employment based on the assumption that they are able to withstand delayed wage payment. While some migrants are available for employment, others must stay in villages in order to support the availability of active migrants.

MARRIAGE AND LABOR REPRODUCTION

In Faming some women, like Auntie Lou, return to the village to support the migrations of others, while others, like Wang Fei, become permanent migrants. Generational dynamics and social capital shape the distinction between those who return and those who migrate; younger women are more likely to settle in urban regions than are older women, and those who have linkages to the brokerage class are more likely to have the resources to invest in vocational training, entrepreneurial ventures, and other activities that facilitate settlement. However, in Faming Village, because so many households have intertwined interests, with the Gao brothers relying on migrant men to keep their contracts afloat, the community exerts normative pressure on younger women to return to the village and maintain the households that will help migrants withstand delayed wage payment. In particular, marriages between young villagers have become subject to increased scrutiny, since they establish the conditions under which men can underwrite the risks of migration.

Though young villagers are increasingly apt to find marriage partners while working in cities, several older Faming women still attempt to provide informal matchmaking services to young villagers. Little Deng's wife Yue-na was known for making several auspicious matches between young migrant men and village women. Elderly villagers often approached her with hopes that their daughters would marry high-earning migrant men. Those with sons consulted with Yue-na to find good farming women who would refrain from labor migration and run effective households in the village. Older villagers also urged their own children to marry suitable partners who would reproduce a status quo that would provide them with support. One older woman, living alone while her thirty-one-year-old migrant son had neither returned home nor remitted wages for five years, approached a local matchmaker with a direct appeal: "Find me a good village girl who will convince my son to return home more often!"

Yue-na had once been one of these good village girls. She met and married her husband Little Deng in Faming Village. She had been working in a furniture factory in Chengdu City, to the north. She met Little Deng when he came to Faming from his natal Landing Village while working with his brother-in-law, Boss Bo. Little Deng was working in a coal mine near Faming. Six months into working at the mine, Deng asked his older cousin if he knew of any single girls in Faming the cousin could introduce him to. Deng and Yue-na were introduced in the village by an older village woman.

Yue-na was initially resistant. She was from an impoverished family, her parents both being farmers who had never left the village. She was one of three daughters and was not interested in being courted by a man who would expect her to relocate to his home village, as was expected according to patrilineal marriage custom in rural China. Early on she signaled to Little Deng her intention of staying on her family land rather than relocating to his village. "I am from a poor family," she told him. "We have troubles; you might see what you can do about them. We walk half an hour to the nearest river for drinking water; we have no cow for plowing the rice paddies."

Several months later Little Deng responded by pouring his savings from the mine into hiring local villagers to dig a drinking well on Yue-na's parents' land and buying an ox for plowing. Yue-na was eventually moved to accept his proposal of marriage, under the condition that he cohabit with her and her parents on their land in Faming. After they married, the couple built a house on the family land, a split-family house with a newer, tiled portion for themselves attached to the older, brick-and-mortar farmhouse of Yue-na's parents.

Yue-na was well known in Faming for her success in securing for her parents the financial support of a wage-earning migrant. It was on this basis that, for example, she was approached in 2007 by the Huangs, an elderly farming couple who hoped that their three daughters would also marry similarly well. Mr. Huang had long before suffered an accidental injury that ended his wage-earning capacity, and he expressed his hope to find a migrant son-in-law who could remit wages to supplement his household income. Yue-na had such a migrant in mind for the Huangs: her husband's nephew, a thirty-year-old man named Deng Guang, then living in Landing Village.

Deng Guang was seeking a wife. At thirty, he was considered old for the marriage market, and he was painfully shy, but Yue-na assessed him to be of good moral constitution. Deng Guang had spent some time in Faming Village with Little Deng. The two men worked and migrated together nearly every year, and Deng Guang had taken to spending many of his Lunar New Year holidays with Little Deng. There was another reason that brought him to the village year after year, the idea that he too, like Little Deng, might settle down in Faming. The land in Faming was plentiful, and Deng Guang liked the feel of the place.

Deng Guang had another reason for wanting a wife in Faming Village. Back in his natal Landing Village, he had heard rumors of unpredictable changes in land policies. A former neighbor had lost his land rights and had been forced to relocate elsewhere. It was unclear what these policy changes actually were or why they were happening. But Deng Guang spent so much of his time living on construction sites that he had little time to find out more. What he did know was that when he spent time in Faming, he had the growing sense that life there would be more stable.

Yue-na thought that if one of the Huang daughters were a suitable match for Deng Guang, he could settle on the land of the Huang household. A good wife and a good piece of land could provide the support and stability that he needed to shield his household from the risks and debts of construction work. The eldest daughter, Huang Rong, age twenty-five, was at that time away working in a garment factory in Shenzhen, China. Yue-na set up a meeting for the next Lunar New Year and returned to Deng Guang with instructions:

> Don't get your hopes up. Don't set high expectations. I don't know their family so I can't vouch for them, but I liked what I saw. They are not rich, they are quite poor. But the girl can do farmwork, and she feeds the pigs every day. The parents are good people.

When the two finally met, Huang Rong's parents were overjoyed. Three years later, Deng Guang had proposed and the couple began building a new house on a plot of Huang Rong's family land in Faming. To build the house, Deng Guang sent nearly 58,000 RMB—his entire life savings, accumulated over a decade of construction work—to Huang Rong's parents. It would be a modern two-story house, complete with accommodations for her parents.

The most tenuous part of their marriage negotiation, however, was the basic division of labor the couple would share. Deng Guang would continue sending remittances, but he wanted Huang Rong to quit her factory job and farm the village land that would be the source of their security. Huang Rong, however, worked in a factory in Guangzhou, and she relished the job. She continued working in the factory during the entire period of their courtship, and when she occasionally returned home to Faming, it was usually for a short while. She had a coterie of girlfriends in the nearby county seat with whom she often stayed. Frequently, when she returned to Faming Village it was only for a few days to help her mother at harvest time; she then scampered off to the nearby county seat. One of her middle school classmates worked as a shop girl in a beauty salon, and Huang Rong stayed with her in an empty bunk in the storeroom behind the salon, where the shop girls slept.

This was a matter of particular consternation to Yue-na. When Yue-na had introduced Deng Guang to Huang Rong, she had been under the impression that Huang Rong was, as the girl's mother had reassured her, a "good village girl" who was suited to farming and domestic work. But during the engagement Huang Rong began to voice reservations about her future. "How do I say this?" she began one day. She was in a teahouse in the county seat near Faming Village, surrounded by several classmates from middle school. "I'm not excited, I'm nervous. I always knew this was coming. But I am not sure what to do." Later, she lamented her situation in private:

My mother, she is the one who is making me marry Deng Guang, she is from that old generation, where as soon as a girl gets married she has to stop working in the city, she is locked in her house like a prisoner. Doing farmwork, feeding the pigs, cleaning the house and cooking all day, that's what married women did in the old days. I want to still be able to go out to work in the city after I marry. I have a friend who married last year and she had a baby but she still works in the city. Her mother takes care of the baby. I plan to do that too.

Huang Rong was stuck in a difficult bind. She was an eldest daughter in a household with no sons, and her aging parents needed remittances from a migrant son-in-law in order to subsist. The house Deng Guang had built, combined with the remittance income he would provide, would support her parents and make for a more comfortable life than most in the village.

But the relationship was not to last. Soon unpleasant rumors began to circulate. One village woman told Yue-na that Huang Rong had been unfaithful to Deng Guang. Huang Rong had returned to the village in a "bad way"; a rumor circulated that she had surreptitiously gotten an abortion in a hospital in the county seat. Yue-na was furious: "When I first introduced Deng Guang to Huang Rong, I did not know what kind of girl she was. None of us did. She only became like this in the last several years. She learned poor habits in the city." Yue-na explicitly linked Huang Rong's "poor habits" with her exposure to city life, implying that had Huang Rong quit her factory job during her courtship, she would not have strayed away from Deng Guang.

After her abortion, Huang Rong bought a one-way train ticket and fled, along with a middle school classmate, to Guangzhou, where she sought work in another factory. Back in Faming, Huang Rong's parents, unable to pay Deng Guang back for the cost of the house, instead offered him the hand of another daughter in marriage. Deng Guang waved off the offer and went back to work. He chalked up the cost of the house as collateral damage. Huang Rong eventually returned to Faming Village, when her funds ran low. She found a job as a shop girl in a cosmetics store in the county seat and became romantically involved with a villager from the next town over.

The fact that many marriages in Faming were orchestrated around the risks of migration indicates the central function villages play in labor reproduction. Viewed from the perspective of origin communities, migration has a contradictory dynamic. On the one hand, migration exposes people to modern influences, and initial migrations tend to beget later migrations, as migrants accumulate experiences and social capital for future journeys. On the other hand, exclusionary policies in destination sites make migration a risky proposition, and employers capitalize on migrants' political vulnerabilities by instituting precarious employment arrangements, which migrants can only withstand with the support of households in origin communities. Thus, when labor reproduction functions are outsourced to origin communities, communities exert pressure on younger migrants to uphold old modes of support—through marriage and agrarian work, for example.

RURAL WELFARE STATE

The maintenance of a labor force requires that support flow in two directions, namely from those left behind to wage-earning migrants and from migrants to left-behind communities. Remittances from migrants pay for housing; inputs for fertilizer, seeds, and agricultural machinery; and increasingly, pensions for adult migrants anticipating underemployment in their twilight years. Moreover, because pensions for old-age support were not made available to migrant workers before 2009, many households must contend with channeling support to ballooning numbers of elderly members. Auntie Luo and Luo Guangleng, for example, saved their wages for ten years; then in 2000 they built a house for 70,000 RMB. In 2010 the couple finally finished paying off their house loans. Once their house was paid for, they began channeling support to their three elderly dependents: Luo Guangleng's parents and an unmarried uncle.

The New Rural Social Pension Scheme was only established in 2009; before then, rural residents relied on only two means-tested welfare programs for support. Neither the Rural Minimum Living Standards Scheme nor the Five Guarantees Scheme provided Luo Guangleng's elders with subsidies. This was because in Qianwei County, those with wage-earning migrant children were disqualified, on the assumption that they could receive a portion of migrant remittances.

In Faming, the number of aging farmers reliant on their migrant children for support was staggering. Leader Cha himself spent much of his time fielding a large and growing number of livelihood-related complaints from the village elderly. When these grievances came in, he encouraged villagers to apply for low-income welfare subsidies. But even those villagers who qualified for support received scant amounts: 82 RMB per month per qualifying member. Inevitably, Leader Cha would then summon adult children or next of kin to contribute resources to elder support. His directives, moreover, always assumed the availability of migrant remittances for contribution. "When old people come to me and say they have no livelihood source," Cha told me, "I require their children to come up with a certain amount of money to cover the elderly people's medical expenses and their consumption and subsistence needs." If this support was not available, he called for a portion of rice to be contributed to the elderly. But his usual assumption was that there was nearly always a kin relative, usually an adult child, who could channel remittance income to the elderly.

Even when the rural pension scheme is implemented, it too provides only scant support. To gain substantial benefits, enrollees must begin paying into the pension scheme more than fifteen years prior to retirement or otherwise contribute premiums far larger than the norm. Luo Guangleng's parents only began paying premiums a few years before retirement; as a result, they received a baseline, minimum level of pension support: 55 RMB per month. This problem of late enrollment is rampant. In 2015 the average pension benefit in the rural pension scheme, nationwide, was only 120 RMB per month.[6]

Only those who begin contributing to their pension fund early in their wage-earning years can expect pension benefits substantial enough to yield sufficient old-age support. All others who are unable to gain full support from pension benefits must rely on current migrants for support. The launch of the rural pension scheme thus created extra burdens for working-age migrants, who must purchase pensions for their own retirement while supporting older generations who receive insufficient state support. After Auntie Luo and Luo Guangleng had saved enough wages to pay off their house loans, they began to channel Luo Guangleng's wage remittances toward purchasing pension insurance for themselves. In the meantime, however, they had to continue to farm their land, which would provide subsistence for their elderly dependents.

The timing and overlap of these various financial burdens often delayed rural pension enrollment dates for migrants. Luo Guangleng and Auntie Luo, for example, spent so long paying down their housing debt that they were just beginning to pay into their pension at the time of this fieldwork. Their neighbors, Little Deng and Yue-na, were in a similar situation. Yue-na in particular felt panicked about the situation. She had attended several village meetings on the rural pension scheme and was so determined to enroll for the pension on time that she was considering taking out a loan from the Postal Savings Bank so that she and Little Deng could enroll, despite the fact that for the time being, most of their earnings was going to paying back villagers who had lent them money to build their house. She explained her thinking on the issue to Auntie Luo:

> The way the pension works, you are supposed to buy the pension and begin contributing very early, when you are in your thirties. But we farmers can't

afford that. The best we can do is buy it in our forties or fifties, and by then, it's too late to contribute for very many years. So we have to contribute the full amount every year. This loan is the only way to do this. Otherwise, if we buy the pension late in life and only contribute a very little amount for very few years, then we might as well have not bought the pension at all.

But when Auntie Luo told her husband Luo Guangleng about this idea, he was convinced that borrowing for pension enrollment was a swindle:

> The interest is so high that it will take you even longer to pay the sum off. It is a rip-off. You are taking on debt to create a pension, which is a loan from today to tomorrow. We farmers can't earn enough every year to support present costs, let alone make a loan toward tomorrow. They tell us to buy these pensions, but in the end if we can only take out high-interest loans to be able to buy them, then that should tell you something. It should tell you we should not be buying these pensions. We cannot afford them.

Yue-na was insistent, however: "You have the wrong idea. You have the old-fashioned idea. The system is different, they design it so that you can pay off the loan right before the pension begins paying you." Yue-na did not end up borrowing money for pension enrollment, partly because Little Deng's employment had become uncertain, and she was unsure they could meet the loan repayment schedule. The idea of borrowing to meet the payments necessary for pension enrollment had come to her via word of mouth from other villagers. Most in Faming were aware of the importance of pension enrollment but were themselves unable to make the payments due to overlapping financial burdens. The rural welfare state has spotty coverage. Welfare subsidies are available only for those without wage-earning kin, and the pension scheme works only for those able to enroll early in their wage-earning years.

PAYING FOR ACCESS TO CITIES

The incompleteness of the rural welfare and pension systems created a generational dependence in Faming, with many older residents relying on support from wage-earning migrants. This dependence exerted a centripetal pull on migrants, obligating them to remit wages and establish households in the village. Yet other reforms ongoing in cities were lowering the bar for migrants to transition to cities.

Would these new reforms create a viable alternative path for Faming migrants to resettle in urban regions? Since the beginning of urbanization reforms, the central state has been lifting *hukou* restrictions and funding vocational training and urban schools for migrant children in cities, thus opening the option of raising children in cities.[7] Yet obstacles to assimilation are still far more substantial in big, first-tier, coastal cities than in smaller, inland cities and county seats. In first-tier cities such as Beijing or Shanghai, migrant children can attend designated public schools and gain vocational training, but only if their parents attain the requisite temporary residence cards and proof of stable employment.[8] Even then, students are still barred from taking nationwide senior high school entrance exams in any city other than the county seat nearest to their place of birth. They must travel back to their hometowns to take this exam, and their parents must make the requisite arrangements for them to do so. One study has found that as a result of these disruptions, migrant children who accompany their parents to cities are less likely to be actively enrolled in school than nonmigrant children in either origin or destination sites.[9]

The education system requires rural children to enroll in high schools near their birthplaces, but the job market offers migrants far better opportunities in coastal, first-tier cities in greater proximity to foreign investment and global trade. Thus, even when migrant families break with the dual strategy of subsistence farming and migrant labor, they are rarely able to bring their children to the cities where they work. One villager in Faming, a thirty-year-old woman named Shu Li, is a case in point. Shu Li met her husband, Weimin, while working on an assembly line in a factory in Shenzhen City. Weimin came from northeast China—Heilongjiang Province, north of Beijing. Both of them found informal jobs in Beijing, she as a hotel maid and he as a construction worker. They were ambitious, and they rented a ramshackle hut on the outskirts of Beijing, commuting into the city. With his first paycheck, Weimin bought a desktop computer that he used to track stock prices for companies he heard were on the rise, such as Alibaba and JD.com.

When the couple had a son, they initially left him in the care of Weimin's parents in the northeast. After he reached school age, they enrolled him in a migrant school on the outskirts of Beijing. Shu Li was proud of the fact that her six-year-old son spoke standard Mandarin with precision. She enthusiastically embarked on a quest to learn what she could of navigating *hukou* regulations and Beijing-area middle schools. What were the differences between the Heilongjiang and Beijing senior high school entrance exams? Was it easier to test into a Beijing university from a Heilongjiang high school? Could they finagle a way for her son to attend high school in Beijing despite *hukou* restrictions? Shu Li spoke of fostering her child's creative impulses and enrolling her son in art and music lessons. She and Weimin planned to save their earnings for an apartment in a municipality in Heilongjiang.

In the meantime, however, Shu Li and Weimin tasted bitterness. They lived in an unheated, ramshackle hut in a migrant shantytown on the outer edges of Beijing. They cooked their meals outdoors on an electric hot plate, which they had hotwired to a stray wire connected to a faltering electricity source. Only one public bathroom served the shantytown, which housed hundreds of migrants. Shu Li and her husband kept their expenses in Beijing low. They had no safety net to fall back on if they suffered wage arrears. Shu Li was not like Wang Fei; she did not have a high school education, a formal, salaried job, or a father who was a labor broker. Weimin was not like Boss Bo; he was an ordinary worker, not a broker.

What Shu Li did have was the ability to observe rules in a changing game. In the hotel where she worked, she cleaned the rooms of international businessmen, and she tried to pick up some English to interact with them. She socialized with other young migrants she met in various workplaces, and once she learned about the range of jobs available to vocational school graduates in Beijing, she began sending money home to help her parents pay tuition for her brother to enroll in a vocational school in the Qianwei County seat.

Back in Faming, however, villagers were skeptical of Shu Li's affairs. Older villagers such as Auntie Luo looked askance at the fact that she did not support her farming parents in the usual ways. She did not cohabit with them, and she had not helped them update their dilapidated, stone farmhouse. Shu Li's parents farmed a full crop of rice to sell at the county market, and she did not return home to help them during harvest time. Yue-na was Shu Li's middle school friend. They had shared a desk for years, and she could see no difference between Shu Li and herself, neither of them having tested successfully into high school. Why should Shu Li be capable of chasing such lofty goals when, as far as she could see, it was only those who were entrepreneurial, like Boss Bo, who had the capital to purchase urban apartments and send their children to urban high schools? In casual gossip with other village women, Yue-na reduced the social ambitions of her old friend to a mere preference for urban living:

> [Shu Li] is not really a city person but she likes to enjoy the pleasures of city life. You see her parents live in that dilapidated house, and she doesn't yet have a house in [Heilongjiang] where her husband lives, but they like to treat these years in the city as a permanent thing when it is actually temporary. If I were her I would save the money for a house in the village, but then everyone is different.

Yue-na was unaware of how *hukou* transfer policies worked or what middle school options were open to migrant children in cities. She only knew that her own husband regularly encountered difficulties in the labor market, and it seemed naively hubristic for Shu Li to desire an urban apartment and an urban education for her son. In Faming only wealthy bosses could afford such things.

Still, when Shu Li returned to Faming with her six-year-old son, Yue-na could not help but compare her life with her old friend's. Shu Li wore designer sneakers with slim-cut jeans, and she and her son got off the bus at the township station carrying rolling luggage that she delicately lifted over the muddy piles of cow dung scattered through the fields along the walk to her parents' house. She gave her son daily homework lessons and listened to classical music with him. Yue-na's own parenting included purchasing daily vitamins she hoped would help her spindly son grow taller and stronger so he could handle migrant labor and tasking him with the daily chore of climbing barefoot into the pigsty to shovel out the feces. Privately, Yue-na thought that Shu Li was giving her son a confused upbringing, moving him to a city where he had no guarantee of high school eligibility.

STRADDLING RURAL AND URBAN SOCIETY

Shu Li was one of the few villagers in Faming who had moved her child to Beijing with her. Most villagers worked in first-tier cities such as Beijing or Guangzhou for the relatively higher wages but left their children with relatives back in the village until they could establish residence in a county seat near Faming. There they could qualify for urban *hukou* status and guarantee themselves a more permanent residence in a school system where their children would not face discrimination, be placed on an interminable waiting list for enrollment, or become subject to arbitrary fees.

Luo Jun, a construction worker in Faming Village, married a woman whose natal village is near Zunyi City, a midsized municipality in nearby Guizhou Province. Luo Jun has continued to work construction on various projects in Beijing and other cities, and until his daughter reached schooling age, she lived with her mother in the village near Zunyi. At that point Luo Jun's wife took a job as a shopkeeper in Zunyi City, and the family rented a small room there so their daughter could attend a middle school in Zunyi. While that particular school admits migrant children, it charges them an extra 600 RMB per school term, and in the past Luo Jun has faced arbitrary changes in the fee schedule.

Zunyi is a third-tier city, with lower requirements for urban *hukou* registration than Beijing. In Zunyi, rural *hukou* holders who have purchased property and worked in the city for five years are allowed to register under urban *hukou* status. So Luo Jun found work in Zunyi, and the couple purchased a high-rise apartment on the outskirts of the city. After five years he registered himself and his daughter as urban Zunyi residents, ensuring that she would no longer have to join the long waiting list of migrant children waiting to receive an urban education.

However, Luo Jun's wife retained her rural *hukou*, which is still registered with her natal household in the village near Zunyi. This was a deliberate decision. The down payment for the apartment exhausted the couple's savings, and the burden of subsequent mortgage payments made unaffordable the monthly premiums necessary for enrollment in the urban pension system. In lieu of a pension, Luo Jun and his wife plan to relocate to her farm land when they become unable to work and rely on agriculture for their livelihood. "I am not a labor broker," Luo Jun explains. "I cannot get rich doing migrant labor, but I can improve my family's conditions. Right now the important thing for us was to buy a house in the city, and I have this capability right now, to buy the house, so we did it." As for his retirement, Luo Jun reflects: "We'll think about the rest later."

In China the constituent parts of urban citizenship—access to education and a pension—have been administered as market transactions, made contingent upon successful buy-in. The awarding of Chongqing *hukou* status to Landing residents, for example, is contingent on proof of property ownership or formal employment, making *hukou* registration in a direct municipality accessible only to those with a firmer foothold in the urban labor market. These requirements exist to ensure that full admission into urban citizenship is only available to high-value migrants with desired skills and capital. They create a tiered hierarchy of mobility, according to which migrants must divert their resources toward gaining employment and purchasing property in cities before they relocate. As Luo Jun's case illustrates, the real difficulty of becoming urban is not in gaining admission to urban social programs, but rather in relinquishing rural land as security, given the out-of-pocket costs of urban social welfare.

Luo Jun was an ordinary migrant, one whose work still exposed him to risks of wage arrears, and this made the upward ascent into urban citizenship difficult. However, in Faming many brokers, like Chen Lehai and Boss Bo, accumulate earnings more rapidly and can handle the simultaneous financial burdens of property ownership, pension payments, health insurance, and school fees, attached to urban relocation. However, even brokers are still reliant on access to the village labor market for their earnings. Chen Lehai, for example, used brokerage earnings to pay for his daughter Wang Fei's vocational training. She now works as a receptionist at a real estate agency in Leshan City and will attain an urban *hukou* registration through marriage. Meanwhile, Chen Lehai and Wang Ting continue to rely on their rural land rights to support their subsistence farming and to provide a base from which they can continue to recruit laborers from their kin network in Faming Village.

Like Chen Lehai, Boss Bo has only partially moved into the urban world. Boss Bo accumulated enough to purchase, in early 2011, a commercially developed (non-public-housing) apartment unit priced at 544,000 RMB, in the center of the county seat near his home village of Landing, where he hopes real estate values will grow (see figure 5). The apartment sits empty for much of the year. The couple still owed 225,000 RMB in outstanding mortgage payments by the end of 2011; to meet these

Figure 5. Boss Bo's wife, Deng Liwen, posing in front of her farmhouse in Landing Village. Photo by author.

expenses, Boss Bo travels among his various contracts in Beijing or Chongqing. His wife, Deng Liwen, still lives in their farmhouse in the village (see figure 6), where she does not cultivate much of a crop, but she does keep up a public profile in the village to facilitate her husband's recruitment activities. They plan to keep their rural *hukou* registration for the rest of their lives, retaining their house in the village in case one of their two sons marries and wants to move into the apartment.

Even younger migrants whose livelihoods are unconnected to the agrarian economy are careful to retain their linkages to the village as a source of social support. Most relocate to third-tier cities and townships near their home villages so that they can still rely on support from kin in villages. Faming Village has five young migrants who have received higher education beyond high school. Among them are two who, like Wang Fei, attended vocational school, and three others who enrolled in universities. One recent college graduate described declining the opportunity, made

Figure 6. Deng Liwen in the county seat apartment she and Boss Bo purchased in 2011. Photo by author.

available upon university enrollment, to register for *hukou* papers in the city of his university. He was unsure whether he could get a job there, he explained, and wanted to keep open the option of returning to his parents' household during periods of unemployment. "The *hukou* is not important for me because I do not have a family," he said. Thus, he was not overly concerned with educating children or about his pension.

Another recent college graduate explained that most of his rural peers chose to transfer their *hukou* registration to county seats near their village homes. "Most of us buy apartments in the county seat nearby," he explained. "Then we can register for urban *hukou* and send our children to the urban county school. Even if we work in the next city over, we can leave the children with the grandparents in the countryside nearby and can go home very often." Such a solution makes available to migrants urban entitlements such as health care and schools without cutting them off from the support of the elderly rural generation.

REDRAWING THE *HUKOU* DIVIDE

The construction labor recruitment structure tethers laborers and brokers alike to villages, where functions of the labor reproduction process are located. Those who cross the rural-urban divide enjoy upgrades: better-funded pension schemes, higher quality schools, and access to superior health care. But the prerequisites for rural-to-urban *hukou* transfer are rigorous. Since the inception of the 2011 New National Urbanization Plan, municipalities administer a point-based system that awards eligibility for urban household registration based on applicants' property ownership, job tenure, educational background, and special training and skills.[10] To qualify for urban *hukou* eligibility in most municipalities, applicants must be formally employed at a salaried job, either in the private or the state sector, for at least five years. In the absence of a formal private sector or government job, rural residents may instead purchase property to demonstrate an intention of long-term settlement. Then, once resettled in cities, new urban *hukou* holders must also begin paying into the urban social pension fund before the age of forty-five in order to reap the primary reward of urban citizenship: a retirement free of farming labor.

This creates a double burden of paying off housing debt and covering pension premiums, all while leaving enough to cover the higher living costs of urban residence. Moreover, these cost burdens do not take into account the additional responsibilities of supporting the previous generation or investing in future generations. It is no wonder that Chen Lehai and Wang Ting exhausted their resources on their daughter's urban education and rural pensions for themselves, or that Boss Bo and Deng Liwen could purchase a county-seat apartment but refuse to exchange their rural land for an urban pension. They had little left over after one pricey investment and could not afford to lose their last source of security, their rural land. Recent research has documented the unwillingness of many migrants to trade their rural *hukou* for urban *hukou*. A 2012 survey conducted by the National Health and Family Planning Commission shows that although many migrants planned to stay in cities, very few intended to transfer their *hukou*.[11] A survey by Sichuan's Bureau of Statistics conducted in 2014 found that 90 percent of migrant workers did not want urban *hukou*.[12]

Hukou reforms therefore do not diminish the rural-urban divide; they merely redraw it elsewhere. Two factors exacerbate the difficulties of rural-to-urban transitions. The first is the construction subcontracting structure, in which financial risks devolve onto all migrants—brokers and laborers alike—and which they must withstand by relying on their land. Laborers such as Luo Guangleng and Little Deng still require their land for retirement, and even brokers such as Boss Bo and Chen Lehai must abstain from *hukou* transfer in order to retain their access to the village labor market. Construction creates a rural elite, but this rural elite rises on the condition of access to village markets. Therefore, even when the gateway to urban citizenship is opened, few migrants in Faming are able to cross over.

The second factor in redrawing the rural-urban divide is the contractualization of urban citizenship. When rural residents register as urban *hukou* holders, they are eligible to enroll in new pension and health insurance schemes, recently revamped under the welfare reforms of the 2000s. Yet migrants without formal employment face higher prices of enrollment with fewer benefits, since most pension and health insurance programs rely on employer contributions to subsidize costs assessed to the enrollee. For example, enrollment in urban health insurance requires application through an employer, a condition out of reach for entrepreneurial and informally or self-employed migrants.[13] Most rural migrants are employed in informal sectors such as construction or manufacturing, in which employers engage in widespread subcontracting practices, and which rarely provide benefits such as health insurance or pensions.

RURAL-URBAN DUALISM

Agrarian marriage norms still encourage women to return to the land, thus preserving the labor reproduction function of the village. In villages, recent pension reforms have created a generation of older migrants who enrolled too late to receive pension benefits sufficient for substantial old-age support. Working-age migrants therefore face pressure to remit their wages to kin left behind in villages. Despite current urbanization that has opened legal pathways for rural residents to secure access to the urban welfare state, few migrants in Faming are able to become urban. This reluctance to transition into urban citizenship is due to the contractualized character of the urban welfare state, as access to urban pensions, education, and health insurance is increasingly administered through market transactions, contingent upon successful buy-in. In particular, formal employment is a prerequisite for urban entitlements. Employer contributions to urban pensions and health insurance greatly reduce out-of-pocket costs for migrants. However, migrants are still excluded from the formal sector of urban employment, since many formal jobs in cities still require applicants to hold urban *hukou* status, and the industries that utilize rural labor are also highly susceptible to subcontracting. Informal employment confers few of the benefits that would otherwise ease the transition from rural to urban society.

Are opportunities for upward social mobility more prevalent in rural sites where the dominant industry is not structured around exploiting the symbiosis between migrant labor and subsistence farming to suppress wages? In Shuang-ba Village, the prosperous wholesale farming village north of Faming, migrants are few and households rarely consent to relinquish their land in exchange for urban *hukou* status. "Land is too important here," a Communist Party secretary in Shuang-ba offered by way of explanation, "so we do not buy urban pensions here." Instead, rates of enrollment in the rural pension scheme are far higher in Shuang-ba Village than in Faming. Even older villagers who were beyond the cut-off point for enrollment in the pension scheme could afford to pay higher premiums in order to compensate for their relatively short pay-in period before retirement. The majority of households in Shuang-ba reported income sources that included agriculture, but many ran small shops as well as engaging in market-oriented farming, and these ventures did not impose strict retirement.

Living standards in Shuang-ba reflect most households' long-term investment in village residence. Most houses are newly renovated and have modern appliances. Roads are paved, and villagers have running water and modern sewage systems. Higher rural industrial revenues mean that middle schools in Shuang-ba Village are better funded and have higher graduation rates than those in Faming. These improvements to rural life diminish the appeal of relocation to more urbanized locales.

Young, university-educated villagers in Shuang-ba, like their counterparts in Faming, strategically retain their rural *hukou* status as a fallback option. Of the villagers I met in Shuang-ba, I found only one with plans for urban relocation. Fan Bing, the noodle entrepreneur with a business in Shenzhen, is saving for a down payment on an apartment in the Qianwei County seat as well as an urban social pension that he and his wife will rely on for retirement.

Like Faming villagers, Shuang-ba villagers too face obstacles to urban relocation. Many are also informally employed and thus face exorbitant fees in cities. However, unlike Faming villagers, Shuang-ba villagers do not face pressures to remit wages to support older farming generations. Rates of migration in Shuang-ba are lower, and even nonmigrants are still able to pay into the rural pension scheme. Relatively less normative pressure is placed on young women to cease migration, since migration does not require households to function as bases for the maintenance of workers in precarious markets. In Shuang-ba, farming is seen as an entrepreneurial venture in which men and women alike engage in agricultural labor, negotiate prices with market buyers, and strategize product development. Farming is dynamic in Shuang-ba, but stagnant in Faming.

The dualism between subsistence farming and construction growth that developed in Faming is regionally variable, secured through a highly specific set of political and institutional dynamics. In Faming the closure of rural industries and the incidental arrival of Boss Bo in the 1990s created a path-dependent trajectory toward employment in construction. Over time norms surrounding marriage and migration solidified to accommodate the precarious labor recruitment practices in construction. Furthermore, because labor recruitment is localistic, with brokers relying on kin networks to yield a trustworthy and reliable labor source, exploitative labor practices gradually normalize within the local community. In Faming, unlike its neighboring Shuang-ba, an unequal symbiosis between the rural farming economy and the urban labor market has coalesced through the spread of construction work.

What are the costs of exiting this cycle of symbiosis? In Faming departures from collective norms inspire contradictory responses. Some villagers morally disparage migration practices that depart from the norm. One of Faming's residents, a former construction broker named Chen Zhong, was known for having severed all ties to the village economy. After net-working with urban construction subcontractors, he secured a formal, salaried job as an electrician in the electric company of the nearby county seat. After he secured the job, Chen Zhong stopped brokering labor and rented a room in the county seat. Several years later he purchased an apartment in Leshan City—a municipality located several hours away by bus. His land back in the village lay fallow.

Many women in Faming, however, saw Chen Zhong not as a success but as a cautionary tale. Chen Zhong had married a village woman before he became a broker; after his wife raised their two children, the couple divorced. At that point Chen Zhong relocated to Leshan, where he remar-ried. To Yue-na, for example, Chen Zhong's ascent into urban society was an abandonment of both his family and the rural community that had once supported him. "His ex-wife was from the village, but after he left her for another city woman, she started working in another city," Yue-na stated. The detail that shook her seemed to be the fact that Chen Zhong's ex-wife now had to support her children through migrant labor. "Now she doesn't come home often either," Yue-na added. Another woman in the village was quick to point out that when young Faming migrants, some Chen Zhong's former recruits, sought him out to ask about job opportuni-ties in the electric company, Chen Zhong rebuffed their inquiries.

Chen Zhong's departure broke with norms of reciprocity that govern the relationship between migrants and brokers, with migrants relying on brokers for protection and brokers depending on the reliability of their migrants to secure construction contracts. Unlike Boss Bo and Chen Lehai, Chen Zhong fully severed his reliance on the village market. His salaried job at the electric company was unique, as it provided him with a private urban pension plan with employer contributions and obviated the need to return to his land ever again.[14] Chen Zhong intended to file for a rural-to-urban *hukou* transfer in several years.

Publicly, however, villagers—particularly the men—were respectful of Chen Zhong. When he returned to Faming to take care of some paper-work, a gathering of men in the village market surrounded him. Chen responded only minimally, nodding at the crowd and raising his arm in reply. I stood at the edge of the scene, where Big Gao nudged me. "That is Boss Chen," he said. "He is the big boss in our village. He is the richest man in the village." Chen had helped the Gao brothers get started with their own construction brokerage business by introducing them to subcontractors in western Xi'an City with whom he had formerly worked. It was still to their advantage to continue currying Chen Zhong's favor, as who could know when he might one day recommend one of them for a job or contract in the industry.

LEWIS TURNING POINT

When migrants maintain households in the village, the village as a whole serves a labor reproduction function, providing a site where workers can return during periods of unemployment or retirement. Thus the continuation of the Arrighi developmental path, in which capital accumulation occurs in the absence of wholesale dispossession, is contingent on social policies and demographic shifts that keep migrants tethered to sites of labor reproduction. In addition, a range of sociostructural factors—gender, village organization, and age demographics—also mediates the relationship between those who migrate and those who stay behind. In Faming, the combination of high and uncertain educational costs in cities, incomplete welfare reform in the countryside, and a traditionally gendered division of household labor has ensured the continued availability of migrants able to withstand low wages.

The continued availability of surplus labor in rural China is in fact subject to substantial debate. Based on anecdotal observations of rising industrial wages combined with labor shortages in coastal cities in the mid-2000s, many scholars have posited that China has reached the Lewis turning point, a moment when the surplus rural labor supply is exhausted.[15] Some scholars have attributed this phenomenon to demographic changes, primarily the one-child policy, which has produced a shrinking share of the working-age population relative to those who have retired.[16] Others suggest that this labor shortage is created by a trickle-down effect of previous generations of migration, leading to increased education among future-generation migrants and a falling share of migrants entering the labor market through informal, blue-collar employment.[17] Another hypothesis is that as agricultural productivity rises through rural modernization initiatives, agricultural wages will rise relative to industrial wages and compel potential migrants to stay in the countryside. The low migration rates in Shuang-ba Village relative to Faming Village support such an argument. Finally, one argument suggests that the inland migration of capital, combined with *hukou* reforms that permit rural residents to relocate to urbanizing townships and counties near their origins, has pulled potential coastal migrants back inland. The labor shortage, in other words, is limited to coastal regions and is counterbalanced by an unobserved increase in surplus labor inland.

In Faming many potential coastal migrants are pulled inland by *hukou* reforms that make accessible urban residence in counties near their origins. This chapter thus provides anecdotal evidence for the latter argument on coastal labor shortages caused by new routes of upward social mobility for migrants in inland cities. But most of all, this chapter reveals the significance of social mechanisms of labor reproduction that are occluded in economic theories of labor supply, which simply assume the availability of labor given sufficient demographic supply. Changes in the availability of rural labor, in terms of both who is available and under what conditions, are shaped by localistic and path-dependent dynamics of village organization. For example, Faming Village supplies labor migrants, mainly men, for construction employment due to the development of localistic recruitment networks, while its neighboring Shuang-ba Village does not, due to policies that have increased agricultural productivity. In industries such as construction, the sourcing of labor is clustered, predicated on a social infrastructure that ensures that migrants receive support and access to public services that allow them to withstand risky migrations.

CONCLUSION

For a migrant labor force to be maintained and reproduced over time, laborers must be embedded in a community organized to help them withstand the risks of migration, and they must also be systematically excluded from substantive rights in their places of employment. This chapter has shown how this equilibrium is maintained. New pathways to urban citizenship come with high-cost barriers to entry. Costs of attaining urban *hukou* in cities are especially high for migrants without formal employment, since urban citizenship is becoming increasingly contractualized, with access to education, pensions, and health insurance contingent on employer contributions or other market transactions. At the same time, the rural welfare state offers incomplete coverage, with older residents past their working years by the time the pension scheme was launched largely relying on migrant children for support. Both factors contribute to keeping migrants tethered to the rural economy, even when they have ambitions to leave.

What factors have altered this equilibrium? The changes that are influencing the character of rural labor come from above, as rural governments face deficits and turn toward land development for fiscal recovery. Chapter 5 spotlights Landing Village, where the guarantee of rural land rights as a part of the rural social contract has eroded. A wave of rural modernization has overtaken the county, and the central source of profits in this rural modernization is village land: its expropriation from rural households and its sale to private developers.

5 Urbanization and the New Rural Economy

Early in 2011 Little Deng brought me to the home of Boss Bo to spend a year living in Landing Village. Little Deng had come to Landing to look after his parents, farmers who still lived in a farmhouse on a craggy cliff. He brought his cousin, Deng Guang, who had lost his savings on the house he had built for his former fiancée, Huang Rong. The two men were concerned about rumors they had heard the previous year. Just before Lunar New Year 2011, Boss Bo had called Little Deng with news. He had heard that a list of household names had been posted in the township store, and according to hearsay, these households held land that had been earmarked for expropriation. It was an early harbinger of what was to come.

In official parlance, rural land expropriation is often referred to as "trading land for welfare" (*tudi huan shebao*). This very phrase evokes the Polanyian concept of land as a part of nature whose commodification dislocates the livelihoods of those who rely on it for sustenance.[1] In China, where a socialist legacy made universal rural land-use rights into a part of the rural social contract, the revocation of rural land rights means the disruption of livelihoods, which the state mends by expanding the urban welfare state. Yet the urban welfare state, as villagers discover, does not confer benefits equally on residents who are dislocated from rural land.

In the countryside, rural *hukou* status guarantees use rights to land, but although land provides security, it is also a yoke, confining rural people to a subsistence-oriented farming economy that is considered outside of the purview of state responsibility. Rural land rights are the reason that entitlements such as unemployment benefits are not available to rural residents. In the eyes of the state, the rural unemployed can always retreat to farming during periods of unemployment.[2] Therefore, land rights, in the words of T. H. Marshall, are "not . . . an integral part of the rights of the citizen, but . . . an alternative to them."[3] The admission of rural residents into the urban *hukou* regime is therefore considered an upgrade, reflected metaphorically in the policy makers' reference to rural-urban integration as a way of "letting farmers upstairs" (*rang nongmin shanglou*).

The rescinding of rights to land is the crux of the ongoing transition from a mode of development based on the commodification of rural labor to one based on the commodification of rural land. Previously the state upheld collective rural land rights, leaving land values untapped, in favor of establishing a reserve army of labor. Now the Qijiang County government has terminated collective rural land rights, largely by upgrading the rural residents who live on this land to urban *hukou* status. However, this presents a problem for governments intending to use land commodification as a revenue source. As the population of urban-registered households increases, the cost of delivering public goods and welfare provisions to the urban population grows. As this chapter shows, local governments often minimize funding to urban welfare programs by changing eligibility requirements and lowering subsidies for recipients. This dynamic dilutes the value of urban citizenship. Whereas land was a yoke that made rural people available to work for below-subsistence wages, now welfare has become an unreliable support, provided at rates too low to compensate households for the real costs of urban residence.

REVERSALS IN FORTUNE

Little Deng was part of a large clan in Landing. His parents were farmers, and his brothers were migrant workers. His sisters, on the other hand, had done well for themselves. One sister, Deng Liwen, was married to Boss Bo, and the two had purchased an apartment in the center of the Qijiang County seat. Another sister, Deng Yaoli, was also an entrepreneur. She and her husband helped their son run a noodle restaurant servicing migrant workers in coastal Zhejiang Province. Deng Yaoli and her husband lived in a rented apartment above the restaurant, and though they rarely returned to Landing Village, they had purchased an apartment in the Qijiang County seat.

One peripheral branch of the Deng family tree had a different experience. Little Deng had two cousins who, unlike the rest of the family, had attended high school and college. One worked in the Qijiang Post Office, and the other, a woman named Deng Shaoli, held a government job in the Qijiang County Land Reform Office. Both sisters married men with urban *hukou*, changed their own *hukou* status to urban, and lived in the Qijiang County seat, the urban center of the then-rural county. Although Deng Shaoli earned far less in her government job than Boss Bo earned as a labor broker, hers was a formal job with a steady employer, which conferred on her benefits such as an employer-subsidized pension and health insurance.

Rural modernization schemes upended the social hierarchy of Landing Village. For decades migrants had devised particular strategies to reap the hidden benefits of exclusionary *hukou* policies. They maintained households in low-cost villages while investing capital in cities and kept their rural *hukou* papers as a social safety net, which guaranteed them an idyllic farming life in retirement. But after their rural land rights came under siege, it was villagers such as Deng Shaoli whose formal employment guaranteed their access to employer-subsidized urban welfare programs.

Entrepreneurs such as Boss Bo, who were previously at the top of the social hierarchy of the local economy, were also adversely affected by land expropriation. In Landing, unlike Faming, a large stratum of entrepreneurs had emerged, largely due to the village's long legacy of migration and the village's close proximity to Chongqing. Moreover, the village's proximity to Chongqing enabled migrants to establish business relationships with other entrepreneurs in the city, and many entrepreneurial elites had largely relocated to nearby urban centers.

For example, among the most successful entrepreneurs was Wu Guangming, known locally as Landing's "big woman boss." Wu Guangming ran an automotive supply shop in Chongqing City, which she launched with the help of a relative who had been a labor broker. Most other entrepreneurs launched business ventures that drew from the resources of the village community. For example, Wu Minjian, a former farmer, had set up a contract farming arrangement that pooled individual farmers across many regions to share costs of shipping and to coordinate sales prices of their products for agricultural market middlemen. Wu Minjian and his associates established a network of rice producers who coordinated a simultaneous fall harvest and hired trucks to transport large quantities of husked and market-ready rice to vendors in Chongqing food markets.

For entrepreneurs such as Wu Minjian, land expropriation represents a major upheaval. It endangers the livelihoods of anyone who is reliant on the ecosystem of the village. Even entrepreneurial villagers who, like Deng Yaoli, had purchased property in the Qijiang County seat, are affected. Even if they are to relocate to urban centers, they cannot receive favorable terms under urban pension schemes, which by the late 2000s had moved toward an employer-contribution financing model. Formal employment is becoming an increasingly necessary condition to qualify for favorable terms in the urban health insurance and pension schemes. Because most Landing villagers are informally employed, even successful entrepreneurs such as Wu Guangming who are able to meet the requirements for urban *hukou* registration in a first-tier city such as Chongqing are exposed to the shortcomings of the urban welfare state.

HUKOU POLITICS AS A GROWTH ENGINE

Land is a central pillar of the village economy, and few villagers who own it are willing to relinquish it voluntarily. Because of this, the Qijiang County government took special measures to ensure that land expropriation was implemented on time and with minimal pushback from villagers. In 2009 Landing Village's parent county, Qijiang County, successfully applied for qualification as an official BNSC site of modernization and received permission from the Sichuan Ministry of Land Management to lay out a three-year plan for redeveloping Landing's collective village land. Qijiang County was then suffering heavy fiscal deficits, and county officials believed they could recover more quickly if the county were incorporated into the jurisdiction of Chongqing Municipality. At the time the county was classified as a rural territory just outside the Chongqing jurisdiction and therefore received fewer fiscal transfers from Chongqing than its neighboring urban districts, which had already been subsumed into the municipality.

The plan to modernize Landing Village, along with all of the villages of Qijiang County, involved converting rural land to higher-value, revenue-producing uses. Officials determined that land use should be geared toward maximizing the region's tourism appeal, due to Landing's proximity to Chongqing and its scenic, mountainous topography. A modernized township, which I call "New Land Township," was slated to be built atop village land, and local officials rezoned this land for the construction of luxury real estate—hotels and restaurants—intended to serve an urban middle-class clientele from Chongqing. Officials were fully empowered to create in New Land Township a rationalized plan for profitable development. One employee in the county development office I spoke to likened the process of building New Land Township to "drawing on a clean sheet of white paper," in the sense that "there are no obstructions to rational development."

The construction of New Land Township conferred various benefits on the Qijiang County government. Profits from rural modernization came in the form of administrative fees, most significantly a land transfer fee that is levied when rural, collective land is legally converted to state ownership, and is paid by the private developers who will contract this land for use. Land transfer fees increase with land values—in Chongqing's central business district, land transfer fees reached 90 million RMB per square kilometer—and are shared by local and central governments alike, making centrally located land extremely attractive for expropriation. Furthermore, rural land, once expropriated, can also be used to as collateral for land-backed mortgages and other forms of state bank credit to fund urban construction. Finally, under the BNSC campaign, county governments can receive matched fund subsidies from the center to help fund projects aligned with BNSC goals, such as irrigation construction, aquifers, and public housing construction.

The customary way that local governments expropriate land in rural China is by preemptively changing the *hukou* status of land rights holders from rural to urban. This juridical change in citizenship status shifts residents to a new, ostensibly upgraded category of citizenship, one that no longer conveys land guarantees. In many locales, before carrying out planned land enclosures, county and township officials deliberately incentivize, through gifts and financial rewards, voluntary *hukou* transfers from agricultural to nonagricultural status, targeting prominent village leaders in order to obtain widespread compliance. Only after transfers are complete do state officials begin to expropriate land forcibly. This prior *hukou* incorporation delegitimates claims to lost land, an entitlement attached specifically to agricultural *hukou* status, and amplifies juridical divisions among evictees. Some of these will already have relocated to townships while still holding agricultural *hukou*; others remain in villages yet hold nonagricultural *hukou* status.[4] *Hukou* incorporation has the added benefit of creating a growing ledger of urban-registered households, useful for a county government wishing to prove to the municipality that it deserves reclassification as an urban district. Finally, voluntary *hukou* transfer programs were designed to appeal to younger residents with greater labor market viability. These programs were intended to minimize potential future resistance to land expropriation by clearing out of villages market-savvy residents who might otherwise launch resistance to land requisitions more forcefully than the older farming generation.[5] Such is the strategy that Qijiang County officials pursued in land expropriation in Landing Village.

Just after Little Deng and Deng Guang returned to Landing, in March 2011, township Communist Party secretary Zhang held a town meeting. There, he distributed glossy pamphlets, printed by the Qijiang County Public Security Bureau. They advertised rural-to-urban *hukou* transfers— all voluntary, the officials assured readers—for all Landing residents. The pamphlets illustrated, on successive pages, sanitized images of newly urbanized lives: an elderly retired farmer seated in a well-lit modern apartment, a young family walking hand in hand through well-clipped green hedges. They advertised township welfare eligibility as one of many benefits of *hukou* transfer, as well as access to township schools, health care, and urban pension funds. Secretary Zhang added an extra detail: beginning immediately, in Landing and its surrounding villages the county government would be offering a 500 RMB bonus payment to any villager who would volunteer to transfer rural *hukou* to urban status— specifically, the transfer to a registration as a nonagricultural household.[6]

What was not communicated as clearly to villagers, however, was that any villagers who traded away their rural *hukou* would also lose user rights to their allotted village land within three years.

In general, *hukou* transfers have two outcomes. First, as the pamphlets assured villagers, they incorporate rural residents into the urban welfare state. Second, made less explicit at Secretary Zhang's town meeting, is that they terminate residents' use rights to village land. The process of rural-urban integration is meant to coordinate this two-part transition, with residents first relinquishing land rights, then gaining access to urban social support. The offer of *hukou* transfer was meant to front-end the benefits of land loss by advertising the upgrade to urban citizenship that would accompany the transition. Though local officials had already earmarked all residents' land for eventual forcible expropriation and return to state ownership, they decided that it would be more effective to present the voluntary option of a land-for-welfare trade before making involuntary land requisitions.

This approach to land expropriation alienated some of Landing's farmers. After hearing about the *hukou* transfer program, one elderly farmer, Zhou Wenbing, was suspicious of the monetary incentive that was attached. "They think we village people are too easy to fool," he said, trudging on the dirt path from the township to his village house. "Dangle 500 RMB in front of our faces and we will reach for it." Even more disconcerting to villagers was the fact that *hukou* transfer was being made available at a moment when the situation surrounding village land was also changing:

> Some old people, you see they are eager to . . . transfer their rural *hukou* to urban *hukou*. But what will they do if they have already changed their *hukou* and then their house gets demolished? They become homeless; who has the money to buy one of those apartments in New Land Township?

Zhou Wenbing was rightly fearful that the *hukou* transfer would be a direct road to land dispossession.

MONETARY COMPENSATION FOR LAND

Another state tactic for land expropriation was wide advertisement of the monetary compensation available for those who relinquished their land.

Those villagers whose land plots were located in advantageous positions, obstructing key infrastructural projects in the township center, for example, could receive large compensation payments if they volunteered to relinquish their land. At the same March 2011 town meeting, two township officials and Secretary Zhang announced the commencement of voluntary "land transfers" authorized under the BNSC campaign.[7] Volunteers relinquishing both their land and their housing could receive a one-time compensation payment of 10,900 RMB per mu for their land, and an additional compensation payment for their housing, with rates varying based on the quality of materials used to build the house.[8] One important condition, however, was that only those villagers who could provide proof of purchase of a government-subsidized apartment in a nearby town or a photocopy of a property contract belonging to a relative who had agreed to allow them to cohabit were permitted to relinquish their land under these favorable compensation arrangements.

The offer generated intense speculation and excitement among Landing villagers. Eager to obtain economic concessions, many immediately began devising plans to "trade in" their fallow, nonarable, and inconveniently located land plots, retaining their best plots for continued family farming. One villager, who lived on steep land located on the ridges of a valley, hoped to relinquish his undesirable land, then squat in a long-vacated house on a more desirable plot registered to a long-absent migrant worker. Another set of households hoped to relinquish their farming land yet set aside a hidden remaining plot on which they could rebuild a new house for joint residence. But these were wishful plans, made by villagers who, whether by their own lack of attention or the intentional vagueness with which policies were promulgated, misunderstood the terms of the exchange.

The initial excitement in the village over the *hukou* and land transfer programs soon deteriorated into cynicism and disappointment. Most households that expressed interest in trading in their land did not receive the compensation money they expected. That spring, of seventy-five households in Landing, nineteen expressed interest in trading in their land for compensation and *hukou* upgrade. Of these nineteen, three did not have the paperwork to show proof of access to new housing. After more information was provided on the house demolitions, however, two households, nervous about whether remuneration for housing demolitions would be sufficient, backed out. Many signed up for land transfer but later learned their land was not zoned for New Land Township construction, and they would therefore receive scant monetary compensation for their land. In the end, only eight households received the promised compensation for relinquished land and demolished housing.

What was not immediately communicated to the villagers was that monetary compensation of land was tied to the type of use for which the land would later be contracted to developers. In New Land Township, for example, redevelopment plans were focused around high-value ventures, such as a five-star hotel, a natural park designed for tourists seeking a respite from city life, luxury real estate development, and commercial space. Residents occupying land that would later go for real estate development and infrastructural construction were compensated at the highest rates, usually determined on a case-by-case basis by county officials. Residents occupying land that would be consolidated into large agricultural enclosures to be contracted to private agribusinesses would receive the 10,900 RMB per mu that was quoted at the town meeting. This rate was set by the Chongqing municipal government under the parameters of the BNSC campaign, which oversaw agricultural modernization.

However, many residents occupied land that would be used to build the natural park, to be located near the center of New Land Township (see map 4). This land was not requisitioned for state ownership, since local officials could requisition the land using a recent series of environmental protection campaigns, such as the "Open Up the West" and "Sloping Land Conversion Project," which called for returning pastureland to restore forests and grasslands (*tuimu huancao*). Under these environmental protection campaigns, local governments could force rural residents to cease using their land indefinitely and pay them a low annual payment in exchange, without having to return the land to state ownership.[9] The Qijiang County government used these environmental campaigns to clear off rural land that would be used for aesthetic yet noncommercial purposes, since it sidestepped the land transfer fees. In New Land Township a centrally located enclosure of land was placed under environmental

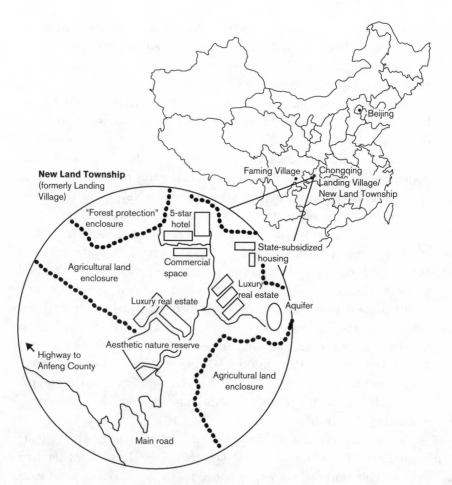

Map 4. New Land Township. Map by author.

protection in order to create an aesthetically pleasing park directly adjacent to the five-star hotel under construction.

CONFUSION AND MISINFORMATION

For all of the warnings from village leaders about the coming changes, villagers still did not know whether the land seizures would be completed, specifically whether they would continue until all villagers were evicted in their entirety. Villagers noted variation in the ongoing changes underway in neighboring regions; in some villages, evicted residents received rates of land compensation much higher than those stipulated in Landing Village. In others, only some residents were evicted, the majority later being allowed to retain their land-use rights due to last-minute changes in the zoning of the township development. Many villagers, particularly those older residents who remembered receiving a guarantee of secure land tenure made after decollectivization in the early 1980s, were convinced that the land seizures would be reversed in time.

Not long after the town meeting in March, a list of households was posted on the wall of the village general store. This list was a second phase in the unfolding of BNSC campaign construction in New Land Township. Households with land directly obstructing township construction projects were listed and told they would be forcibly removed from their land on a near future date. These households would receive monetary land compensation and *hukou* upgrades on the same terms that Secretary Zhang had outlined at the March meeting. The difference, however, was that they had no choice but to submit.

In the midst of this confusion, Secretary Zhang began making personal calls to households, whether or not they were affected by phase two evictions. During these calls he offered affected households the option of *hukou* transfer as a way to secure a three-year eviction postponement while they made arrangements for relocation. If they gave up their rural *hukou*, he informed them, they would receive a guaranteed three-year grace period before losing their land. If they did not, they risked losing their land before they were fully prepared to relocate.

This ploy also pressured many households unaffected by the eviction notice to give up their rural *hukou*. Secretary Zhang also suggested to unaffected households that they were likely to find their names on an eviction list in the near future, advising them to consider signing paperwork allowing them a three-year grace period so that they might "protect" their land rights for a guaranteed three years. This sleight of hand was confusing to older villagers easily misled by subtle changes in policy. When Secretary Zhang suggested to one bachelor farmer and his father that their land, located on a hill, was likely to be confiscated and "returned" to forestland in the near future due to a high risk of landslides, the men were so flustered, and then so relieved to hear they could safely continue using their land for three more years, that they signed away their rural *hukou* on the spot. Only after they had completed the necessary paperwork did they realize they had signed away rights to their land after three years:

> They only told me, when I asked, that I could keep farming the land. I did not ask how long. I thought that it was better not to ask too many questions. I cannot afford to relocate, so I want to avoid drawing attention to my household. Secretary Zhang told me the land was susceptible to landslides but I did not have to relocate yet. I don't know what that means but I collected my money and I went home.

Misinformation was rampant, particularly among villagers who were older and lacked information sources on these new modernization policy programs.

Villagers with more substantial connections to county officials, however, were more wary, and they attempted to alert others to the importance of making preparations to vacate. One village-elected leader named Pen Gang traveled to neighboring villages to ascertain the state of their land-use rights. He reported back to villagers:

> To the south, there are two villages that have already been cleared for development. Those villagers have already been asked to leave, immediately. Here in Landing, this month the officials gave us a document that said that we have a three-year grace period. . . . However, we should not take these three years lightly. The state will [still] ask us to leave the land.

Pen Gang also warned villagers about the sparse state support during the three-year period of transition. He had heard many Landing villagers surmise that they might qualify for welfare payments in successive years or that additional new public housing units would be built to accommodate more villagers, notwithstanding that public housing available in New Land Township had an extensive waitlist by the end of 2011. Pen Gang visited Landing households one by one with an admonition:

> We cannot expect much. Always they have left us to rely on ourselves. Pension? We must buy it ourselves. Land? We must farm it ourselves. We should not be surprised that they leave us to fend for ourselves these three years.

But warnings like this were only partially useful. Though most villagers were duly warned, many, like Luo Xianyu, had no means to make necessary preparations.

Another villager, an older woman named Wang Deihua, had heard similar reports. Her daughter was Deng Shaoli, who worked in the Qijiang County Land Reform Office, and she had distant relatives living in a village to the north, near the township of Sanjiao. Wang Deihua's relatives had been evicted from their housing and land to make way for aquifers to be built on their village land. Through conversations with her daughter, she had gleaned enough awareness of the fiscal interests guiding land conversions to know that the benefits of urbanization accrued disproportionately to residents of higher-priority urban localities. Her relatives lived on land near the Qijiang County seat, and she reasoned that what was under way in Sanjiao would soon occur in Landing. In a conversation with Little Deng and his sister Deng Liwen, Wang Deihua broadcast her concerns and predicted that evictions would soon be taking place in Landing:

> You think about this: that's what they're doing in Sanjiao. Sanjiao Township is closer to the center of Qijiang District than New Land Township. So Sanjiao will always be superior to New Land Township in what kinds of subsidies and treatment villagers get. That's why Sanjiao is doing their land reform now, before New Land Township. It is closer to the city center.

Wang Deihua's instinct was correct: Localities closer to the center anticipated higher growth in land values; therefore, construction and land redevelopment in these regions was implemented first.

Moreover, as Wang Deihua intuited, the resources that Qijiang County had earmarked for public housing, social programs, and monetary compensation for lost land were finite. Villagers who were dispossessed early had better access to public housing in particular, which was being sold at a subsidized rate and was limited in supply. Wang Deihua feared that by the time the county government began dispensing services in New Land Township, many fiscal resources for public housing and welfare subsidies might be exhausted. Moreover, she herself knew that her relatives in Sanjiao Township were already voicing complaints about land compensation monies that were slow in coming. "If villagers are already having problems with the compensation money in Sanjiao, then you can imagine what kind of problems we will have here. I tell you, nobody is going to get rich and move to the city on their compensation package."

CUTTING COSTS IN THE URBAN WELFARE STATE

As the "land-for-welfare" trade unfolded, the Qijiang County government continued to interact with villagers through village-level proxies such as Secretary Zhang. Zhang served as a necessary conduit for the state, smoothing villagers' transitions from rural to urban citizenship. This role was necessary because urban citizenship, as it was implemented in New Land Township, was a bundle of entitlements under revision. Between 2011 and 2014 three million rural residents in the Chongqing region were converted to urban household registration status, thus freeing approximately 520 square kilometers of rural land to be added to the urban territory of the municipality. These *hukou* transfers cost the city government an estimated total of 180 to 240 billion RMB.[10] Public, nonemployee retirement pension support for the elderly was estimated at 18 billion RMB. Government contributions to public housing, education, social services, and employment training added up to another 30 billion RMB.

Some of these costs are covered by private parties. For instance, the Yufu Asset Management Group, a local government financing vehicle that borrows from state banks to fund urban construction, contributes 15 to 20 percent of its annual profits to the municipal government to help finance social welfare programs and public housing construction. A portion of public goods provision is funded by allocations and fiscal transfers from the center. Education, for example, has been funded almost entirely by transfers from the central state since the education reforms in 2009. Similar reforms to the pension and health-care systems have made employer contributions a major source of funding for the urban welfare state. What is not paid for by the center or by employer contributions, however, must be covered by government revenues. In order to cut enrollment costs, many county governments, like Qijiang's, began to narrow the eligibility requirements for some welfare programs.

Some social programs that were advertised at the start of the land requisitions, such as plans for a reemployment center, where farmers could

retrain for nonagricultural occupations and inquire about new job opportunities in the township, were simply never implemented. Other existing
welfare programs, such as the Minimum Livelihood Allowance Guarantee
(MLAG), a nationwide, low-income program that supplies poor residents
with monthly cash subsidies, and the Rural Minimum Living Standards
(RMLS) cash transfer program, had their eligibility requirements nar-
rowed substantially. In interviews, Qijiang officials explained this change
as the result of funding logistics, in that both programs are funded through
provincial expenditures determined on the basis of population census data
collected during previous years. During the previous year the township
census had simply failed to account for the recent expansion in township
residents. Hard budget constraints and growing numbers of unanticipated
supplicants had forced Qijiang County officials to narrow the low-income
social insurance program's eligibility requirements.

Recent studies have shown wide variation in local government implementation of national welfare policy. In regions facing budget deficits,
local governments tend to treat welfare programs as a form of temporary
assistance for the elderly, the disabled, and the infirm that often disquali-
fies the able-bodied unemployed from eligibility. However, in better-
funded regions these same welfare programs are treated as universal wage
supplements for the working poor.[11] In Qijiang, local government officials
require applicants for these welfare programs to report a household
income below a certain level, even after accounting for the income of adult
children. Because many of these welfare applicants are elderly farmers
whose adult children live apart from them but deliberately left themselves
registered at their natal household as a way to claim rights to land during
their own retirement, this new requirement affected a large number of
villagers.

For example, one older farming woman Liu Zhaoyin had for years
received a monthly subsidy of 80 RMB under the Rural Minimum Living
Standards cash transfer program in Landing Village. After she found her
husband's name on the list of households whose land would be expropriated, the two of them re-registered under nonagricultural *hukou* and were
told they were still eligible to qualify for the urban Minimum Living
Allowance (MLA) subsidy that would be implemented in New Land
Township, where the subsidy was available to households earning less

than 750 RMB monthly. Liu Zhaoyin and her husband were farmers, and their son worked as a bank teller in Qijiang County. His job paid 1,200 RMB per month, and he had recently gone through a divorce. He slept in a dormitory for villagers in the county seat while his young daughter, over whom he had sole custody, lived in Landing with Liu Zhaoyin and her husband.

When Liu Zhaoyin applied to qualify for MLA subsidies, county officials required the couple to report the income of any adult children still registered to their household. At the meeting she attended on the new welfare programs in the township, an official from the county welfare bureau emphasized this new requirement to villagers:

> All households must register their circumstances and the annual income of each member registered to the household. This means, and this is important, that you must report your children! You must report all children that are listed as household dependents in the *hukou* registrar. Each person registered to your household in the *hukou* must be accounted for. Where are they? What do they earn? You say your son is not a filial son? We cannot help you there. You still must report his circumstances and his income. You say you have not seen your son for five years? Your son has not returned home for ten years? You still must report his income.

It was on these grounds that Liu Zhaoyin lost access to these subsidies. Her son was still registered to the household, and his income, though insufficient for even his own livelihood needs, disqualified his farming parents from receiving state support.

Implementation of this new rule created a large group of villagers who were bereft of state support during the land-to-welfare transition. One way that local officials dealt with temporary shortages in welfare support was by encouraging such villagers to rely on extended family. Landing Village leader Zhou, for example, had long dealt with complaints and grievances from older villagers whose children failed to send them remittances. He at one point attempted to institute a fine of 10,000 RMB on households in which elders who could not care for themselves were left alone in the countryside, yet the policy became impossible to enforce. When county officials descended on the village to address concerns of welfare support for aging villagers forced to leave their land and their homes, officials took a similar tack:

We advise for each household that migrant children remit 20 percent of their income to their elderly parents. If your children do not remit this amount, then you tell them that it is a state-mandated responsibility to care for their parents. Keep this in mind when you talk to them next. Tell them they must remit 20 percent of their income home to you.

The new policy recast the failure of the welfare state to provide full support to elderly villagers lacking labor market viability as a private, not political, concern.

Not only was it now more difficult to qualify for welfare programs, they were also offered at different rates in different regions. Whereas land had been distributed in equal portions to all rural residents, welfare subsidies were calibrated to match local cost of living; therefore, welfare subsidies in Chongqing City and the Qijiang County seat were far more generous than those in New Land Township. However, urban *hukou* status in these urban centers was conditional upon formal employment and property ownership. Most villagers who had lost their land were given urban *hukou* status in New Land Township. Only entrepreneurial villagers such as Wu Guangming and Boss Bo or villagers with formal employment such as Deng Shaoli were able to relocate to urban centers with more favorable social programs.

In the Qijiang County seat, for example, the government had made available temporary rental apartments for newly dispossessed residents who were unable to buy property. However, applicants for these apartments were required to have transferred their registration to local Qijiang urban *hukou* status. Moreover, the county had established a requirement that all applicants for Qijiang urban *hukou* show either proof of formal employment or a certificate proving property ownership in the county seat.

In addition to welfare reductions, a housing shortage plagued the new citizens of New Land Township. Housing was perhaps the most significant determinant of successful relocation to New Land Township. Housing units in New Land Township were available initially at government-subsidized rates ranging from 70,000 RMB to 120,000 RMB per unit. But even with these subsidized rates, relocation to the township required considerable personal resources, even on top of government assistance in the form of land and demolition compensation payments. One elderly farmer, Xia Sihua, was one of the few Landing villagers whose land qualified for compensation under the favorable terms of the BNSC rates. He received a total of 50,000 RMB, which still fell short of the costs of state-subsidized apartments in New Land Township. The villagers who could afford to secure a township apartment quickly did so. High-rise apartments in New Land Township grew scarce before long, and the Qijiang County government's development plans did not leave room for the construction of supplemental housing.

With a housing shortage looming, collective anxiety became widespread. For most elderly villagers, both *hukou* and land transfer programs elicited fearful responses. Once they realized that public housing would be difficult to afford even if they could access a unit in time, many older villagers resisted participating in any modernization programs, opting instead to remain steadfastly in place. Elderly farmer Zhou Wenbing, for example, abstained from the *hukou* transfer program out of fear of land loss. None of his four sons had accumulated enough earnings to secure housing in the township for their own families, let alone relocate an evicted father. Zhou Wenbing stayed in place and declared that the land policy seemed to "change every year or so, first they announce this rule, then later it will change and they'll announce another."

Another elderly villager vacated his land and moved in with a wealthier brother, yet professed his lack of trust in the township welfare regime and kept his rural *hukou* in hopes of one day reclaiming his land. "I will try to keep my rural *hukou* and my rural house. I think nothing has changed. The township welfare provisions are very low, not much higher than those of the village, and this way one day I might be able to make a claim for my land again." Finally, one elderly farmer scoffed at officials' suggestion that villagers fall back on family support and understood it to be justification for a cost-cutting welfare rollback:

> The officials are just going to tell everyone to try to move in with their children in the city so they can demolish their houses. That is the purpose of these meetings. They are worried that we rural people will have problems if we stay in the village, because they are forcing everyone to move out. But they do not actually want to solve the problem of rural subsistence. They want us to rely on our children, put the burden on our own families, and move out. This way the farming population will not be a problem they have to use state funds to solve.

This farmer's own children could not help him, and he had no extended kin with whom he could cohabit when his home was demolished. When villagers learned of others who had acquired housing in the township, they became anxious. Chen Yi, an elderly farmer with little experience in wage labor, became agitated when he heard that his neighbor Xia Sihua had already registered for housing demolition; he had not known that his friend had the resources to relocate. Xia Sihua had purchased a high-rise in a public housing complex being built near New Land Township. His son, Chen Yi knew, was an entrepreneur, and it was with his help that Xia Sihua was able to relocate:

> I heard that a lot of people have already started to register their names to have their houses demolished. . . . At market today I heard that Xia Sihua has already registered to have his house demolished. He already bought a government-subsidized apartment in New Land Township! Someone said the apartments are going fast. There is a lot of competition for them.

Chen Yi, on the other hand, had three sons who were ordinary migrant workers, unable to help him come up with the capital for a down payment for public housing. In New Land Township, early surrender of land for money became an advantageous strategy, allowing residents to purchase scarce urban apartments before government subsidies ran out. This strategy favored younger migrants who had accumulated wages in off-farm employment, leaving bereft those older farmers reliant solely on land for their livelihood.

A MARKET RHETORIC OF RIGHTS

In the transition from rural to urban citizenship, issues of public goods distribution are increasingly resolved through market mechanisms rather than state channels.[12] Land rights are replaced by one-time monetary land compensation payments, and subsistence becomes an individual concern to be resolved through market engagement. For example, when government-subsidized housing units ran out, residents were instructed to cohabit with extended family members or use their compensation payments to purchase pensions and market-priced housing units. Yet unlike land, which defrays housing and food costs year after year, monetary compensation is a one-time cash infusion, and residents require employment to meet new expenses.[13]

Living expenses in New Land Township, moreover, escalate over time. One young entrepreneur, thirty-three-year-old Li Bing, was part of a household that received an usually large, one-time land compensation payment of 83,500 RMB for his household's land plots, which were expropriated for urban construction. Li Bing used a portion of his land compensation payment to purchase a large truck, with which he began delivering materials to the very construction subcontractors who were building the highway through his land. After construction was complete, he went on to transport crops for the agribusiness subcontractors operating on the edges of the township.

But even entrepreneurs such as Li Bing found it difficult to sever their ties to land. Li Bing's trucking business was more profitable during the height of township construction; once the construction activity slowed down, his business would suffer. Moreover, even the agribusiness subcontractors operating on the edges of the township were appointed by county officials, and they employed Li Bing only during a busy ramp-up period as they imported the machinery and materials they needed to build their agribusiness facilities.

Meanwhile, Li Bing's cost of living continually increased. With what remained of their land compensation payment after Li Bing's truck purchase, Li Bing's parents made a down payment for a mortgage of 90,000 RMB on a state-subsidized apartment in the township. They shared the cost with two siblings—all three families would cohabit in the township apartment. But after they spent the entirety of their land compensation payment on the down payment, they soon realized they needed a new cash flow to keep up with mortgage payments and food costs in the town market. Li Bing's aging parents eventually sought work in factories to meet these new costs, and Li Bing himself eventually had to sell his truck and seek migration opportunities in coastal cities.

Township residence presented rural residents with new costs. They now paid household taxes and fees for public utilities and faced higher food costs. Furthermore, many public goods previously available to village residents were unavailable in the townships. As many villagers learned, welfare, unlike land, is a subsidy that is conditional and can be revoked. For these reasons, Landing villagers were generally unwilling to relinquish land-use rights in exchange for urban *hukou* registration and the welfare entitlements it conferred. This finding has been confirmed by survey research in other urbanizing sites on the peripheries of expanding cities in inland and coastal regions alike. In a survey of one thousand households in the urbanizing periphery of Chengdu City that gave up their village housing land for public housing units, researchers found that on average, residents' household income increased by 20 percent, while their expenditures increased by almost 60 percent.[14] These new expenditures included payments for pension insurance and new food and mortgage costs that were previously defrayed by production from land and housing plots.[15]

Moreover, in Landing Village as at other sites, it was not just villagers with no foothold in the nearby urban economy who were reluctant to relinquish land. Even some households that had plans to relocate to urban townships and county seats were unsettled by the prospect of land loss. For example, based on a survey of 133,653 households in 106 cities, researchers found that despite the willingness of one-third of the respondents to transfer *hukou* to destination cities, once surveyors clarified that they would have to permanently relinquish use rights to contracted village land, those voicing willingness to transfer *hukou* decreased from 35 percent to 12 percent.[16] Another survey of over 7,000 migrants in twenty cities undertaken by the Development Research Center of the State Council found that only 9 percent wanted to return eventually to their home villages; the majority were not willing to relinquish their farming and housing plots.[17]

In the face of popular reluctance to relinquish land, county officials launched a broad ideological campaign to reframe the land-for-welfare trade as a modernizing reform. Monthly "ideological re-education" meetings were held, which targeted older residents, whom officials identified as a potential problem population, given their relatively diminished labor market prospects. At one meeting, a county-level official proclaimed:

> [Converting farmland to] forestland will prevent landslides. Fallow land is simply a waste of public resources. We are not taking land-use rights from villagers when we request that they return their fallow land to forest state. We simply offer them an annual compensation payment in exchange for their promise not to farm the land. They can use this payment to buy the food and rice they need, instead of growing it themselves.

By suggesting that evictees could simply "use [compensation payments] to buy the food and rice they need instead of growing it themselves," local officials recast the issue of subsistence rights wholly in market terms. Yet these compensation payments, set at 240 RMB ($40) per mu annually, were far too small to cover food costs, let alone housing costs.[18] By prioritizing the "efficient" use of land over the needs of its inhabitants, officialdom subsumed subsistence as a secondary priority in a larger project of rationalized land use. As a whole, the comment frames the transition from peasant production to a market-oriented economy as a shift from principles of "subsistence" toward virtues of "efficiency" and prioritizes land's exchange value over its use value precisely by discursively erasing the needs of those who rely on it for subsistence.

This is sleight of hand at the heart of the land-for-welfare exchange. Compulsory rural-urban citizenship transfers were framed as a means of efficient rural development incorporation; the narrowing of urban social entitlements, such as the provision of land expropriation compensation payments far lower than subsistence levels, was conveyed as a means of weaning farmers off the dole. For example, New Land Township officials portrayed the modern township lifestyle as one of self-responsibility, juxtaposed implicitly against the backwardness of land dependence. Secretary Zhang complained after one township ideological meeting of elderly farmers with intractable ties to the land:

> Many old farmers are reluctant to give up farming. . . . [S]ome of them relocate to [the township], but they remain backward in their thinking, and try to re-create their old lifestyle, planting vegetables on any available piece of land in town. We . . . [must] re-educate them on proper forms of land-use.

Another Qijiang County welfare official took a longer-term perspective on the BNSC campaign as a natural transition "matching" the evolving lifestyle choices of younger, increasingly urbanized villagers:

> Of course, some older villagers will not be willing to move. They lived their entire lives in the villages. . . . [B]ut they are the last generation to farm the land. The younger generations, they are not accustomed to living in the countryside. So, of course, this reform is slow and gradual, but it is designed to complement the natural desires of rural people. As older people become

too old to farm, they can move to the towns to rest. And this way younger migrants who go to work in the city can live in the city as well.

Finally, another New Land Township official framed those resisting township relocation as "lazy" subjects unwilling to adapt to the demands of a market economy: "Before the transition, you still saw a lot of younger people stuck in the village. These are the people who have trouble transitioning. Most of them were in the village because they are lazy. . . . They don't know how to think, how to find money in the city."

Secretary Zhang often responded to disgruntled villagers by encouraging them to follow the example of younger entrepreneurs who had found ways to profit from the process of rural modernization. For example, one young man, Li Bing, used his land compensation money to buy a large truck, which he used to deliver building supplies and materials to various construction sites around the township for a generous fee. A former electrician, Zhou Changwei, supplemented his income by lending his services to private businesses in the township. Li Bing and Zhou Changwei were upheld as model examples of entrepreneurial and striving individuals, whose "successful" modifications to their livelihoods, enabling their relocation to New Land Township, undermined grievances regarding insufficient state support for relocation.

Mutual competition for employment widened existing inequalities between evicted villagers. Many wealthy migrant workers and local entrepreneurs spent their savings as seed capital for small businesses, such as motorcycle repair shops and food stands, in New Land Township. They hired kin relatives to maintain and run these small businesses, which often generated income supporting their entire clans. Other farmers, lacking such advantageous kin connections, struggled to find work in the new township. Complaints from those who failed to find stable sources of work were, however, met with blame.

A NATIONWIDE RACE TO URBANIZE

By the end of 2011 Qijiang County had applied successfully for administrative promotion from Chongqing Municipality, and it was eventually awarded reclassification from a rural county to an urban district through a merger with its neighboring Wansheng District. This political promotion was awarded based on Qijiang's now majority-urban population, its construction of vital urban infrastructure, such as an aquifer vital to the Chongqing water grid, and its forecasted high revenues from increased tourism and commerce. As an urban district, Qijiang could exercise more autonomy in doling out tax waivers and land deals to lure potential capital investors. This process of administration promotion—counties becoming districts, townships becoming county seats—produced a win-win scenario for state and market actors alike.

Priorities of capital accumulation trumped responsibilities to administer social programs in places such as Qijiang. There, officials were desperate to enter a commercial network among Chongqing's districts from which it had previously been shut out. After promotion to district status, officials could apply for funds for development directly from Chongqing Municipality rather than appealing first to the nearby prefectural district, which would then allocate funds it had received from the Chongqing Municipality. In an interview, an official in the Qijiang City Ministry of Civil Administration described how an administrative promotion would cut bureaucratic red tape in Qijiang's commercial dealings with its neighboring regions:

> Our development projects will become more high priority. And finally, district status will put us on level ground with all the other districts within Chongqing Municipality. This will greatly facilitate inter-city trade and commerce. It creates less paperwork and tax hassles when we need to transport goods and construction materials from district to district.

Administrative promotion came with a long list of economic advantages in China's hierarchical and decentralized governance structure, in which local governments must bargain with provincial governments for fiscal transfers and compete with neighboring counties and districts for resources.

Both central and local state bodies benefited from the urbanization of previously rural land. Revenues from land transfer fees accrue to all levels of government, with the center claiming 30 percent and provinces and prefecture-level cities receiving 20 percent, leaving the remainder to county-level governments and lower entities.[19] As fiscal extraction has shifted away from the traditional industrial tax base, which had accrued to provinces, toward land-related transactions, which accrue to the center, scholars have noted a strengthening of the extractive capacity of the state. County governments possess both eminent domain over state-owned land and rights to land transfer fees, but in order to extract revenues from land conversion they also must fund a series of public services, for example, the financing of urban infrastructure and the provision of public goods. In other words, dispossession requires local governments to expand the scope and scale of state activities, in terms of both personnel and expenditures. China scholar Yuen Ang has argued that aside from the traditional administrative units of the government, a "sprawling periphery of extra-bureaucracies" has emerged, consisting of parastatal units that are privately contracted to perform services of the state but do not receive budget allocations from the government.[20]

These trends in urbanization are visible in many regions of rural China. In 2011 I visited an additional site in northern Sichuan, Yilong County, which had undertaken urbanizing reforms concurrently with Qijiang. Unlike Qijiang, which focused on developing its tourism sector through urbanization, Yilong adopted an urbanization model based on manufacturing. The county had devised a long-term development plan centered around luring industrial investors away from coastal SEZs such as Shenzhen and Dongguan, where rising wages and land rents were putting downward pressure on profits. After securing an investment from a mid-sized Sino-Taiwanese joint high-tech enterprise, Yilong Party officials put together a package of land subsidies, tax waivers, and labor recruitment programs to attract further industrial investors to the region. Land-use allocation plans in Yilong were designed to maximize potential rents from a future consumer base expected to arrive along with investment in manufacturing jobs. Officials cordoned off large swaths of land to be allocated gratis to coastal investors for assembly and manufacturing facilities, with surrounding land reserved for built housing for the migrant laborers from neighboring regions who would one day work in these facilities. On fringe land even farther outside the county center, officials placed public housing for local residents who were dispossessed from seized land.

How generalizable is this trend of urbanization as a means of generating growth and boosting fiscal revenues? Since their introduction in 2006, rural modernization programs such as the BNSC campaign have become so commonly used by local governments as revenue vehicles that subsequent policy updates were added to curb runaway capital accumulation through urbanization. For example, in 2007 the Ministry of Civil Affairs promoted a policy called New Rural Community Building, which intended to improve public goods delivery by creating a new unit of administration for public services, and in 2008 a new Urban and Rural Planning Law mandated that plans for cities, counties, townships, and villages be coordinated and implemented hierarchically. The combined effect of these policies has been the concentration of housing and services in so-called central villages. Finally, in 2014 a New-Style Urbanization Plan was passed to replace the BNSC, emphasizing the extension of welfare benefits to landless residents. It was a necessary addition to the BNSC, which was passed under conditions of ambiguity that allowed local governments to frame the policy as a way to accelerate the process of urbanization without limit.

Acceleration in the rate of rural land expropriation also prompted the center to pass policies that attempted to limit the rate of land conversion. Annual quotas on the amount of arable land that can be converted for urban construction use have been levied on provinces in an attempt to address fears of food insecurity due to overzealous land expropriation. Because of this, urbanizing counties such as Qijiang usually maximize the agricultural productivity of arable land by contracting land-use rights to large-scale agribusinesses. In many regions, officials can terminate farmers' land-use rights contracts without requisitioning land back to state ownership and simply issue new contracts for use of collective land to agribusinesses. In other words, quotas on land conversion do not prevent termination of farmers' land rights.

Finally, the central state has also attempted to discourage speculative urbanization beyond the limits of demand by enforcing laws that have historically prohibited local governments from borrowing from state banks for urban construction. Yet this regulation has merely prompted local governments to create parastatal units, which use jurisdictional state-owned land as collateral to obtain mortgages, bonds, and other debts. These financing platforms act as proxies for local governments, which are themselves barred from borrowing from state banks for construction, but then hold the debt until local governments can raise sufficient revenues for repayment.[21] Chongqing City, for example, established the Yufu Asset Management Group to register two hundred square kilometers of newly expropriated rural land as collateral for credit to build urban infrastructure. Such debt is kept off the local government records, but a recent study by Moody's estimated total debts held by local financing platforms to fund urban construction as nearly 40 percent of China's GDP in 2016.[22]

WHAT EXPLAINS REGIONAL VARIATION IN LAND POLITICS?

There is one limiting factor in the spread of urbanization as a growth strategy for local governments. In regions such as Qijiang, the termination of small farming has triggered an agrarian transition, wherein residents turn wholly to industrial employment over agrarian production. Yet because this transition is taking place through land capitalization, and nearly all surpluses and profits generated by the transition are being captured by local government, popular grievances over the distributional outcomes and legitimacy of land expropriations are unbridled.

In Landing Village, state strategies of *hukou* transfer have allowed officials to demobilize claims to land without experiencing consolidated protest around land loss. This demobilization can be attributed to the gradual timing and sequencing of land expropriation, whereby officials first presented land transfer as a voluntary option, only later communicating the compulsory nature of land requisition, followed by the enlisting of key village officials, such as Party secretary Zhang, to act as intermediaries among villagers. Another factor that contributed to the lack of claims making in Landing Village was the status of the village as a longtime migration-sending site. By the time of land expropriations, many members were geographically dispersed, many younger residents already residing in townships and county seats. Due to the high level of rural-urban integration in Landing, with many residents already residing in nearby urban sites, the last remaining villagers to be evicted from their land were primarily members of older farming generations, those lacking social connections or with minimal experience of wage-work. These stragglers were easily framed by state officials as backward subjects ill adapted to a modernizing economy.

Yet different outcomes of land expropriation have been recorded in other contexts. Because collective land ownership rights are defined ambiguously under the law, with no specific actor identified as the owner, townships and village collectives may manage land in different contexts.[23] In some coastal regions, many village collectives have grown savvy to the strategies of developers and county-level governments and have corporatized their villages, registering them as limited liability corporations. In such "shareholding" or "corporatist" villages, village collectives transfer collective land ownership rights to a land shareholding company, and shareholding companies then auction land-use rights to private developers.[24] In another configuration of village corporatism, township governments are the managers of collective land, issuing sublegal land-use certificates on their own, which they can auction to private developers.[25] Regardless of which government body manages land revenues, residents relocate to nearby townships, where they usually transition to urban *hukou* status, while malls, real estate offices, factories, and commercial buildings appear on former village land. Revenues from these land development projects are redistributed back to residents both in the form of income and also as social benefits negotiated by village collectives. For example, scholars have recorded villages in Guangzhou where shareholding companies provide subsidies for elderly medical care, living expenses and funerals, nursing homes, day-care centers and schools, and even scholarships for local college students.[26]

In other contexts, landless residents have organized in a more direct manner, making demands on the county government on the basis of the illegality of land expropriation. In a well-known case in 2011, evicted farmers in Wukan Village, Guangdong Province eventually won back confiscated land and compelled the resignations of local officials by exposing the use of sublegal land sales certificates by township officials without central state approval.[27] Some demands about land have succeeded in stalling or outright stopping demolition, while others have simply ended in violence and submission. Many scholars have suggested that the political organization of villages shapes the outcomes of land politics. In sites where village leaders share kin relations with many of those who are expropriated, villagers can exploit lineage ties to recruit the support of village leaders who might otherwise be tempted to trade rural land for kickbacks and political positions promised from above.[28]

CONCLUSION

Urbanization creates new revenue streams for local governments, yet it also requires that villagers be uprooted from villages and rehabilitated in new townships. The work of expropriation is bureaucratic, requiring a forced change in the citizenship status of evictees, and the work of rehabilitation is ideological, producing a rhetorical shift in the categories of personhood through which evictees claim urban entitlements.

The expansion of urban citizenship in China is not straightforward. Although the international media and the Chinese central state itself have promoted a socially progressive framing of comprehensive *hukou* reform and rural-urban integration, the expansion of urban citizenship does not incorporate landless rural residents into a category of personhood that is substantively equal.[29] Instead, urban citizenship remains differentiated, with first-tier cities selectively choosing the residents they permit. Only in third-tier counties and townships such as New Land Township are dispossessed rural residents allowed to re-register as urban residents.

This differentiation is, of course, by design. The central state adjusts *hukou* policy in deliberately graduated fashion to admit skilled migrants while preserving social order. Citizenship reforms, in fact, are particularly effective in silencing potential grievances among urbanizing residents. For example, in many cases "nail households," residents who refuse to vacate housing marked for demolition, gain leverage by attracting media attention that puts public pressure on local governments to slow down land expropriation. Yet in Landing Village *hukou* and welfare policy is redefined in ways that create demobilizing divisions among the aggrieved, for example, making some eligible for welfare and housing subsidies and creating competition among residents who relinquish their land in time to acquire public housing and those who stubbornly hold out in hopes of retaining land rights. A central condition for this mechanism is China's localized welfare state. County governments can autonomously adjust conditions for welfare eligibility, as well as ideological categories determining who is deserving and undeserving of state support, to facilitate land expropriation and maximize land-based revenues and acquiescence to both.

Chapter 6 explores the distributional consequences of this shift, in particular its interaction with an informal economy of migration that previously coevolved with labor-intensive production priorities of employers in cities. To do so, it returns to the life of Landing Village, itself embedded in a larger informal economy of labor recruitment, its residents linked by blood and association to those of nearby Faming Village. Though urban *hukou* and welfare policies have shifted, and rural land entitlements have gradually dissolved, Landing villagers still rely on livelihoods and social networks established throughout the 1990s. In this intermediary period, as villagers transition away from reliance on land, the tensions between two mechanisms of development, one channeling labor into cities and another monetizing land in the countryside, become apparent.

6 Paradoxes of Urbanization

Farmer Luo Xianyu of Landing Village hanged himself in his home during a late-afternoon rainstorm in 2011 that had most villagers, including Luo's wife, distracted and playing cards and *mahjiang* in the homes of others. Word of the suicide spread instantaneously after his wife returned home that evening to find Old Luo strung up in the storage room of their old farmhouse, hanging from a rafter by a thin string of rope. His death was an act of desperation, deliberately timed, as Luo Xianyu's house had been scheduled for demolition the next day.

By late 2011 Landing Village had been razed nearly to the ground, its territory redrawn to fit the development priorities of Qijiang County, soon to be Qijiang District. Villagers made various preparations for their rapidly approaching evictions. Luo Xianyu, for example, had four sons, all of whom worked in factories in coastal cities. Ever stubborn, he had refused to go along with county officials' instructions to transfer his *hukou* to urban registration; he had refused to vacate his land even when informed that it would be forcibly seized on a specific date. Luo Xianyu had kept his struggles over his land secret from his sons in order to save them from anxiety, and when they heard word of their father's death, they hurried home in shock.

This chapter examines the distributional outcomes of land expropriation in Landing Village. While some villagers, particularly those with a foothold in the urban formal economy, such as Wang Deihua's two daughters, were smoothly absorbed into the urban district, those working in the informal economy, whether they were successful informal entrepreneurs such as Boss Bo or ordinary laborers such as Little Deng or Deng Guang, found their lives upended.

The reason for this bifurcation is Landing's legacy of labor migration, which enriched an entrepreneurial elite while forcing ordinary laborers to rely on subsistence farming as a wage supplement. Without this wage supplement, and without housing or welfare programs sufficient to support the evicted, villagers had to fall back on kin support, or worse, face hard times seeking jobs in an industry that is still organized around the assumption that laborers have support from farming households.

THE LABOR OF URBANIZATION

One assumption commonly held in the literature is that urbanization, whether in terms of the in-migration of people or an expansion of urban space, leads to growth of the middle class. One mechanism for this is job creation, the employment of labor to perform the actual task of building urban infrastructure and the ensuing wage increases and falling unemployment. Harvey, for example, has argued that the process of urbanization provides a means of stimulating flagging economic growth. It allows the absorption of labor and raw materials that typically become redundant and unused during stagnation and creates a new consumer outlet for new construction and commodity production.[1]

In China, however, the jobs created by urbanization do not typically employ local residents. Instead, local governments manage the process of urbanization and contract construction enterprises to undertake the work of building infrastructure. These construction enterprises, moreover, recruit employees through their own subcontracting networks. In addition, because most county-appointed subcontractors are not natives of the region, they bring in work teams through their own personal networks, which are invariably based in villages elsewhere.

Harvey's supposition that urbanization will create jobs that will fuel consumption makes an assumption that is faulty in the Chinese context: that jobs must be going to the very people who will become new urban consumers. In Qijiang County, for example, local officials developed infrastructure to anticipate growing tourism and consumption from urbanites in Chongqing seeking weekend respite from the city. They built this infrastructure using rural labor, however, and due to the intensive subcontracting practices that make construction profitable despite a lack of bank credit, wages for construction jobs had not increased. China's emergent cities and townships create jobs, but these jobs are more likely to go to nonlocal rural laborers, not to the residents displaced from the land on which they are built.

This mismatch—those who build cities are not the people who consume within them—is generated by the capital structure of urbanization in China. As in many urbanizing contexts, local governments benefit more from high-value urban construction, that is, luxury high-rises over public housing. What makes this revenue-driven urbanization unique, however, is its interaction with the preexisting political economic context of China's labor-intensive development. A hierarchical citizenship system, localized welfare state, and decentralized fiscal governance system have all intersected to produce widespread wage suppression in cities. This wage suppression requires the employment of rural labor, and typically, rural laborers have collectively organized themselves both to seek irregular employment and to withstand the delayed wages that come with them.

What jobs were available to villagers in Landing? Early in 2011, handwritten signs were posted on streetlights in New Land Township advertising jobs that would shortly be available to local Landing residents: openings for a cook in the luxury five-star hotel that would open in two years and a pipefitter for the new high-rise apartments being built. Yet of the Landing residents, only a handful successfully secured these jobs, and even then, those who did were successful only for political reasons. One woman hired for the coveted position of hotel cook, for example, had a son employed in a Qijiang County government office who was well placed enough to secure the job through personal channels.

Many local labor brokers returned to Qijiang to try negotiating labor delivery contracts with the subcontractors the county had staffed to build New Land Township. But county officials had already appointed construction enterprises to take on these projects, and the managers of these enterprises were uninterested in hiring local labor. From their standpoint, the employment of labor teams composed of newly landless and potentially aggrieved locals was an unattractive option, presenting risks that these enterprises were not willing to take. Because many of the private developers funding construction in Qijiang had gone into arrears to pay land transfer fees to the Qijiang County government, they contracted enterprises to carry out labor recruitment and materials purchases under low-cost conditions. While some had access to local government financing platforms that could generate credit flows by using newly state-owned land as collateral for mortgages, most of this credit was reserved for infrastructural and agricultural modernization projects rather than for the private real estate projects.[2] Construction related to private real estate development in these newly urbanized regions conformed to the same low-cost labor practices as before.

Most brokers and subcontractors in the Landing region were similarly unable to successfully solicit work opportunities from the county government. Most had developed their existing networks and industry connections in nonlocal regions, where wages were higher and brokerage more profitable. Boss Bo, for example, often traveled to cultivate his social relationships with urban labor contractors, and he maintained regular labor contracts in Beijing, Tianjin, and Xi'an in the north, as well as Chongqing and Guangzhou in the south.

This recruitment structure is the reason urbanization is unlikely to absorb the local unemployed. Even in rural construction sites in peripheral regions such as Qijiang County and New Land Township, subcontractors come from far away and bring laborers recruited from their own regions.[3] In Qijiang County, for example, government officials draw up building contracts with a construction enterprise in Chongqing, and many of the laborers that eventually arrive in New Land Township are from Hubei Province to the east of Chongqing. These construction enterprises and contractors directly appointed by county officials are so important to the urbanization process that they are regularly referred to as "businessmen of urban management" (*chengshi yuying shang*), delegators of the work of urban expansion, and are given full latitude to recruit laborers from their own preferred sites. Furthermore, because the work of urban expansion is supported directly by the local government, state resources meant for migrant workers are often channeled not to local residents but instead to nonlocal labor in-migrants. For example, temporary migrant dormitories erected in the Qijiang county seat were initially touted as livelihood relief for Landing residents without housing, but in the end, most units in fact housed nonlocal migrant laborers who were recruited by subcontractors to build the new infrastructure of Qijiang.

Similarly, much of the land in Landing was expropriated to form large enclosures for agribusinesses to farm. Yet these agribusinesses, like the construction projects, were run by government-appointed rural subcontractors, who relied on localized networks to seek work teams from their own communities. Landing villagers could work as contract farmers for these agribusinesses, but most believed that such jobs were risky, since rural subcontractors were likely to prefer promoting laborers they hired from their own villages. Like the subcontracted construction workforce, the contract farming workforce was recruited locally, with brokers hiring from their home communities rather than the local community.

So few jobs were available to the Landing villagers awaiting eviction that late in 2011, when county officials offered to pay some villagers to help demolish village houses and level off expropriated village land, many accepted the work. County officials further allowed the villagers to keep for themselves any building materials they were able to salvage. Yet without land to build on, such materials were of little value. Many elderly villagers who were unable to find work outside the village were enticed by the offer, some even volunteering to demolish their own houses and level their own land.

Of course some local residents were able to access jobs and special favors through state connections. Many Landing residents, for example, were quick to point out that Party secretary Zhang had purchased a township apartment in the township even before it became New Land Township. Several of his close kin were in conspicuously fortunate circumstances since the urbanization. His sister, Zhang Shiqun, obtained a coveted job as a cook in the large flagship hotel recently built at the center of New Land Township, one of the only jobs advertised explicitly to attract local residents. It struck many villagers as at least odd that the best job in the new township went to the sister of the party secretary. But most villagers, politically cautious, were quick to attribute her job to resourcefulness. One reassured me, immediately after mentioning her job, "[Zhang Shiqun] is very resourceful, always looking for opportunities."

There were more direct suspicions of corruption that villagers harbored but did not voice. Secretary Zhang had a distant cousin who faced the pending eviction with no support; her husband worked for Boss Bo, and she herself had been a farmer for years. Her side of the family was not on good terms with Secretary Zhang, and she in particular often chafed at the good fortune that somehow befell those kin he favored: "[My cousin] bought an apartment there in the township before anyone else. Prices were probably lower then. But he is Party Secretary. Who knows what kinds of income he has?"

When I reacted to her implication that Secretary Zhang had alternative and informal sources of income, she quickly clarified: "I mean that he does some local business with other men. . . . I don't know where Secretary Zhang gets his income. But I will say he is better off than one would think." If any capital did trickle down from the state-led urbanizing process to villagers, it flowed only via political channels and accrued solely to those with state connections.

A SURGE IN MIGRATION

Instead of relying on the government to generate jobs during modernization, Landing residents turned to their preexisting migration networks for employment. With the news of eviction, there came a surge in migration, as residents scrambled to find jobs through their informal, local networks.

The Deng household had four *hukou*-registered members: Little Deng, his older farming brother, and his elderly parents. In 2011 the Dengs transferred their *hukou* to urban status in New Land Township and received a notice that in three years they would lose access to their land and receive a one-time payment totaling 43,600 RMB, compensation for lost housing and land, some of which had been earmarked for agricultural enclosure and some for environmental protection. The payment was insufficient for the purchase of either a pension or a public housing unit in New Land Township.

Each of the Dengs embarked on various strategies for making a living after learning of the land loss. Little Deng still had access to his wife's land in Faming Village, but he had the responsibility of trying to help his nephew Deng Guang find work. Deng Guang had also lost his registered land within the three years limit, and he was having trouble finding work.

Moreover, since it was Little Deng's wife who had introduced him to Huang Rong and instigated the series of events that led to the loss of his savings, Little Deng felt compelled to help Deng Guang. Little Deng had assumed that his brother-in-law Boss Bo would rehire him and Deng Guang as he had so many times in the past. But during a prior migration, Little Deng had served as a foreman for Boss Bo for a team of Faming laborers he had recruited to work in Beijing, and Boss Bo had been dissatisfied with his performance. Moreover, Boss Bo was inundated with requests from other Landing residents for work, and he told Little Deng he had no room on his contracts. Little Deng then went back to Faming Village to seek work from the Gao brothers, but they refused to hire him out of suspicion that he would simply poach recruits for Boss Bo.

Unsuccessful in seeking work through his usual outlets, Little Deng then began to cultivate a relationship with another labor broker, Boss Zhou, from Jiulongai Village, directly adjacent to Landing. Boss Zhou needed a foreman to help him recruit a team of workers for a construction contract in nearby Chongqing, and Little Deng persuaded Boss Zhou to hire him.

Little Deng included his older brother on the team roster along with a motley crew of several other villagers. Among the junior workers on his team were a couple in their fifties, who had two school-aged children, no savings, and no posteviction plans for where they would relocate in three years. Another farming couple working for Little Deng lost their land in exchange for a slim compensation payment of 10,000 RMB in total and could not rely on help from their son, who had relocated to the village of his wife and did not offer help. These villagers were the only laborers that Little Deng could scrape up in Landing by late 2011. They were stragglers, those left behind after a frenzied rush to find work earlier in the year. Most villagers had launched extensive searches for jobs and new residences after the announcement of upcoming evictions.

Although pending evictions created a surge of interest in migration, this interest largely came from inexperienced migrants. Labor brokers such as Boss Bo found themselves inundated with requests for work but were often dissatisfied with the quality of available labor. For example, Deng Liwen fielded many requests for work on behalf of her husband. One afternoon she was summoned to the home of Luo Xianyu, where several older farmers, Zhou Wenbing among them, beseeched her to ask her husband for jobs on their behalf. Some of the men were first-time migrants, one was an older woman who had lost an arm long ago in a factory accident, and none were accustomed to migrant labor, and Deng Liwen knew they would be of minimal value to her husband's work team. But she called her husband anyway, and Boss Bo again agreed, out of sympathy, to connect them to another local broker, Boss Liu.

The farmers were unaccustomed to even the most basic logistics of migration. They were staffed on a project in Chongqing, a mere three-hour commute from Landing Village, but still they were flustered over how they would locate the worksite. Luo Xianyu had no cell phone, and so Deng Liwen wrote down Boss Liu's cell number on a large piece of paper and instructed him to locate a pay phone once he had made his way to Chongqing, to get directions to the worksite. Land expropriation had now forced the last of the village's population into migration.

However, Boss Bo's subcontractors in Chongqing expressed displeasure with the ragtag team he sent them. That spring, coinciding with the first phase of evictions back in Landing Village, members of this team began to launch grievances. Some made requests for time off to return home, others requested loans and cash advances to send back to kin. All of these requests stemmed directly from anticipation of land loss and new attempts to acquire subsidized housing in New Land Township.

Despite the sudden surfeit of Landing laborers, therefore, Boss Bo was losing income. He had employed some older farmers who were untrained and inexperienced, and his subcontractors in Chongqing had even rejected a number of these recruits outright. At the same time, other recruits were demanding advance payments for aid in relocation, and in some cases he provided these workers with sizable loans. Finally, one of his subcontractors in Chongqing canceled his contract for the year in March, shortly after receiving Boss Bo's delivery of twenty workers. The team, he was told, was not up to Boss Bo's usual standard.

DIVERTED CHANNELS OF RECRUITMENT

Land expropriations thus disrupted the profitability of labor brokerage, and this disruption was damaging to brokers such as Boss Bo, who were themselves subject to rising costs of urban relocation. But Boss Bo could

Map 5. Boss Bo's recruitment and contract sites. Map by author.

always hire workers from elsewhere to replace Landing villagers if they became troublesome. By 2011 Bo was recruiting labor from four villages in the Sichuan-Chongqing region. Over the course of his career he had dispatched labor to seven cities in all: Beijing, Tianjin, Shanghai, Guangzhou, Shenzhen, Xi'an, and Hohhot in Inner Mongolia (see map 5).

Boss Bo could send laborers from these four villages even from a distance. In 2011, when he had a sudden shortage of fifteen men at a worksite in Chongqing, he placed a cell phone call to a villager at one of his four sites and dispatched the men almost immediately: "I just make some calls. . . . They all know where I am. It's very easy, I am short fifteen men, I just call a couple guys here back at home and tell them to get on a bus. No problem. Right away."

Since his forays into Faming and three other neighboring villages, Boss Bo had become less reliant on Landing laborers and as a result more cavalier in his business dealings with them. In general he found Faming villagers expedient replacements when Landing workers performed poorly.

They were accustomed to lower wage levels than Landing laborers, given their relative inexperience in migration. Boss Bo noted his own surprise at this fact, when he first traveled to Faming Village:

[In 2007] I started going to Faming to find workers. . . . I brought about ten men from Landing to Faming and then I hired about twenty from Faming. The Landing men, we all earned about 80, 90 RMB per day. Back then that was a lot. But the Faming men, they were satisfied with 20 or 30 RMB.[4] I know now that if I ever need to find some men who will work for cheap, I just have to go to Faming.

Faming villagers were cheaper to employ than Landing laborers, and importantly, they also still held land plots, which allowed them to withstand delayed wage payment without complaint.[5] They became his primary labor supply in 2011, when his own troubles with recruitment in Landing were just beginning.

Indeed, Boss Bo did have a large number of labor contractors in his network. But he also expended much effort and resources in their cultivation and maintenance. The reason for this is that labor subcontractors and contractors are usually intermediaries working for managers in construction enterprises, and they enter into agreements with rural brokers only on the basis of long-standing trust and reciprocity. Boss Bo frequently took his subcontractors in Chongqing out for pricey dinners but expressed consternation at the high cost of maintaining these social connections:

Last night I [took my subcontractors out] to eat at a hot pot place in Chongqing. . . . Spent 500 RMB in one night! . . . In the city, money goes fast. You can say I earn 5,000 RMB a month, but it goes away very fast, I can only save maybe 1,000 or 2,000 RMB every month. People like us, we make 50,000, 60,000 RMB in the city every year, but it still goes very fast.

Given the high costs of greasing employers' palms, the loss of a contract, as had happened with his Chongqing subcontractor, was a disastrous event. After that incident, Boss Bo had his own personal crisis. He bemoaned in particular the costs of his ongoing relocation to Qijiang. By late 2011 Boss Bo still owed 225,000 RMB on his mortgage in Qijiang District:

I have to pay 300 RMB a month to maintain the apartment, for water and garbage pickup, these "community fees" that the apartment complex requires. That's not even mentioning the mortgage I still have!

He calculated that he would need to keep brokering labor for fifteen additional years to pay down this debt. But at age fifty-two, Bo worried he might not last that long in the business. Though he did not do bodily labor as a broker, the job was nevertheless physically strenuous, and his wife Deng Liwen often worried about his health.

Replacing Landing laborers with Faming laborers, however, was a costly and difficult task. Prior to land expropriations, Boss Bo had been willing to pay relatively higher wages to Landing laborers, because he could leverage village-based relationships with their families to guarantee their reliability. Replacing Landing laborers meant sending a team of trusted kinsmen with workers from a village where he had fewer substantial social connections.

Despite Boss Bo's boasts that he could assemble a team from Faming Village with a single cell phone call, his initial attempts to broker Faming labor met with resistance. Some Faming villagers became aware that they were being paid considerably less than Landing laborers. One man even overheard a cell phone conversation between Boss Bo and his wife and learned of a sizable mortgage Boss Bo had recently taken on in the purchase of real estate in New Land Township. This man spread a rumor among the other Faming replacements linking Boss Bo's financial situation with their lowered wages:

> [I could tell that Boss Bo] had just spent a lot of money in 2011. He was only interested in keeping costs to a minimum. . . . He made excuses, he told us we were inexperienced workers and had to work a year before we could get a raise. But actually, we found out later he was just shortchanging us because he didn't have the money.

Another Faming villager from that work team corroborated this view:

> [Boss Bo] had just come off a bad investment. . . . He had no money, no savings that year. But he hid that information from us. So, when it came time to give us our weekly living allowances, he was very stingy, only 100 RMB per 10 days. That is far less than what we usually get in a city like Beijing. It's usually 30 RMB daily. . . . And at the end of the year, we earned very little. Nobody said it at the time but I think he kept more for himself than he should have.

One of Boss Bo's first teams of laborers from Faming Village eventually launched a protest about their low living allowances and refused to work, idling in the dormitory during their work shifts to protest their unequal pay arrangements. After they had spent only one month on the job, Boss Bo's subcontractor canceled the contract and sent all of the migrants home.

Nonregional labor recruitment, in which a group of kin-related villagers work for an outsider broker not of their origin community, is uncommon within China's rural workforce. In most migrant workplaces, labor recruitment remains localistic and is conducted via long-standing, trust-based social networks in origin communities. In factories, for example, researchers have depicted separate assembly lines operating using distinct linguistic dialects.[6] In migrant enclaves in Beijing, entrepreneurs maintain regionally distinct, informal banking networks, mutual aid groups, and networks of buyers and suppliers.[7] In Zhejiang Province, a coastal region known for its flourishing informal markets, each informal industry—shoemaking, cigarette lighter sales, counterfeit cellular phone sales—has become monopolized by rural entrepreneurs from the same province.

In construction, regionalized labor recruitment is an accepted norm specifically because subcontracting practices have created informal employment arrangements in which guarantees of wage payment are difficult to enforce legally. Brokers who attempt to recruit and deploy labor from nonnative regions therefore face skepticism and lack of trust among workers who are accustomed to working exclusively for locals. They also encounter perceptions of competition and encroachment among local brokers. Boss Bo's foray into Faming Village, for example, posed a threat to the Gao brothers, who themselves had a stake in monopolizing labor recruitment there.

Distrust of outside labor intermediaries was widespread in Faming Village. One previous year, when a team of Faming workers agreed to work on a contract in Beijing negotiated by Boss Bo, villagers in Faming blamed their foreman, Little Deng, for wage nonpayment. That year, one villager had returned home to Faming before receiving his pay for the year, assuming that Little Deng would simply pay the workers after he too returned to the village. When he went to Little Deng to ask for his wages, however, he began to suspect that Little Deng had collected the team's total wages from Boss Bo but decided to keep the money for himself:

I went to Little Deng to get his money, and Little Deng told me, he said, "I haven't gotten my money either, so how can I give you your money?" And then I came home for the Lunar New Year and still there was no money. . . . [Little Deng] said he hadn't gotten paid either. But how can I know whether Little Deng got paid or not? The labor contractor was Boss Bo, who is Deng's brother-in-law. Of course, Little Deng probably got paid.

The worker never received his wages for that year. But according to Little Deng, neither had he—that was the year that Boss Bo removed Little Deng from his post as foreman and refused to pay his back wages. Still, Little Deng was Boss Bo's brother-in-law, and the villagers' perceptions of nepotism were difficult to dispel.

Despite these difficulties, Boss Bo eventually diverted all of his labor recruitment activities away from Landing Village, where evictions had made his labor supply untenable. Many of the Landing villagers who had previously worked for Boss Bo were unable to withstand the wages he normally paid them, since their families were unable to subsist through farming during the year. Some requested that their wages be paid up front, so that they could make down payments on public housing in New Land Township. Several Landing laborers paid visits to Boss Bo's wife, Deng Liwen, to beseech her for loans for children's school fees, regale her with the troubles of their aging parents bereft of welfare support, or ask for time off so that they could return to Landing Village to handle paperwork for their land compensation and *hukou* transfer. Boss Bo could not afford to raise wages, extend loans, or give laborers time off; neither could he afford to lose another subcontractor due to underperforming laborers. As difficult as it was to recruit labor from Faming and other non-native villages, he maintained a healthy network of construction subcontractors to whom he could deliver labor.

CLASS STRATIFICATION AFTER EVICTIONS

Broadly speaking, land expropriation exacerbated an already stratified class structure in Landing Village. It created new differentiations among villagers, whose livelihood strategies had largely assumed that land rights would remain intact. For example, even Boss Bo himself had not planned on having to relocate to the Qijiang county seat, where living costs were higher than in the village. Indeed, many entrepreneurial villagers had adopted hybrid strategies of investing in nearby urban centers by purchasing real estate or starting small businesses there, while still residing in villages where they could continue farming to subsidize food costs. Therefore, when evictions took place, even these entrepreneurial villagers had to alter their plans.

Landing's local class structure had long been bifurcated. Some households had begun migrating early and parlayed saved earnings into entrepreneurial activities, whether labor brokerage or otherwise; others had remained wage laborers, their labor to be brokered by intermediaries. Entrepreneurial households that had completely shed their ties to the village economy fared well during rural modernization. For example, the well-known "woman boss" Wu Guangming, for example, had relocated to a migrant enclave in Chongqing, where she ran an automotive repair shop and purchased an apartment. Her reported income from her business, combined with property ownership, had made her eligible to qualify for Chongqing *hukou* status. Her means of livelihood was not even indirectly affected by the land expropriations in the way that Boss Bo's was; she made no adjustments to her lifestyle after the transition.

For households that engaged in wage labor, on the other hand, eviction triggered a downward trajectory, introducing a new riskiness to already risky migrations. Although migrations were still possible after land loss, the removal of land as a fallback solution made some migrants less willing to take on more distant or risky migrations. Deng Guang, for example, backed out of a work opportunity in Inner Mongolia when he heard a rumor that the subcontractor for whom he would be working had stiffed villagers on wages in the past. In the town market only a week before he was scheduled to depart for the job, he met another migrant who had heard a secondhand rumor from other migrants who had worked for the same subcontractor. "That boss, if he comes up short, he just pays everyone less money than agreed on in the beginning," the migrant told him. "The year the other villagers were there, they were paid 1,000 RMB less monthly than what they agreed on in the beginning."

Deng Guang had been hoping, like Little Deng, to use this work opportunity to begin building some work experience as a foreman. He had heard about the job from an old acquaintance from his working days in Beijing who had become a subcontractor in Inner Mongolia and was in need of a team of workers. After making some calls, Deng Guang had decided he could fill that contract by bringing along his brother and their mother, who would work as a team cook at the site, and five other middle school classmates he would bring along as recruits. But the rumor about the Inner Mongolia subcontractor had unnerved him. Deng Guang could not expose his mother and brother to such risks now that his savings were wiped out and their land rights no longer guaranteed. He got a refund on their train tickets to Inner Mongolia and instead made plans to work with Little Deng on Boss Zhou's contract in Chongqing. The job was a relatively low-paying one, 60 RMB per day as opposed to the 100 RMB daily that had been promised with the Inner Mongolia job. But it was lower risk, with wages paid by the month rather than at year-end.

The process of job searching created distinctions between longtime migrants with greater social capital, such as Little Deng and Deng Guang, and less experienced migrants who had spent most of their lives farming, such as Zhou Wenbing and Luo Xianyu. Deng Guang could draw on an extensive network of contacts in the construction industry during his job search. Less experienced migrants took what jobs were available and sometimes could not discern the difference between high- and low-risk migrations. In fact, after Deng Guang turned down the Inner Mongolia job, he referred the job to a distant cousin, a fifty-five-year-old man named Wang Sanbu. Wang Sanbu was a farmer who also worked as a pig butcher during the Lunar New Year, when most families returned to the village for the holiday and customarily butchered several pigs for the feast. He had occasionally worked for Boss Bo on local construction contracts in Chongqing, but he had never ventured beyond the province for work. In 2011, however, Wang Sanbu had learned his house would be demolished by the end of the year, so he accepted the Inner Mongolia job, taking along with him a younger brother.

The two men found that the rumors were grounded in truth. After they arrived in Inner Mongolia, Wang Sanbu and his brother were promised a monthly wage of 2,800 RMB, to be paid at year-end, and a monthly living allowance of 360 RMB, which would later be deducted from the wage. The job started out well. Wang Sanbu was particularly pleased to find that costs of food and housing were gratis, not deducted from their wages. However, halfway through the year the subcontractor disappeared from the worksite, before paying out any wages. Wang Sanbu and his brother returned that summer with only 800 RMB each, which they were given by a foreman who divided up among the workers the little that had not been pocketed by the subcontractor.

Villagers were well aware of the differences in social capital that shaped different posteviction outcomes. Deng Guang, for example, explained that the job search process favored younger villagers, as they were more likely to have spent more time building social connections outside of the village:

> The truth is that the Wang brothers do not have much experience working. They are usually just doing farm work at home. So, they do not have many connections [outside the village]. They must take what they can get. For most of us younger people, we work construction on local jobs every year so we all know each other. It's easier for us to find jobs because we know people and we know their reputations.

There was some truth to the perception that younger migrants assimilated more easily to living conditions after the land expropriations. But this view also elided the difficulties that even experienced young migrants had when working for subcontractors they met outside the village. Finally, it was not always the case that villagers in possession of a wide social network or entrepreneurial skills were safe from precarity after evictions. The farming entrepreneur Wu Minjian, for example, was widely respected in the village for the large contract shipping network he had built, which coordinated the harvests of nearly a dozen small farmers in the Qijiang region. Yet when the land expropriations came, none of Wu Minjian's painstakingly built business relationships with agricultural buyers in Chongqing were of use. He found himself in a situation much like Wang Sanbu's once he lost his land: in need of work and forced to take any job that came his way.

Nevertheless, the perception that hardworking migrants were better prepared for eviction than risk-averse farmers was difficult to shake. Many villagers had internalized and personalized this view, even to the point of blaming older villagers for their inability to adapt to a migratory livelihood. Wang Sanbu and his brother had a wealthy eldest brother, Wang Sanzai, himself a former construction worker who had accumulated enough seed capital to open a small automotive repair shop in Qijiang County. Wang Sanzai was able to take out a large bank loan and purchase property in Qijiang. When the eviction notices came, he and his wife relocated to Qijiang. In the past he had sent Wang Sanbu money, but his support dwindled as he began to see his brother's predilection for the farming life as a weakness:

> He has no way to earn a better living. So, he can only work locally for Qijiang labor contractors. But it is no way to make a living. These days, we have to go far from home in order to make a better living. My brother has never been able to do that.

In response to these perceptions, Wang Sanbu was able to offer only a feeble defense. Wang Sanzai had begun accumulating wages at an early age, and this had given him starting capital to invest later in life. By choosing to spend his youthful days on the farm, Wang Sanbu had missed out on an opportunity to accumulate wealth. "I would be lying if I didn't say that it was easier for [my brother]," he said. "Once one person has money, they can take out loans and invest in property and then it is easier for them to start businesses."

STRATEGIES OF SURVIVAL

By the end of 2011 villagers began enacting strategies for preparing for eviction during the three-year grace period. Some, such as Deng Shaoli and Wu Guangming, were sheltered from the changes, as they had already relocated to cities and were now engaged in livelihoods that were fully autonomous from the rural economy. The loss of land had no effect on their ongoing livelihoods. But for the rest, whether they were brokers or laborers, eviction was an event that necessitated extensive preparation.

Most labor brokers weathered land loss by diverting labor recruitment to new sites, but without the local village as a community of subsistence farming, brokers were bereft of a central location where workers could congregate, disseminate information, and exchange small loans. When Bo had recruited local Landing labor, he had relied on his wife, Deng Liwen, to leverage her village relationship with Landing laborers' wives to smooth over disagreements with his laborers. But after he began to hire Faming laborers, Bo could no longer leverage village ties for labor mediation.

Faced with these challenges of nonlocal labor recruitment, Boss Bo began to seek out investment opportunities in entrepreneurial activities less connected to the rural economy. This had long been a common strategy in Landing Village, where the most enterprising entrepreneurs started off in construction but later transitioned into other informal sectors. Such a strategy was particularly attractive to Boss Bo, for it would shield him from the repercussions of land expropriation, which had disrupted his labor brokerage business. When two distant nephews approached him with a proposal to open a noodle shop in New Land Township, he agreed. Bo provided a seed loan of 50,000 RMB to the nephews, under the condition that after the noodle shop began to turn a profit, he could begin expecting a regular cut of profits. Should his labor brokerage activities fail or in case he needed to retire early, he could rely on this investment for his livelihood.

Similar calculations among brokers became the basis for the emergence of a small class of entrepreneurs. These were the kin of brokers, who survived land loss by launching supply stores, restaurants, automotive repair shops, and lithium battery replacement shops. They concentrated their activities on the edges of Qijiang District or New Land Township, where rents were lower and urban tourists often stopped for meals and repairs. They made back their monthly rents and accumulated savings. With their profits, many took out high-interest bank loans to acquire state-subsidized housing units. Moreover, they relied all along on close relationships with brokers, who helped them grease the palms of local party secretaries and other political figures responsible for procuring the necessary business permits and licenses.

Boss Bo's cousin Boss Zeng also had made such a calculation. In 2008 he provided financial sponsorship to another entrepreneur in Landing Village, a middle-aged woman called Manager Wang, who was a distant cousin. She had long worked as an apprentice in an automotive repair shop in Chongqing before land expropriations. He gave her a loan, enough to cover rent, materials, and machinery to open her own auto repair shop in Qijiang County in 2008. For three consecutive years, her auto shop failed to turn a profit. Boss Zeng, whose assets were heavily leveraged in real estate by then, was tempted to stop paying her rent. But he nevertheless persisted in making her rent payments, though it meant missing payments on his mortgage on his own Qijiang high-rise apartment. Such was the importance, for aging labor brokers, of maintaining an ownership stake in township businesses.

Villagers who lacked the accumulated capital necessary to engage in entrepreneurship found other ways to detach themselves from reliance on the rural economy. Many families pooled their savings to put together down payments on the state-subsidized public housing available in New Land Township. When villagers could, they sought out old connections to other rural regions. Many older villagers could move in with migrant children who had earlier married and relocated to other villages where land rights remained intact.

Older farmers generally cohabited with their children. The village leader Pen Gang, who had warned villagers of the evictions to come, made plans to cohabit with a son who had purchased an apartment in Qijiang District. Wang Deihua and her husband relied on their college-age daughters, who had relocated to the Qijiang county seat. Deng Shaoli had known for years about the upcoming evictions; in preparation, she and her sister had purchased a subsidized apartment in New Land Township and a state-subsidized pension for their parents. Their mother, Wang Deihua, provided an informed explanation of the older couple's retirement plans: "In several years, after the government pays us compensation money for the land and for this house," Wang Deihua gestured to the spacious, two-story stone house she lived in. "Then we will move to New Land Township and retire from farm work. We are about that age."

Finally, there were villagers whose children had relocated to other villages who could now extend help. One farmer, Wu Minwu, and his factory worker wife Zhou Zisu were among the unlucky few who had signed away their rural *hukou*, and along with it their rural land, before they realized they could not qualify for welfare.[8] However, their eldest son had married a woman from a remote farming village in Guangxi Province, two provinces away. At the time of that marriage, Wu Minwu and Zhou Zisu had been disappointed that their son consented to relocate to her household's plots of village land. This decision meant the young migrant couple would provide more remittance support to her parents rather than to them. But now the younger couple, who worked in factories, offered to take them in, and they were glad he had made that decision. Wu and Zhou moved to their daughter-in-law's household in Guangxi, where they cared for their grandchild and tended the land.

Any claim to land in other villages became useful to villagers who were in a rush to make living arrangements. After he was laid off by Boss Bo, aging migrant worker Zhou Kai and his wife Liu Jingnian discovered that their savings were not enough for the necessary down payment for state-subsidized housing in New Land Township. Luckily his wife was from a village in neighboring Guizhou Province, and when she married Zhou Kai she had neglected to re-register her *hukou* in Landing. Now Zhou Kai was thankful for the oversight, which meant she still held rights to a small plot of land in her natal village. His wife and daughter relocated to her natal home, where they cohabited with his mother-in-law in Guizhou and farmed her mother's land while awaiting his wage remittances from working as a migrant laborer.

Finally, another aging farming couple found unexpected good fortune when their son relocated to another neighboring village that was similarly scheduled for demolition. Their thirty-three-year-old son, a lowly concrete pourer who once worked for Boss Bo, had been introduced through distant kin relatives to a woman whose family lived in a nearby village close to Chongqing Municipality, and he had married her. He had kept his *hukou* registered at his parents' household in Landing. But when officials in his wife's village announced that her parents' household would be demolished and their land absorbed into the Chongqing city limits, he moved his *hukou* registration to join the household of his wife's parents. Monetary compensation for land expropriated so near the city center was expected to be far more favorable to households than for more remote land, and the once-lowly concrete pourer now found a way to help his parents. He and his wife collected their compensation package for their eviction, then put a down payment on a subsidized apartment built to house villagers in Chongqing City. Once the down payment was accepted, he invited his aging parents in Landing to cohabit with him and his wife.

FRACTURED KIN NETWORKS

This strategy of cohabitation with other rural kin became especially popular after state-subsidized units ran out and the remaining villagers were priced out of the township housing market. It allowed villagers to re-create livelihood conditions that they had previously enjoyed, namely access to land for farming. Yet kin relations were also strained by these various negotiations. For every villager who received help from a more fortunate relative, there were also kin groups wrenched apart by unmet expectations and miscommunication.

A long-standing feeling of discomfort often ran through extended families whose members spanned the rural-urban divide. These feelings often overwhelmed Wu Minjian, for example, a farmer engaged in a large-scale rice production network around neighboring villages. Wu Minjian had an older brother named Wu Mindian who was a primary school teacher with urban *hukou* registration in a town near Landing, a status he owed to an assignment to a socialist work unit in the 1970s. Wu Mindian had kept his distance from his two farming brothers since escaping village life during the bad years of hunger before postsocialist reforms. Their relationship was strained; Wu Minjian could not forgive his brother for what he saw as abandonment of the family. His response to these feelings of abandonment was to become self-reliant; he determined that he would lift his children to circumstances above those of his brother.

Wu Minjian had a son who married well. Long before, Wu Minjian's wife had sent their son to work in the factory of a distant wealthy uncle, who ran a business on the outskirts of Zhengzhou, a boomtown to the east. While there the son had not only impressed the distant uncle, but also met and romanced a distant cousin, daughter of this rich uncle. They married and settled there, in a village near the factory, where he managed sales for the factory that his father-in-law managed.

Wu Minjian counts among his life's major accomplishments the success of his son, whose career he takes as evidence of the value of hard work and a rural upbringing: "I always say, you look at my son and you know what real smarts are. My son didn't go to school but he has street smarts. He knows how to talk to people, how to think, how to get things done. You don't learn that in university." On one of the few occasions when he had seen his brother Wu Mindian in the past decade, Wu Minjian had felt proud. His own son was now outearning the son of Wu Mindian, who worked a similar job in sales at a factory in Chongqing.

Because Wu Minjian's son was doing so well, he assumed that upon eviction he and his wife could cohabit with their child in Zhengzhou. But just prior to the arrival of his actual eviction notice, Wu Minjian's son called with bad news. He had proposed the idea of his parents relocating to Zhengzhou where they could cohabit with his family, but his father-in-law had vetoed the plan. Afterward, Wu Minjian could not bring himself to beseech Wu Mindian for help. It would mean forgoing dignity before a brother whom he could not forgive.

Many families were like Wu Minjian's, in that they had long been estranged by the rural-urban gap, even before the onslaught of evictions. The Deng clan, for example, was economically diverse. Deng Liwen had married a labor broker, while her brothers were ordinary construction laborers. Her aunt Wang Deihua was the most fortunate of all, with daughters who were now government employees, possessed a township apartment, and could rely on a government-subsidized pension in the posteviction future.

Even when members of the Deng clan tried to offer mutual aid, this aid was often limited. Little Deng hired Deng Guang and his brother for his team of men working for Boss Zhou in Chongqing after Deng Guang decided against traveling to Inner Mongolia. But Deng Guang's mother had been hoping to work as a cook on the dormitory site as well, and Little Deng was unable to help her. Similarly, Deng Liwen tried to convince Boss Bo to hire Little Deng and Deng Guang, but Boss Bo was uninterested in hiring the Deng men and eventually diverted recruitment to Faming Village instead.

Moreover, the rural-urban divide had long shaped villagers' values about the proper channels of social mobility. Deng Liwen and Wang Deihua, for example, bore mutual resentment as a result of their different class trajectories. Wang Deihua often spoke of Boss Bo and Deng Liwen as rough and uneducated and their wealth as ill-begotten. Deng Liwen, for her part, thought it reprehensible that Wang Deihua thought herself so superior when it was her daughters who had married well, while she herself remained a lowly farmer. She also believed government officials were corrupt and saw Wang Deihua's daughter Deng Shaoli as a traitor to her kin for participating in the affairs of the Land Reform Office.

These tensions often became impasses in personal relationships that could have otherwise led to useful outcomes such as information sharing or cooperation. Wang Deihua, for example, had privileged information on the land expropriations. She knew long before any of the other villagers that all of the village land would eventually be expropriated, and she knew the relative rates at which lost land would be compensated. Most significantly, she also knew that the welfare programs in New Land Township were going to be diminished. Yet when she shared this last piece of information with Deng Liwen, she did so in a way that multiplied resentment over her privileges:

> When we all get to the township, you'll see. There will be very few people who will qualify for welfare aid, and the welfare payments will be . . . so small! [My daughter] told me, "Don't fight over the scraps and leftovers with the rest of those villagers, just wait," she said. Anyway, my daughters will buy pensions for us anyway, so there is no need to worry about such little money.

The disclosure only magnified antipathy among other villagers. "Let other people fight over the leftovers?" Deng Liwen commented later on Wang Deihua's statement. "Is she so much better than the rest of us that she doesn't have to worry about livelihood?" Existing class tensions, in a context of deliberate misinformation over state policy, had elevated mutual resentments into real social divisions. Rather than consult with Wang Deihua to glean privileged information from her, villagers brooded over the coming changes in isolation.

MIGRATION WITHOUT LAND

Finally, how did migrants unable to preserve their access to rural land fare in the labor market? Migrants such as Wang Sanbu, who continued to engage in long-distance, high-risk migrations under the protection of unfamiliar, nonkin, and nonlocal labor brokers, were the most vulnerable to financial risk after evictions. Some among them, such as Deng Guang, were young and experienced migrants and were able to find work with brokers and subcontractors with whom they had some work experience and a basis of trust. But those worst off, such as Luo Xianyu, the farmer who hanged himself, had been farmers their entire lives before the evictions.

There were two suicides in Landing Village during evictions. The first was Luo Xianyu, whose death, it was speculated, was meant to diminish the burden he feared he would place on his children. The second was the death of Wang Sanbu, who returned from Inner Mongolia with his brother with only 800 RMB for half-a-year's work. By the time he returned, other work opportunities were hard to come by, since the hiring season had long passed.

When Wang Sanbu's life began to come undone, he put out various calls for help. He asked Deng Liwen to secure for him a job with Boss Bo, but Boss Bo declined to hire him. Rebuffed, he asked Deng Liwen for small loans for food. But further misfortunes befell him: a serious stomach illness of an unknown nature and hospital bills for the year totaling over 1,500 RMB. He was unable to plant a crop that year. As his eviction date approached, Wang Sanbu himself knew that things were serious. He felt increasingly isolated, and he became depressed. He knew that his situation was deteriorating fast:

> I have to get out of here. But it has been three months working [construction] in Qijiang and I have saved so little. I will probably need at least 15,000 RMB to build a new house, but even then I have no land to build it on. I have to move. I am beginning to feel it is not safe here. At night there are no sounds, the day too is silent down here, and if something happened to me, I would be all alone. There are no neighbors to help me. The fact is, I know that my situation is bad.

Wang Sanbu's house was finally demolished by December 2011.

In September 2011 Wang Sanbu had found a job at a construction site near New Land Township under a state-appointed subcontractor. The job had seemed a windfall opportunity at the beginning. But it was a short-term, temporary contract arrangement, calling for workers to perform interior renovations on properties after major construction was complete. The other workers hired on the job, moreover, were local commuters, mainly well-connected new township residents looking for extra side money. Wang was the only laborer there fully dependent on this job for his livelihood.

When he arrived, he found that the worksite dormitory and cafeteria, which had previously accommodated the migrant workforce carrying out major construction, had been dismantled. Wang Sanbu found himself in an awkward position: His wages, as usual, were not to be paid until year-end, yet his house in Landing had already been demolished, and he had no access to food or shelter. In desperation, he approached distant kin and other villagers for small loans to cover the costs of renting a month-by-month bunk bed in a group shelter for migrant workers in Qijiang County. At the end of the year he collected his wages, but he remained in arrears, still owing 3,900 RMB to relatives for his room and board for the year.

Debt imposed a high psychological cost on Wang Sanbu. Wang was proud of his self-reliance despite his struggles, and though he could have called upon his eldest brother Wang Sanzai for assistance, he chose not to. At one point Wang Sanzai returned to Landing Village on a brief visit to hire some local villagers to plow his fallow land flat, according to state regulations for relinquished land. Wang Sanbu offered his services to Wang Sanzai for a small sum, 90 RMB a day. In 2012 Wang Sanzai returned to the village to oversee the transfer of his plowed land to the Qijiang government.

The meeting between the two brothers was tense. Wang Sanzai wordlessly offered Wang Sanbu a cigarette. The two sat and smoked silently, little passing between them despite their not having been in contact for nearly a decade before the land expropriation. After several minutes had passed, Wang Sanzai asked Wang Sanbu about his plans for the upcoming land seizure. Wang Sanbu did not answer immediately. When he eventually did, his tone was curt. "I have plans," he said simply. "You don't have to worry. I still have the certificates for my land. When the time comes I will return it for the compensation money as well." Another pause. "I will call you when your land is ready to return. You should take your land certificates with you for now. Then when it is ready, you can go straight to Qijiang District to submit the paperwork and not trouble yourself with coming all the way back here." Wang Sanzai left for the Qijiang county seat the next day and did not return.

When Wang Sanbu walked off the edge of a cliff near his demolished home several months later, most villagers were too busy making arrangements for their own families to dwell on the reasons for his death. Many villagers attributed the deaths of both Wang Sanbu and Luo Xianyu to family drama rather than land loss. Deng Liwen, for example, had long viewed Wang Sanbu's struggles as the result of his status as an unmarried bachelor. Several years before evictions began, Wang Sanbu had been jilted by a woman in a series of events similar to those Deng Guang had experienced with Huang Rong. During a long engagement to Zhang Liaoyi, a forty-year-old woman who lived in a neighboring village, Wang Sanbu poured 30,000 RMB, the entirety of his savings, into building materials for a house the couple built on Zhang Liaoyi's natal land. Then their relationship disintegrated, and Wang Sanbu faced the land expropriations with little kin support and no savings. Similarly, many believed Luo Xianyu, long widowed after the loss of his wife to illness, had hanged himself out of loneliness rather than as a resistance to eviction. While marriage might have alleviated the psychological stress of economic hardship after eviction for both men, it is difficult to deny the role of sudden, oppressive economic precarity in their deaths.

HOW GENERALIZABLE IS LANDING VILLAGE?

Can we understand the outcome of evictions in Landing as representative of the consequences of land expropriation across rural China? In Landing Village many residents are employed in the informal economy of construction labor recruitment, in which a delayed wage payment structure has forced households to rely on subsistence farming while they await wages. The impact of land loss has been amplified by the exigencies of this particular labor market, as without land families awaiting end-of-year wage payments have become unable to subsist while waiting.

If this study had been conducted in another village, would the results have been different? Residents who work in other industries, for example manufacturing or the service sector, do not rely so heavily on rural-based kin networks to find work and guarantee on-time wage payment. In manufacturing, wage arrears do occur, but not to the same extent as in construction. In the service sector, wage arrears are rare, but pay is generally lower than in manufacturing or construction. For example, the son of Liu Zhaoying worked as a bank teller in Qijiang District. His job paid 1,200 RMB per month, enough to cover rent for the bed in a migrant dormitory in the county seat and his personal expenses, but not child care or other fees. Losing land depleted his savings, since he now had to pay rent year-round rather than maintaining a house on collective village land. And it deprived him of the option of returning to the village during periods of unemployment or in retirement. In a village where manufacturing and service industries were the modal source of employment, land expropriation would have created economic precarity, but possibly not the levels of homelessness and debt that it created in Landing, where construction jobs were geographically mobile and ended so often in wage theft.

Had land expropriations occurred in Faming Village, on the other hand, consequences would have been far more dire. Landing Village was a mature migrant-producing site, where many households had accumulated sufficient earnings from construction work to transition into entrepreneurship. In Faming, however, migration had knit together two distinct economies: a subsistence farming system and an economy of labor brokerage. In Landing, these two systems had become delinked. This delinking, moreover, was enabled by a diversification of economic activities. While some households still relied on farming to supplement their wages, many had invested savings in real estate or informal economic activities such as Boss Bo's nephews' noodle shop, which generated supplementary income separate from the land.

URBANIZATION WITHOUT WORKING-CLASS FORMATION

The case of land expropriation in contemporary rural China runs parallel to the classic case of England's industrialization in the eighteenth and nineteenth centuries, which Polanyi ([1944] 2001) understood to be emblematic of the close relationship between social immiseration and capitalist growth. In England, a system of common lands left over from feudalism sheltered the working classes from the turbulence of markets, providing a means for them to supplement income by grazing domestic animals. The later enclosure of these lands, combined with the abolition of a parish system of relief for the poor, then spurred a sudden migration of laborers into cities, where unemployment rates rose precipitously.

What were the consequences of the English land enclosure, and how does the contemporary Chinese land enclosure differ? In 1795 the so-called Speenhamland Law was established to create a welfare subsidy by providing an allowance system indexed to the price of bread. But this system had the effect of allowing employers to lower wages below subsistence level, and it also tied laborers to their local rural parishes, where these subsidies were administered. Deeply unpopular at the time, this law was eventually lifted in 1834. Its cancellation marked the beginning of a national labor market with full labor mobility, and it forced laborers to face head on the full impact of market turbulence. It inaugurated a period of great social upheaval, in which labor protests and political mobilization became a response to turbulent markets that had been destabilized by free trade, wide fluctuations in grain prices, and a rigidly enforced gold standard. Polanyi's interpretation of the Speenhamland case is that it birthed, through violent means, a politically mobilized working class, one that eventually launched demands for social and legal protections for labor from the state.

What are the political dynamics of land enclosure in rural China? Like the English land enclosures, the expropriation of collective rural land in urbanizing regions has terminated the ability of many working people to supplement their income. Like the Speenhamland Law, the *hukou* system continues to tie rural people to their local townships, which administer their access to schools, welfare, and other public goods. Yet unlike the Speenhamland Law, which created a universal bread subsidy available to the working poor, *hukou* reforms in China have restricted welfare access to those unable to work. Most important, unlike the English case, the enclosure of rural lands has not created the full mobility of labor in China. Municipalities enforce a points-based system of *hukou* admission, granting residential rights only to those with formal employment.

In effect, the spread of rural land expropriation has removed the farming supplement enabled by collective land rights, without creating a fully free national labor market. From Chinese policy makers' perspectives, this gradual reform will prevent the formation of a concentrated underclass in megacities, instead channeling the newly landless to small cities and townships where few jobs are available. Rather than launching a violent process of proletarianization that will end in the creation of a politically empowered working class, these continuing regulations on population mobility have simply made rural land available for profitable development, while keeping rural laborers tied to townships and counties.

By dismantling the village communities that previously supported labor migration, land expropriation destroys the social institutions that traditionally protected laborers from market risks. Because townships such as New Land Township do not provide employment for the newly landless, land expropriation in Landing Village created a surge in migrants in dire straits, most of whom were inexperienced, elderly, or first-time migrants who were unattractive recruits for local brokers. Even if they were young and able-bodied, the fact of their landlessness was itself a deterrent to labor intermediaries looking for workers whose families could withstand delayed wage payment practices. Instead, labor brokers turned to other recruitment sites such as Faming Village, where labor migrants remained unaffected by the trauma of land expropriation.

This diversion in patterns of labor recruitment has created friction for laborers and brokers alike. In China's informal rural labor market, recruitment operates via regional social networks of trust and reciprocity. Given the associated risks of wage nonpayment in construction, migrants are reluctant to be employed by labor intermediaries from elsewhere. Thus, while laborers in Landing struggled to find work after eviction, so too did brokers struggle to recruit labor from elsewhere. In both cases, migrants and brokers alike found themselves adrift as the village community and subsistence farming economy were dismantled by rural-urban land conversions. Evictions disembed both migrants and brokers from the local networks of migration that guarantee brokers will reciprocate migrants' trust with protection, and to which workers contribute diligence and productivity in exchange for a guarantee of pay. When labor brokers such as Boss Bo become disembedded from the rural subsistence farming economy, they cannot secure the trust of their recruits, and when workers such as Deng Guang are disembedded from it, they cannot secure the guarantee of pay from their brokers.

Polanyi considers institutions that facilitate trust-based networks necessary for the long-distance transactions foundational to the making of human labor into a saleable commodity. Brokerage networks, which leverage kin-based relations of trust and expectations of reciprocity in order to compel on-time wage payment and loyalty, preserve the viability of labor over time. Women's village-based networks, such as Madam Gao's credit network in Faming Village, also contribute to the sustainability of labor delivery networks over time, since they help families withstand periods of wage nonpayment and meet large living expenses. Without these networks, Polanyi suggests, when workers are "shoved about, used indiscriminately, or even left unused," they will starve, and the commodity value of their labor will diminish.[9] Urbanization in China does not create a fully free, politically mobilized workforce, as it has historically done in Western contexts. Instead, it hobbles the existing workforce, disembedding it from the protective networks of trust and reciprocity that previously guaranteed successful labor transactions.

What makes the pinning of rural people to urbanizing fringes deadly is that elsewhere in rural China, migrant laborers still seek work within the old system of informal labor recruitment, bolstered by land-use rights embedded in village institutions. Landing's landless population is required to reside in New Land Township, where village networks are weakened and social services are scant. Still, they seek work, and when they do, they receive wage levels sufficient for the needs of a farming household, but insufficient to meet the new costs of food and housing incurred in townships. The rural dispossessed, less valuable than the land they inhabited and less employable than landholding laborers elsewhere, increasingly find themselves outside of the informal economy of labor recruitment.

CONCLUSION

This chapter has shown that the transformation of rural residents into urban citizens via a "land for welfare" trade has had devastating effects on many rural residents of Landing. Landing's residents were highly stratified even before the onset of urbanization reforms, as early labor migrations throughout the 1980s had led to the accumulation of remittance income among households engaging in the brokerage of labor. As these households gradually transitioned into entrepreneurial activities, they left behind those of common laborers such as Wu Minjian and Wang Sanbu, who had no choice but to continue subsistence farming in order to engage in the labor market.

The removal of land-use rights forced residents to adopt various strategies of survival, and these strategies produced various outcomes. Entrepreneurial residents, those engaged in petty proprietary activities outside the village, in townships and in county seats, for example, were largely insulated from the effects of land loss. Those entrepreneurs who brokered labor from the village, such as Boss Bo, were forced to move their labor recruitment elsewhere in order to avoid dealing with the disruption of laborers' livelihood troubles and related grievances. Those who fared the worst were laborers whose households still relied on subsistence farming during times of unemployment. These different outcomes reflect what You-tien Hsing calls deterritorialization, or the spatial dispersion of the dispossessed.[10] After eviction, villagers scattered, with some cohabiting with kin in other rural locales, but others struggling to find housing or jobs near their former villages of residence.

The dispersion of the dispossessed is in part a result of the fact that urbanization in China has not created local jobs. Instead, the labor of urbanization is carried out by government-appointed subcontractors, who rely on localized networks to seek work teams from their own origin communities. When these subcontractors do turn to landless laborers in the vicinity, such as Wang Sanbu, they do so only to fill in gaps in production, and such laborers will be dismissed before all work is completed. Those who are newly dispossessed are particularly vulnerable to these precarious employment conditions.

For these landless folks, neither welfare nor work have become viable sources of support. In rural China's transformation, many rural people have fallen by the wayside, neither receiving the entitlements attached to urban citizenship, which would otherwise protect them from unemployment, nor receiving the labor market opportunities that longtime urban residents do. Welfare entitlements have failed to materialize, due to the fiscally decentralized organization of local governments, which cut social welfare costs to divert funds toward profitable real estate development. Meanwhile, landless workers struggle in a construction labor market in which employers are accustomed to hiring laborers at below-market, land-subsidized rates.

Finally, the overall impact of land expropriation on the labor market has not been the creation of a free proletariat. In other words, land expropriations have not inaugurated the transition toward a politically mobilized workforce, one formally free of alternative means of subsistence, "free to work or free to starve." Instead, the wave of land expropriation in China has undermined the ability to withstand existing wage levels for a portion of the rural workforce.

7 The Future of Chinese Development

In the early twenty-first century, economic growth in China has become predicated on the expansion of urban industries, commerce, and real estate development into rural areas. Construction, an industry that both enables and sustains the process of urbanization, is at the center of this expansion. The profitability of construction is bolstered by two conditions. First, the availability of low-cost land, expropriated by local governments from rural households, has lowered entrance costs for investors and developers seeking new production zones, real estate demand, and consumer markets. Second, the suppression of wages by enterprises that also hire rural labor on a just-in-time basis, obviating costs of redundancy, social benefits, recruitment, and training, has driven up profits in construction.

This book uses the construction industry as a lens for examining the mechanisms and consequences of urban expansion, a process of capital accumulation that has become a dominant source of local government revenues. By using ethnography to capture firsthand experience, this study takes the standpoint of the laborers of urbanization: rural people living in a subsistence-oriented farming economy who have contributed their labor to urban industries but are largely excluded from the gains of growth in the form of public goods, higher wages, and urban residence.

Increasingly, as the urban welfare state expands to incorporate rural residents, these laborers have gained new formal rights, such as the option to register as urban residents, to access urban schools, and to purchase high-rise housing. Simultaneously, they have lost household land-use rights in the regions undergoing urban expansion.

As a putatively new, propertied middle class in the making, these displaced rural residents are expected to provide a new consumption base, particularly those among them who are younger and eager to gain new skills as industries scale up toward higher-value production. Yet the sectoral character of China's new growth has interrupted this transition. In the new paradigm of urban expansion, whether in the form of industrial investment in rural regions, rural estate and housing growth, or tourism and service-based expansion, new enterprises create new jobs, but these jobs do not employ the local residents who are displaced for their creation.

This chapter revisits the life course trajectories of some of the residents of Faming and Landing and links their diverging trajectories to a larger structural transformation under way in China. It asks a central question: To what extent can we understand the stories of Faming and Landing Villages to represent an overall trend in the Chinese economy? Elsewhere in the economy, manufacturing wages nationwide continue to rise, younger segments of the rural workforce are becoming more educated, and the service sector is expanding to absorb much of this new workforce. Yet Landing Village has undergone a particularly jobless form of urbanization, with construction employers employing labor recruited from elsewhere and real estate developers marketing properties to upscale buyers from nearby cities rather than from the countryside.

POLANYIAN VIEW OF THE ECONOMY

This book has provided a view of the Chinese economy that is centered on the foundations of production, namely the process by which labor and land are converted into productive capacity within the construction industry. In doing so, it suggests that a large portion of China's economic dynamism can be attributed to its low-cost production conditions, the seeming inexhaustibility of its stores of labor and land. Central to the production of low-cost labor, of course, is an exclusionary citizenship scheme that allows enterprises to offload costs of labor reproduction onto rural governments. The basis for China's low-cost land is a postsocialist legacy, which has created a pool of rural land, temporarily contracted to rural households but always under the control of local governments, made artificially "cheap" by the ease with which it can be seized for commercial development.

Many studies of the Chinese economy have examined the structure of its markets—enterprise ownership rights, the relationship between the state and enterprises, the ways that enterprises have learned from global business norms—to find the reason for its rapid growth post-Mao. Others have looked toward the capacity of the authoritarian state—its use of state banks to underwrite investments, its uniquely competitive federalist structure, its allotment of high autonomy to local governments—for reasons for growth. This study has suggested that the mechanisms for China's economic boom lie in how markets themselves are embedded in society—that is, how factors of production such as labor and land are wrenched from rural communities and readied for commodification.

China's economic boom, I argue, is a product of legacy, politics, and globalization. That is, postsocialist institutions such as the *hukou* and collective land have created a surplus pool of labor and land which, under conditions of globalization, have given China a globally low-cost production advantage. Political characteristics such as fiscal decentralization have created a regionally competitive terrain, boosting rates of land development as governments have pivoted toward real estate development as a growth strategy.

THE "AGRARIAN" QUESTION REVISITED

Another way to describe China's boom is to say that it has deliberately preserved the peasantry in order to create a reserve army of labor in the countryside. This flies in the face of scholarly views about agrarian transitions, which typically argue that agrarian capitalism is a precondition for industrial capitalism. The expectation is that in order to create the surplus labor necessary for industrialization, agriculture must be made efficient through technological advances and changes in production relations. Only after agriculture is modernized, and laborers are freed from subsistence farming, can industrialization take place.

In China, industrialization has predated agricultural modernization. Indeed, agricultural modernization has become a high priority of the central state since the mid-2000s, as policy makers and scholars alike have recognized the low productivity of smallholding farmers and the need to scale up food production.[1] Yet the labor that is freed up by agricultural modernization is not directly converted to an industrial reserve army. Under ideal circumstances, members of the industrial reserve army are landholding and therefore are able to withstand low wages. In the Chinese context, dispossessed laborers displaced by agricultural modernization are ill suited for the labor needs of industry.

Instead, China's agrarian transition is a state-controlled process that has little in common with the agrarian transitions in many other contexts. The state has unfolded a highly regulated plan to promote agribusinesses over small farmers. County governments appoint and subsidize private "dragonhead" agribusinesses, which consolidate land and coordinate contract farming practices. Some forms of agribusiness development even preserve collective ownership forms by allowing villagers to enter voluntarily into agricultural cooperatives and permitting village collectives to retain landownership rights.[2]

Agricultural modernization in China has not meant the introduction of private ownership and market-based pricing. Though agrarian transitions elsewhere have been accompanied by the injection of private property rights into agrarian life, land used by agribusinesses in China remains state owned. Pricing institutions for food and agricultural products remain state controlled and protectionist. The Ministry of Agriculture, for example, has liberalized grain pricing in grain-consuming provinces but has continued to regulate prices in grain-producing regions to prevent large-scale fluctuations in supply.[3]

This state-controlled character of China's agricultural modernization sets it apart from the expectations of the literature on agrarian transitions. Because studies of agrarian transitions have traditionally focused on societies without significant postsocialist legacies, they have assumed that agrarian modernization will necessitate the private ownership of land, thus displacing surplus labor into the industrial labor market. Yet China's legacy of collective land ownership has made the transition of surplus labor from agriculture to industry much more fluid. Surplus laborers with access to collective land are far easier for enterprises to hire and fire upon demand, making agrarian modernization a less significant event in the trajectory of China's industrialization.

LAND DEVELOPMENT AND A NEW MIDDLE CLASS

This book has argued that China's new economy of land development, driven more by debt-ridden real estate transactions than by productive, industrial development, creates distributional outcomes that are more unequal than in the past. In the old regime of labor-intensive development, the allocation of universal land-use rights to rural households created a farming subsidy while yoking direct producers to small-scale, subsistence production. The new economy of land-centered urban construction, however, exacerbates rural income inequality, exposing rural workers to high risks of unemployment without concomitant provision of social welfare support.

This new economy also creates a mode of development that is far more speculative. Because governments collect more revenues for allotting land to real estate development than to industrial use, they are highly incentivized to pursue real estate projects. However, real estate land development is far more speculative than industrial land use. Revenues from real estate originate from one-time land sales and land transfer fees paid by developers at the time that land use is contracted. Aside from these one-time fees and taxes collected during land sales, real estate development yields low continuous revenues, particularly since China has no property tax. Because land transfer fees from real estate transactions far outstrip equivalent fees collected from industrial land-use transactions (see figure 7), local governments are incentivized to engage in the continual growth of real estate development.

This preference for one-time taxes and fees associated with real estate creates an uneven spatial terrain of speculation. When real estate deals turn sour, local governments accumulate state bank debt, which is recorded on the books of their financing vehicles and thus hidden from

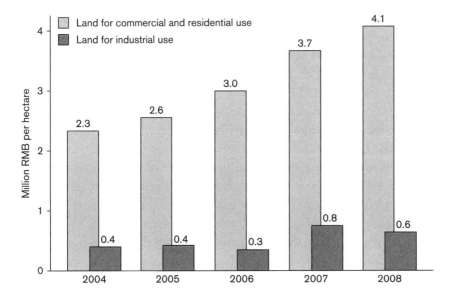

Figure 7. Average land transfer fees by sector. *Source:* Reprinted from Cai (2017). *Note:* Reported data are aggregated at the national level.

official view. More often, however, much of this debt is held by private developers, who have already paid land transfer and sales fees to local governments and can afford to wait long periods for eventual sales to recoup their losses. This, of course, only exacerbates the precarity of employment for construction brokers and laborers such as Boss Bo and Little Deng, whose experiences with delayed wage payment and wage arrears are a direct result of this debt-driven urban real estate boom.

REVISIT TO THE FIELD

What became of many of the villagers whose lives are depicted in this book? Through a brief revisit to Faming Village in 2014 and numerous phone calls, I inquired into the whereabouts of some of the villagers after the end of my research.

Little Deng had continued working construction; by 2014 his son had turned sixteen, dropped out of middle school, and found work in a factory near Chengdu City. With the proverbial nest at home thus empty, Yue-na had begun to travel with her husband. The couple had found regular work in Beijing with one of Boss Bo's subcontractor contacts. Yue-na worked as a kitchen cook in the construction dormitories, while Little Deng worked construction. Despite his ambition to become a labor broker himself, Little Deng remained a middleman working at the behest of Boss Bo. The family continued the life course trajectories on which they had started out.

Boss Bo had continued his business of brokerage. He had continued to invest in his distant nephew's business ventures on the side and had reduced his involvement but not yet retired from his construction business. Boss Bo and Deng Liwen lived in the same apartment they had purchased in the center of Qijiang District. They had at one point been hopeful that their eldest son would soon marry and relocate his young family to the apartment, but their son instead rented a room with old classmates on the edge of Chongqing City. He was dating a young woman but had no plans to settle and start a family, as his mother Deng Liwen hoped.

One family in Faming Village had deviated far from the circumstances I had observed during my research. In 2014 Little Fatty was still working construction in cities but not for Boss Gao. His young wife, Sister He, had left him, a development that did not surprise many villagers, particularly Auntie Luo, who exclaimed on the phone, "We all think it was a good idea for her to go. She had waited for him long enough. He finally came back but did not bring home a single *yuan*. He had spent it all in Emeishan, the tourist town where he had last been working. It was the last straw for her."

The departure of Little Fatty's wife and son had been more distressing to Little Fatty's father, Old Luo, than to Little Fatty. Old Luo and his wife had cohabited with Little Fatty, Sister He, and their son in a rickety farmhouse that Old Luo had built back in the 1980s. Old Luo was counting on Little Fatty to eventually save enough wages to build a new house for the entire family, with a small lean-to on the side to accommodate the older couple. He was also counting on Little Fatty to send remittances so he could retire from construction work and farm the land with his wife.

After the divorce, Little Fatty had returned to work but stopped sending home wages or even information on his whereabouts. According to Auntie Luo, Old Luo was enraged. He and his wife had few savings as a result of Old Luo's having fallen into depression and alcoholism for a decade and thus having accumulated various village debts. Without his son to support him, Old Luo began working construction for Boss Gao. Auntie Luo expounded, "Old Luo must now work like a horse every year. . . . They know they have no other choice for a future: they will eat bitterness for the rest of their lives."

Later, Auntie Luo and Yue-na related to me the sequence of events that followed these developments. One night, in a drunken rage, Old Luo burned his and Little Fatty's house to the ground. After the desertion, and the subsequent drunken rage, Little Fatty's mother moved into her brother's home. Little Fatty's visits home became even more infrequent. Auntie Luo expressed pity for Old Luo's wife, who now had to "live with no face in the home of somebody else." The dissolution of the household reveals the importance of marriage and remittances in the life of the village. Without migrant children to send wages, older villagers suffer, and the social fabric of village life is disrupted.

SUICIDE AS SOCIAL DEATH

There were many households besides Little Fatty's that met with unpleasant ends. Of course the most shocking endings for villagers occurred in Landing Village. Landing's two suicides marked a form of social death— an outcome of alienation and isolation produced by structural exclusion, the end of an agrarian way of life. Wang Sanbu and Luo Xianyu, two bachelors in Landing Village, were exposed to the alienation produced by land expropriation and the dismantling of the village as a site of social solidarity. Though Luo Xianyu's suicide, occurring on the eve of demolition, could easily be interpreted as a direct response to the violence of expropriation, Wang Sanbu's was preceded by a more a gradual process of alienation, the dissolution of an engagement, and abandonment by kin.

A number of scholars have linked suicide with the social conditions that produce alienation during periods of upheaval and social transformation. Emile Durkheim's statistical analysis of suicide in nineteenth-century Europe conceptualized suicide as a detachment from social life, brought on by the disintegration of social norms.[4] Pierre Bourdieu's 1959 ethnographic study of emptying-out villages in the Bearn, a southwestern rural region of France, focused on the alienation of a left-behind group of bachelors, as did Nancy Scheper-Hughes's 1977 study of social disintegration in the disappearing village "Ballybran" in coastal Ireland.[5] Data presented by both studies show that the social violence of rural decline is inflicted predominantly on men. Hypergamous marriage practices exacerbate their social and spatial immobility, tied by land inheritance to rural society, while women can escape through marriage.

Durkheim believed that it was social disintegration, not exposure to events of violence, that prompted suicide. Family and other sources of solidarity, he argued, protect individuals from suicide. Even violent events such as wartime turmoil can be capable of producing solidarities that protect against suicide.[6] In Landing, it was not so much the event of expropriation as it was the unraveling of social relations prior to expropriation that precipitated Luo and Wang's deaths. Luo Xianyu, like Wang Sanbu, had long been separated from his wife. His wife, from a neighboring village just bordering the Qijiang Dam, had left him nearly thirty years before, when their daughter was only fourteen years of age. His wife simply retired back to her natal home, on lower land, and refused to receive visits from members of the Luo clan, who walked down one by one to inquire about the reasons for her departure and implore her, in increasingly plaintive tones, to return.

Over time Luo Xianyu gradually accepted the separation, though formal divorce papers were never fully drawn up. His ex-wife had never moved her *hukou* registration to his household during the marriage, as was typical in the early 1980s, when villagers were only just acclimatizing themselves to decollectivization policies and remained understandably wary of the possible loss of natal land when transferring *hukou* across villages at marriage. Following the divorce, after Luo clan members' visits to the woman's natal village on behalf of spurned Luo Xianyu began to diminish, the Luos lost track of the woman. "She must have gone out to work in a factory in the 1980s," Luo Xianyu's nephew explained. "That is why she disappeared from the village. If she were still here, they would have heard word about her. But they did not hear for many years. I was a boy back then, I only remember what I heard from older relatives. But we never heard about her again. Even today we do not know where that woman has gone."

After the separation, Luo Xianyu never remarried. But he was not alone; he still had his daughter, who later become a migrant worker in a factory in Shenzhen. She married another Landing villager, and she and her husband continued working in factories in coastal China. Gradually, though, she grew tired of the factory and returned to the village to farm their land, leaving her husband to continue working in the city. She farmed the land alongside Luo Xianyu, who was glad to have her company. Eventually, however, her husband strayed. He met a younger woman in the factory where he worked and decided that he had married too early and that this new woman was a more suitable, more attractive partner for him. The split was made public when he returned to the village with his new fiancée, even before his divorce with Luo Xianyu's daughter was finalized.

The divorce created a rupture between Luo Xianyu and his daughter, though not through any fault of their own. Luo's daughter left Landing after her divorce to avoid her ex-husband and to escape the gossip that inevitably followed her. She worked in a factory in Chengdu, returning to Landing Village sporadically to visit her father. She sent wages back to support him, but they were insufficient to meet his full needs. Luo Xianyu still worked construction with local brokers intermittently, and he saw less and less of his daughter.

Social isolation made Luo Xianyu financially vulnerable to the blow of land loss. Like Wang Sanbu, he had few blood kin relations upon whom he could call for help. He had a sibling who worked sporadically for Boss Bo, but the two had long been estranged. Like Wang Sanbu, he was too old to be considered employable in factories. But Luo Xianyu was in many ways less fortunate than Wang Sanbu. He had long suffered health problems that impeded his ability to undertake hard labor, and as a result he had accumulated few social connections to labor brokers. He had often opted out of migration in favor of working his land and supplementing his income with remittances from his daughter. After his death, neighbors suggested that his suicide was intended to lessen the burden he would have imposed on his daughter.

Broken marriages were frequently a factor contributing to social isolation and financial precarity. Wang Sanbu's own broken engagement had cost him precious time and money that he might otherwise have invested in a search for a more stable living arrangement, whether through public housing in the township or cohabitation with kin. Deng Guang was left considerably poorer after the end of his engagement to Huang Rong of Faming Village. In both villages, the general attitude toward such broken relationships was pity and blame. In general, men suffered more from broken relationships than women, due to the patriarchal expectation that men bring to marriages the financial means for building new houses or purchasing township apartments.

Because divorces and other household discord frequently precipitated sudden downward turns of fate, villagers often gossiped and speculated about family dramas. For example, in Landing Village, Deng Liwen often found herself defending Wang Sanbu from vicious gossip directed at his breakup with Zhang Liaoyi. "[Villagers] spread bad rumors," Deng Liwen explained to me. One local woman, He Taikun, had been telling other villagers that Wang Sanbu had continued to carry on his affair with Zhang Liaoyi, even after she had later met and married another man in her own natal village. "Actually," Deng Liwen said, "Wang Sanbu is a good person, a very good person. He is very honest and he would never do the things that He Taikun says he does. He is a moral person. But He Taikun is a gossip. . . . She says things that aren't true."

Deng Liwen herself saw Wang Sanbu as a victim, ensnared by schemes that Zhang Liaoyi had hatched in order to secure a better livelihood for herself and her two children. According to Deng Liwen, Zhang Liaoyi had seen in Wang Sanbu a good provider, before she had found another migrant laborer with even more attractive earning power. "Wang Sanbu was very good to her," Deng Liwen explained.

> She cheated him. He would wake up early every morning to make her breakfast, heat hot water for her to wash up. At night he would tell her, you soak your feet longer, you rest yourself. He cooked for her every day. But she is that kind of woman, she uses men. She got him to build her a new house and then she threw him away. After she married the other man she returned 10,000 RMB of Wang Sanbu's money but forgot about the rest of it. But Wang Sanbu is a good man. He blames himself for all of this. He is sad about it. He Taikun should mind her business and let him live his life.

Because marriage played such a prominent role in shielding villagers from the precarity of landlessness, villagers were quick to construct narratives of blame and victimhood about those without kin. They were aware of the intense normative pressure they placed on men such as Wang Sanbu. "People always talk bad about old bachelors," one village woman in Landing told me. "They see an old man who isn't married and they think it is strange that he has no family. So, they make up stories about them."

In Landing, the breakdown of the subsistence farming economy thrust villagers into such precarity that kinship ties became a last-resort means of support. But is estrangement from kin equally harmful to villagers who do not suffer land loss? In Faming Village too, social isolation was a common enough phenomenon. Many men suffered divorces and bachelorhood in old age and lived alone after their adult children set off to make their livelihoods in cities.[7] Many others were married yet so reliant on their adult children for wage remittances and cohabitation arrangements that they suffered when these children, like Little Fatty, abdicated their family responsibilities. With the exception of Little Fatty's father, Old Luo, few were devastated by these events. Likewise, villagers in Faming engaged in less speculation about and passed less judgment on those in non-normative intimate arrangements, namely those who were unmarried or childless and lacked a nuclear family unit of their own.

Liu Guang, the Faming migrant (see chapter 3) who had made a habit of working for nonlocal brokers, including Boss Bo, never married. In 2007 he devoted his year's earnings to his brother Liu Hong, a miner who asked him for a loan to build a new two-story house for his wife and two sons. Liu Guang himself still lived in a two-room wooden farmhouse that his father had built in the 1980s. He had no reason, he often said, to improve his own living conditions, since he had no wife or children to support. Agrarian norms of household structure placed Liu Guang on the outside looking in, contributing to the construction of a brother's new house yet never building his own.

In Faming, traditional agrarian norms of marrying and having children, then building a house to accommodate these children as well as one's aging parents, formed the foundation of the village social structure. Men such as Liu Guang had an uncertain role in this structure; they were loose agents who were not accountable to women or children in the village. But Liu Guang was childless of his own volition, and he was not socially isolated. He had a wide network of friends and acquaintances whom he often made plans to visit during most of the year when he worked in cities. When he was in the village, Liu Guang made do in his own way, in part by relying on the same brother, Liu Hong, to contribute to him a portion of the crop his wife cultivated. Every Lunar New Year, Liu Guang returned to the village and took meals with his brother's family, and during years when he suffered wage arrears, he received support from them. In lieu of a wife, Liu Guang had other kin to help him withstand the precarity of construction work.

Had his brother not had land, Liu Guang would have found himself rootless, without a source of subsistence aside from his wages. Had Luo Xianyu or Wang Sanbu had a supportive brother, either one of them may not have resorted to suicide after losing their land. The social fabric of rural collectivity was valuable, protecting villagers both financially and psychologically. It was made up of intimate and reciprocal relationships, whether kin-based or otherwise, that were expressed through mutual aid exchanges enabled by landholding.

TRAJECTORIES OF URBANIZATION

Can we understand these snapshots of village life to be representative of a unitary narrative of urbanization? There is, of course, no single urbanization story in rural China. For Little Deng and his nephew Deng Guang, urbanization meant reentering the labor market with few protections, with neither being embedded in the rural economy, entitled to receive welfare benefits or public housing, or able to get formal jobs with benefits. On the other hand, for Boss Bo and Boss Zeng, property owners in county seats, urbanization brought new gains, rising home prices, and an urban policy environment more friendly to rural newcomers. Yet it also interrupted their business affairs as labor recruiters, as it reformulated the structure of their labor pool and necessitated adaptations on their part. Finally, the true winners of urbanization, entrepreneurs such as Wu Guangming, captured not only rents on rising home prices but also a newly urbanized customer base for their small businesses on the margins of growing cities.

Local distributional outcomes of urbanization are significant insofar as they reveal regional variation in the process of agrarian transition, as subsistence agriculture becomes market oriented and industry replaces agriculture as a major source of employment. As discussed in chapter 5, the political process of land struggles has varied across China, with more egalitarian outcomes in politically mobilized "corporatist" villages in coastal regions. Certainly in these regions the transition to urban residence has been far less violent and more egalitarian than it was in Landing Village. Scholars have documented more generously funded welfare programs and lower levels of household reliance on welfare. When households have access to capital via land rents and revenues, they reinvest in entrepreneurial enterprises or accept lower-paying but more stable, protected, and socially desirable jobs in the service sector. The extreme stratification of outcomes noted in Landing resulted from a land expropriation and development process that created rents accruing only to county government bodies and government-appointed private developers and agribusinesses. It is thus notable that all of the entrepreneurs of Landing who accumulated capital for entrepreneurial activities did so by engaging in labor recruitment or by relying on kin connections to capital-rich labor brokers. As discussed in chapter 6, the trickle-down effects of land capital are sparse due to low levels of political mobilization and a process of land commodification that grants the state sole ownership and management rights over land once it has been expropriated from village collectives.

These findings allow us to draw tentative conclusions about the relationship between state politics and the outcomes of expropriation. A recent study of rural land privatization in India has found similar outcomes, with recently dispossessed peasants becoming landless wage laborers, but land and property owners engaging in extreme speculation, serving as middlemen in land transactions with real estate developers.[8] The study's author, Michael Levien, has argued that political factors in the process of land expropriation determine the forms and outcomes of popular resistance to expropriation: the transparency of the privatization process; the class structure of local communities before dispossession; and levels of social capital held by community members, who leverage personal relationships to strategize relocation arrangements or, even better, insert themselves advantageously into land transactions.[9] Individual landowners in India could sell off rural land at market-determined prices, or they could purchase land for consolidation early on from less knowledgeable, small landholders to sell off later at higher prices.

Can such a framework be useful for making sense of urbanization outcomes in China, where a collective landownership system makes local governments the sole proprietors legally empowered to manage use rights to expropriated land? In the India context, dispossessed rural individuals benefit from political connections that create brokerage networks, providing them with an array of information on potential buyers. In China, private individuals are not empowered with rights to own or manage land, and individuals such as Boss Bo and Boss Zeng can capture rising rents only by purchasing property near regions of intense land development and rising rates of land expropriation. It is only local governments that can realize differences between the administrative price of land, determined by land transfer fees, and speculative market rates. Political connections, moreover, matter only insofar as village and township officials such as New Land Township's Party secretary Zhang could be promised financial incentives or political office in exchange for facilitating the process of land expropriation. At the village level, political connections could not open channels for residents to capture rents on land redevelopment.

Both land redevelopment and urban construction are controlled by the state on the local level, and this state monopolization of the process of urbanization shapes on-the-ground distributional outcomes. Because local governments coordinate the supply of labor to enterprises via subcontracting, urban construction projects rarely employ local laborers. The process of urbanization creates new wealth for private developers and local governments, without creating new jobs. In Landing, only petty entrepreneurial and informal sectors generate jobs. Business owners such as Wu Guangming serve the needs of urban residents in the margins of big cities, and long-distance labor brokers such as Boss Bo serve the labor needs of employers in other regions. It is telling, moreover, that entrepreneurs such as Boss Bo's nephew, who runs a noodle shop in New Land Township, and Deng Yaoli, who with her family opened a noodle restaurant near the factory where she once worked in Zheijiang Province, have adapted their businesses to fill niches in migrant enclaves and other sites of rural resettlement. In urbanizing regions, construction capital rarely trickles down, and those who thrive do so only by making themselves useful in serving the needs of other relocated residents.

Instead, land development becomes an instrument for consolidating state power. Once rural land is expropriated from villagers, ownership rights return to the state, creating a competitive terrain of urban governance wherein local governments struggle for control over land as a means of consolidating political power. Qijiang County, for example, was promoted to Qijiang District and now counts among districts of the urban core, enjoying infrastructural, trade-related, and fiscal benefits of its urban administrative status. So much is at stake for rural governments attempting to develop that intrastate struggles between local governments hoping to gain administrative promotion and urban status often become incorporated into developmental policy.[10] After all, even Chongqing City—which in 1997 was approved to become one of five "direct controlled municipalities" in China, thus holding the same administrative status and political priority as provincial governments—leveraged its bid to spearhead construction on the Three Gorges Dam (and thus its need for direct fiscal transfers from the center) as a justification for promotion.

Popular dissent to this state monopolization of the power and resources produced through land development has compelled some limited concessions from the state. In 2008 the Chongqing municipal government, responding to protests over the exclusion of rural farmers from land revenues, designed a land coupon exchange that attempted to confer a proxy of the development rights to land on residents.[11] Rural residents working in cities were granted "land coupons," symbolic coupons valued according to the area of unused farming land their households had in villages. These residents could then sell land coupons to private developers, and these private developers could use these land coupons to purchase permissions from urban governments to use equivalent-sized land plots in cities for construction. Rural residents could negotiate directly with private developers to gain higher prices in exchange for their land coupons. Of note is that in the coupon sales, residents lost their land-use rights back in their villages, and townships and village governments then converted residents' land to farmland for agribusinesses.[12] Though the land coupon exchange was a short-lived experiment and would be phased out beginning in 2016, its introduction was temporarily heralded as a possible mechanism for redistributing a greater portion of land revenues back to rural residents. Moreover, even its brief existence reveals policy makers' awareness of the systematically unequal character of Chinese urbanization, an arena driven by interstate competition and excluding civil society actors, from farmers to workers to residents, from access to gains.

CONCLUSION

This book has captured an unfolding set of transformations: the expansion of urban development into rural peripheries, the inland migration of coastal capital, and the introduction of a market for the exchange of land-use rights among corporate parties.

But behind the backdrop of this single-minded, state-driven growth are smaller stories. In Faming and Landing Villages, the routines of intimate life accommodate the conditions and changes wrought by urbanization and economic growth. Marriages are made to match wage-earning migrants with farming women, each made financially secure by the contribution of the other. Kin groups are mobilized as labor teams, traveling together in search of work. Village gossip revolves around the family dramas and individual tragedies that result when lives and communities have been bent around the needs of capital: demands for migrant labor and a search for land.

Intimate relationships and family life made these economic realities bearable. In the early 2000s in Landing Village, Zhou Kai, a poor migrant, married a village woman living in another nearby village. Yet as it was for so many farming and ordinary migrant men, romance was short-lived and regrettable for Zhou Kai, resulting in nearly irredeemable financial loss when his new wife, weary of the lonely rigors of farming land and forever awaiting an ever-absent migrant husband in an emptying-out mountain village, decamped, first returning to her natal home and then departing for a coastal factory. The story of her desertion parallels accounts of others in Landing. Just as Zhou Kai was abandoned by a wayward wife in his youth, so were Wang Sanbu, Deng Guang, and many others.

Zhou Kai was lucky, however. A Landing elder auntie came to him with a proposition: A cousin in the village had a sister-in-law who hailed from

Guizhou, and she passed on word that a woman from a poor village in Guizhou was in search of a husband. Zhou Kai agreed to a meeting. During a carefully planned introduction, weighted on both sides with expectation, he met Liu Jingnian. The village auntie had told him in advance about this woman who, widowed at an unnaturally early age, had neither abandoned nor been abandoned by her late husband. She had raised a grown son while running a full farm in her natal village. His auntie had warned him in advance: "This woman is neither young, nor beautiful, nor wealthy. In fact, she is quite poor, quite old, and quite plain. But she is a loyal wife, and hard-working. She is not afraid of farm work, and she will not run off at the first hint of hardship like many other women these days." Zhou Kai, a pragmatic man of few words, took heart from this description of the woman he had deep down already resolved to marry.

Liu Jingnian too had arrived at the meeting with great resolve. Before the meeting, she had made one-way travel arrangements from her natal Guizhou village to Landing. She had already said her good-byes, packed her valuables into a single bag, and boarded up her mud house for a possible future return at an undetermined date. If all went well, she would not return to her natal home without a new husband.

During the formal introduction, Liu Jingnian's single bag, containing all her possessions in this world, was left in a separate room, lest Zhou Kai catch sight of it and feel intimidated at the totality of expectations it contained. Yet the bag would not remain hidden for long. Just two days after the two were introduced, they agreed to marry. Zhou Kai was sufficiently impressed with his new bride's rough hands, proof of her willingness to work, and her gruff, laconic speech. She was a good farming wife, exactly what Zhou Kai was seeking after being deserted so unceremoniously by an ex-wife whose desire for town life and discontent with the countryside was revealed too late. He would not make that mistake twice.

Appendix

This book generalizes a trajectory of Chinese development since 1979 based on micro-level ethnographic research conducted among migrant workers in numerous sites across China from 2007 to 2011. It makes a vast analytical leap, from an on-the-ground process of participant observation, to the interactive dynamics within mechanisms of capital accumulation, and then to a broader explanation of Chinese economic growth at large. It encompasses observations of the social processes in the countryside that enable the labor and employment relations prevalent in construction work. Finally, it embeds these labor relations in larger-scale shifts in the Chinese developmental terrain.

In what follows, I describe how the study came about. Specifically, I describe how my travels through China, as both geographical and social terrain, allowed me to move from micro-level observations to macro-level claims on the configuration and internal dynamics of capital accumulation in contemporary China. First, this appendix lays bare the social relationships that enabled me to trace a subcontracting chain from a Beijing construction site to two villages in Sichuan Province. Second, it reveals the slow evolution of my conceptual understanding of Chinese development and how micro-level observations in each physical site expanded my previous analytical understandings of China's labor and land regimes. My hope is that revealing this process will illuminate how I, as a researcher, came to know what I claim to know, and provide parameters for evaluating this knowledge.

MIGRANTS IN THE CITY

As an undergraduate student in 2002, I began considering a topic for an undergraduate thesis. Like many second-generation Taiwanese Americans, I had an interest in China. I also had family ties there. A Taiwanese uncle, my mother's brother, offered to bring me to Shunde City, Guangdong Province, where he had recently relocated the manufacturing facilities for his office supply company. I took my uncle's offer as an opportunity to begin my ethnographic fieldwork.

I did not know it then, but my uncle would be the first of many "insider's outsiders" I would encounter in the field.[1] He was an outsider in China but an insider in the field of production, and his introduction to the situation was informative. Over Skype, in preparation for my arrival, my uncle provided a primer: Beijing was authoritarian and economically stagnant, whereas the coastal South, where tax policies and investment laws were more lax, was the real engine of economic growth. It was because of authoritarian rule, he explained, that the mainland served as an ideal site for investment. He personally disliked his sporadic trips to the mainland, where authoritarianism bred corruption, and he spent considerable funds on political bribes to acquire necessary licenses and permits for exports. It was clear that my uncle understood the dynamics of the internal economy from the outside standpoint of a foreign investor. Later I learned that this view of China aligned with numerous scholarly perspectives on the Chinese economy. Both saw China as a site where low-cost labor and favorable investment policies were produced through the will of the state.

I was picked up at the Guangzhou airport by an associate of my uncle, a Taiwanese owner of a Shunde garment factory. We proceeded immediately from the airport to the Guangzhou train station, where we collected a new worker recruited by a factory foreman to replace a recently absconded girl. She was freshly arrived from inland Hunan Province, fifteen years old, though her permit stated a solid eighteen, and not yet disabused the habit of a chatty guilelessness: "Everybody is 'coming out' nowadays. . . . All of my classmates came out here before me. . . . They say you think of today until tomorrow comes, and then you think of tomorrow. Do you think I'm too much of an aimless wanderer?"

Once settled in the factory, however, I noticed that most women socialized only with other women recruited from their own home provinces, sometimes their home villages. Younger women displayed a relatively footloose quality, often comparing wages with old schoolmates working in neighboring factories and switching jobs frequently. Some carried on romances outside factory gates with men from their home villages; others carried on romances within factory gates with men they had met in Shunde. These latter relationships were looked on with consternation by a minority faction of older women in the factory.

Most of these older women, moreover, viewed the factories with more trepidation than the younger generation. They saw their own employment as an unbefitting prolonging of what should have been a temporary, youthful excursion into bright city lights. They regretted their absence from their rural households. And when their own daughters inevitably turned up at the train station looking for work as well, they considered their efforts a failure and felt regret; in their minds, they had gone to coastal cities in search of work so that their own daughters would not need to.

DOWN THE CONSTRUCTION SUBCONTRACTING CHAIN

In 2007, as a graduate student, I began fieldwork again. This time I entered the field through academic channels rather than family ties. At Tsinghua University in Beijing, I found a cohort of ethnographers and surveyors led by the sociologist Shen Yuan. I began making daily visits with a Chinese colleague, Qi Xin, to a construction site on the Tsinghua campus. Soon we met Boss Zeng, perpetually clothed in an all-black, fur-lined leather jacket. His foreman, Little Deng, was a more passive presence at the construction site. Once Little Deng's wife Yue-na warmed up to Qi Xin, the two of us began spending the majority of our time with Yue-na, Little Deng, and Boss Zeng in the dormitory.

The construction dormitory was revealing of the labor relations of the workplace. Each room of the ramshackle dormitory housed a team of around twenty workers, and each team tended to have been recruited from a single village by a single labor broker. Moreover, each work team tended to have cultivated a single specialty; in one room was a carpentry team, in another a group of steel-and-iron frame workers, in another, concrete pourers. The alignment of workflow and team function with geography and kin ties was expedient for the urban subcontractor who managed the entire construction site. Each team could be brought in just when the construction process required it; they could finish their portion of the work and then be moved out of the dormitory to seek work at other construction sites. Payment would reach the broker at the end of the fiscal year.

At the construction site I conducted semistructured interviews with thirty workers on four separate work teams hailing from Sichuan, Anhui, Shandong, and Hunan Provinces. Some, such as Little Deng, were Boss Zeng's workers, and others worked for other brokers. Unlike the Shunde garment factory, where many of the women had worked at the factory for multiple years, the construction site was a temporary worksite where production began and finished within a few years. Still, there was some regularity in the workforce. The primary subcontractor who managed the site contracted frequently with his brokers on multiple projects, and many brokers had regular recruits whom they brought to their contracts every year. Every year some workers arrived at worksites to find other workers from different provinces with whom they had worked in the past.

Little Deng was an insightful informant, precisely because of his difficult middle position as a foreman and labor recruiter, caught between his broker, Boss Zeng, and the Faming laborers he recruited for Zeng. Faming laborers believed he sided with Zeng, but Zeng evaluated him based on his managerial control over the Famingers. Like many other foremen, he was occasionally defensive about his status, and he often boasted of his indispensability to Boss Zeng:

DENG: Actually, Boss Zeng needs me more than I need him. He depends on me to recruit workers.

QI XIN:But he makes more than you, right?

DENG: If he didn't have me, he would have no workers. I recruited them all for him.

Informants in such precarious positions are often quite accessible; Deng was eager for an outside confidant as well as public affiliation with seemingly resource-rich university students. Through his narration, Qi Xin and I got to see the field site and observe its relationships; our initial understanding was colored by Deng's biases, his loyalties, and his disclosures. This relationship quickly came to feel proprietary; with each disclosure, Deng became more demanding of our loyalty.

When Qi Xin and I began spending time with Boss Zeng, following him on his rounds to other construction sites, Deng became quiet and cagey. This pattern would repeat itself countless times over the next four years. Fieldwork, in any form, requires the constant development of new confidences across adversarial relations. Always, this is a publicly seditious act that severs old loyalties so that the researcher may expand her analytical horizon through the cultivation of new informant relationships. Especially once I had followed Boss Bo and Little Deng to their home villages, I would learn to see each informant as a decoder of new worlds, each decoding as a new data point to be analyzed.

TOWARD A RURAL STANDPOINT

It was largely due to Qi Xin's help that I was able to track down our informants again when I returned to China in 2009. Over the years Qi Xin had kept in close touch with them. She was well-respected by the construction men, who early on discerned her relatively high status within a stratification system distinguished by rural and urban class markers. Qi Xin was a university professor and an urbanite, and she had on more than one occasion secured jobs as campus security guards for construction workers who wished to leave the profession. One of these workers, Wang Jia, invited me to visit his family in his home village in Guizhou. In 2009, during two three-week visits to Wang Jia's village, I found a social reality starkly different from what I had seen in Beijing. These visits would form the real basis for this book.

Packed into a slow train with migrant workers traveling from Beijing to Guizhou for thirty-three hours, I slowly crossed over from city to country. Once in Wang's Guizhou village, I found a mysterious and sui generis world. There the life of the country, embedded in land painstakingly terraced over generations, was continuous and, I soon realized, ever-present in the minds of the migrants. Laboring in the city was but a minor rupture in the continuity of village life. Those who left their villages for reasons other than the immediate needs of family were violators of the unspoken commitment to the life of the village, the land. My first evening in the village, Wang Jia told a harrowing story of an entrepreneur, Fan, whose mother had abandoned him in childhood and only returned after word of Fan's successes had spread: "Twenty years later, though, after hearing that Fan had become so successful that he married and bought a house in the county seat, she came back. No word on her whereabouts for the past twenty years, she just came back. She did not bring a thing for Fan. But she brought two children, around six years old. Whose children were they? Who knows, they could have been fathered by anyone. She always said they were given to her but again there is no way to tell."

In early 2010 I returned to the Guizhou village with my bag packed for a year's stay, ready to begin my real fieldwork. But events conspired against me. Wang Jia had just sold his summer harvest of dried tobacco to a Guizhou tobacco company in the nearby county seat. He had originally planned to return to Beijing to work in construction. Wang's primary broker contact in the construction industry, Boss Xia, a friend from three villages over, had offered Wang a position on his construction brigade. But by January even Boss Xia had returned home; his contracts for the following year had fallen through as well. Wang could not secure work for the year, and in late January he explained the situation to me: "I would rather return home to be with my family, I am tired of working in the city. I *could* work in the city if I chose to, but I choose not to. I will plant tobacco for the year and then in September I will go work again." Just days later, however, another broker from a neighboring village called Wang Jia, and he again packed his bag for the year. He explained the contingent change in his plans with renewed coherence: "The truth is, I only have maybe six good years of hard labor in me. I am thirty-four now, and once I am forty, I will not be employable in construction. I need to work now to save so my family can continue to subsist even after I stop working in the city."

Eventually, once Wang Jia had left the village, I lost official permission to live in the Guizhou village. Village officials had been wary of my presence from the start, and the sealed-and-stamped letters from Shen Yuan did not seem to persuade them. Though I did not know it at the time, neither was Wang Jia's status in the village sufficient to guarantee my trustworthiness to these officials. Finally, the village was home to a large population of Miao ethnic minorities, and as a result, governance issues there were politically sensitive. After receiving a phone call from the Party secretary suggesting that I should leave as soon as I could, that my stay was not welcome, I cut my losses and left.

TRAIN TO FAMING

Discouraged and exhausted, I retreated to Chengdu, Sichuan Province. Meanwhile, back in Beijing Qi Xin, having heard of my predicament, was frantically making calls. In late April she called me with new instructions: I should take a bus to Leshan County, south of Chengdu, and Yue-na would meet me at the township bus station there. Little Deng was still working in Beijing, Qi Xin reported, but I could go to Faming Village for a weeklong social visit. At the end of the visit, she urged, I should ask for permission to live in Yue-na's household for a year. In exchange I would pay rent at a rate roughly commensurate with what she would earn in the city had she sought employment. Under these arrangements, I lived in Faming Village for ten months, and during that time I conducted semistructured interviews with twenty-four villagers and four local government officials.

I conducted a rough survey of fifty households in Faming Village. For each household I recorded brief work histories for registered members, land contract arrangements, and farming backgrounds. This rough survey was useful for contextualizing the representativeness of particular household arrangements in relation to the village population.

In Faming I found a replication of the same dynamics I had found in Guizhou. During my first week there I heard village women disparage an absent village son, in his late twenties, who had gone to Beijing, then Guangzhou, then Yunnan for work. Unmarried and accountable, he had never, in three years spent away, sent any money home. Older village women empathized with his parents for this oversight.

Yet in Faming speculation over absent migrants was less infused with suspicion than it had been in Guizhou. This was due, I soon learned, to the existence of a stable local labor brokerage network in Faming. Famingers, unlike Wang Jia, did not have to search for brokers in neighboring villages. They could go straight to the Gao brothers. Furthermore, once I met the Gao brothers, I realized that whereas the Guizhou villagers had no means of tracking absent migrants, the Famingers had developed an elaborate system of surveillance over departed laborers. Greater livelihood security in Faming, relative to the Guizhou village, created a village culture that was less distressed by risks of abandonment inherent in migrants' departures.

Affiliated with Little Deng, I found myself at the edges of Faming's labor brokerage ring. Villagers were aware of my relationship with Boss Bo, and many tended to keep their distance from Yue-na and Little Deng as well. Seeing the labor brokerage ring from this marginal position, however, gave me a view of its fraying outer edges. It was because of my affiliation with Yue-na that Little Luo, for example, disclosed to me his many troubles with the Gao brothers. Luo Guang also opened up to me once he knew that I was long acquainted with Boss Bo, whom he considered a close friend.

My close relationship with Huang Rong was also a result of my very visible affiliation with Little Luo and Little Deng, both outsiders to the dominant Faming social scene. Huang Rong and I began a close friendship when I visited her home along with Yue-na, in preparation for Huang Rong's marriage to Deng Guang. She invited me to several social outings with her middle school girlfriends working in Qianwei County. On one occasion I met her ex-boyfriend, a tattooed older man who drove a black sedan, who met us after a night of karaoke and watery beers. These outings were always tentative: The girls were dutifully replicating evening activities from their observations in coastal cities, but it was never clear to me whether they were enjoying themselves. When I returned home afterward, Yue-na was always wary. On more than one occasion she warned me to be leery of Huang Rong's friends, as they were wayward girls, and who knew what they were up to.

BUS TO LANDING

In late 2010 I began visiting neighboring villages, among others a wealthy, riverside village to the north, where the village collective had embarked on market-oriented farming, and a mountainous village to the east, where labor networks were less dense and villagers often had trouble finding work. It was not until Little Deng returned to Faming in February and declared that he and Deng Guang would make a trip to their natal homes in Landing Village that I had a real plan. My adviser instructed me to tag along. Little Deng, Deng Guang, and I boarded a bus from Faming Village to Qianwei County, then from Qianwei to Qijiang County, and finally from Qijiang to Landing Village.

In Landing I rented a room for residence in Boss Bo's household. This living arrangement was fortuitous. I soon found that whereas in Faming I had had a view from the margins of village labor politics, in Landing I was positioned at the social center. From the first day I arrived, villagers came daily to Deng Liwen with requests for work to pass on to Boss Bo. Deng Liwen was a capable woman, frank and direct, and she fielded these requests conscientiously, albeit with occasional complaints regarding villagers' neediness.

Later in the year Boss Bo himself arrived home. I had not seen him since a brief meeting in 2007, and though we shared a bus ride from Qijiang County to New Land Township, I did not recognize him at first. He had lost some hair, undoubtedly from the stress of the job, and he had grown slightly more rotund. Like many powerful Chinese men, he conveyed his authority more through pointed silence than through speech. Addressing nobody in particular, he began a long soliloquy on the poor state of transportation to and from Landing Village. I nodded and responded, and it seemed to me that half the passengers on the bus passively nodded as well. After a long silence, he asked after the wife of an older farmer across the aisle, and the old farmer responded with eager smiles and half bows. It was not until we disembarked from the bus and began walking the dirt road toward Landing Village that I recognized this man as Boss Bo of village lore, in person a visage of rural noblesse oblige.

For nearly a year while living in Faming, I had heard villagers disparage Boss Bo, an untrustworthy outsider broker who once had cut living allowances in the city and left many Famingers without wages. When I finally met him, I found that he enjoyed an altogether different reputation in Landing. When he returned, Boss Bo was briefly back from Chongqing, where he had overseen some minor labor disputes. Over the next month I overheard numerous cell phone conversations between Boss Bo and his many village supplicants, all in search of work. When these phone calls came, I was often at Boss Bo's side, where I could hear both sides of each conversation. It is a truism that many older rural laborers, unsure of the efficacy of modern cell phone technology, were in the habit of half-yelling their conversations into the phones. They did this whether they were on noisy trains or in quiet village fields, and truth be told, it made my fieldwork easier, as it allowed me to eavesdrop on entire conversations with ease. Much of the information on Boss Bo's attempts to divert his labor recruitment activities from Landing to Faming was gleaned in this way.

UP TOWARD THE STATE

In Landing just as in Faming, I conducted a rough survey of fifty households, recording brief work histories, land contract arrangements, and farming backgrounds. In the course of collecting information for this survey, I stumbled on the news of planned evictions.

County officials, along with their local proxy, Secretary Zhang, began to appear in the village. These appearances usually occurred at township meetings, which I attended along with Deng Liwen. Rarely did I feel comfortable speaking to officials before or after meetings. It was enough that my presence was not immediately barred. In both Faming and Landing, I had gained administrative permission for village residence by accompanying politically prominent villagers to the county-level Public Security Bureau, where I submitted letters of introduction from Shen Yuan at Tsinghua as well as visa information. In Faming, Yue-na's younger sister served as the village's appointed one-child-policy female leader, as well as my guarantor. In Landing, my affiliation with Boss Bo alone was enough to secure official permission for my residence. Village Party secretary Zhang was aware of my presence, and it appeared that without my directly requesting him to do so, he had vouched for my presence to county-level higher-ups. Nevertheless, township meetings on land and *hukou* reform were undoubtedly sensitive, and I sat inconspicuously in the back during these meetings.

When I realized that my neighbor Wang Deihua had a daughter who worked in the Qijiang Ministry of Land Management (MLM), Xiao Li, I began to curry her favor. She was a difficult subject to cultivate; she sensed my thirst for information and leveraged it to gain my services as a free English tutor for her daughter. After each tutoring session, she fielded several of my questions regarding the New Socialist Countryside campaign and changing land policies. In late 2011 Xiao Li complained of her overbooked schedule at work, due to deadlines for the submission of new blueprints for county land redevelopment to the provincial MLM for review. I finagled a visit to the MLM to see these blueprints for myself.

Near the end of 2011 evictions were well under way. On days when county officials arrived in black sedans to make visits to the village, I avoided venturing out alone, only accompanying Deng Liwen on her own daily rounds. When they were absent, I made my own arrangements to visit certain households and call upon my village informants.

By August I could sense the increasing political sensitivity of my continuing residence in Landing. In late October I received an unexpected cell phone call from Mr. Chen, an official at the Qijiang Ministry of Public Administration. Without any preface or explanation, he began inquiring into my intentions and affiliations—the usual modus operandi of suspicious cadres. When we later met for tea in a Qijiang County *mahjiang* hall, he casually requested a written report of my findings, and I provided one, albeit one focused on "village culture" rather than the process and political economy of land expropriation.

But the exchange was not entirely antagonistic. Mr. Chen also asked questions about my parents' immigration to the United States and answered my extensive questions about the *dibao* system and *hukou* policy. Mr. Chen was the official who explained to me Qijiang County's successful application for administrative upgrade from county to district status. Later I asked Xiao Li about this process, and she provided valuable details as well. Like the rest of my informants, Mr. Chen and Xiao Li were informative and valuable precisely because they saw me as a resource they could manipulate to their own ends. This dialectic relation, with each party manipulating and exploiting the other for particular ends, had been ever present in my research.[2] Little Deng had kept in close contact with Qi Xin in order to exploit any possible job leads in Beijing the latter might have for him. Yue-na had more than once carefully broached the possibility of securing a job in my uncle's factory in Guangdong. Wang Jia, more explicitly, had asked me for a loan of 60,000 RMB so that he might finish construction of his village home. Less explicitly instrumental was Boss Bo, who delighted in a captive audience and enjoyed flaunting his public relations to me when he was back in Landing Village. Always this dialectic was what drove the fieldwork forward.

AFTERWORD

Constant negotiation of this dialectic relation also proved exhausting, and in late November 2011 I left Landing Village. But I kept in touch with Deng Liwen via Skype; I had always felt my relationship with her to be less fraught with instrumental motives than my other relationships. During Lunar New Year of 2012 I called her and Little Deng to inquire after their health. Deng Liwen paused before she answered; Wang Sanbu, she reported, had passed away. It was a long time before she admitted to me how he had died—by throwing himself off a cliff overhanging his demolished village home. It was the third suicide I had encountered during my research, and I was deeply affected by it. I had spent many idle afternoons walking the hills with Wang Sanbu in 2011.

Gradually my calls to Deng Liwen grew less frequent. My academic work and personal life in Berkeley had grown increasingly demanding, and the two years I spent in Sichuan had been reduced to distant memory. Through constant review of field notes I reconstructed, again and again, the world that I had deeply penetrated in 2010. Occasionally I felt the field notes were but a copy of a copy, and that I had lost my original.

Notes

1. Post (2009).
2. Xu Min et al. (2016).
3. National Bureau of Statistics of China (2004, 58).
4. Gallagher (2005).
5. Hung (2009).
6. Hung (2009).
7. International Labor Organization (2013).
8. More precisely, each land plot is, on average, 1.7 mu or .11 hectare in area.
9. Between 1993 and 1998, 34.2 percent of town and village enterprises were privatized, and 15.4 percent were shut down (Brandt et al. 2005).
10. This ownership is made deliberately ambiguous (Ho 2001).
11. By 2010: Pun and Lu (2010); between 2011 and 2013: Swanson (2015).
12. Heilmann (2018).
13. Heilmann (2018).
14. Kelliher (1992).
15. Oi (1999); Walder (1995).
16. Hung (2015); Huang (2008).
17. Han and Lu (2017).
18. Harvey (2001).
19. Luxemburg (1951).

20. Harvey (2003a, 2005).

21. Sassen (2014).

22. Levien (2018).

23. Harvey (2001).

24. Miura (2012).

25. Brenner (2001).

26. Lee (2007).

27. Burawoy (1976).

28. Arrighi et al. (2010).

29. Hart (2002).

30. Hart (2002).

31. Polanyi ([1944] 2001).

32. Landry (2012); Ang (2016).

33. Li and Yang (2015).

34. In 1994, former President Jiang Zemin unleashed a gradual series of deepening reforms, masterminded by his predecessor, Deng Xiaoping, which converted some small and medium state-owned enterprises (SOEs) into share-holding companies and sold off the majority of rural collective TVEs to firm managers at below-market prices (Li and Rozelle 2003; Hung 2015).

35. Bernstein and Lu (2003).

36. Li and Yang (2015).

37. The questions of who pays for social services and who collects revenues have slightly different answers. County governments fund the majority of social expenditures, with township governments and village collectives bearing a smaller portion of costs. Tax and fee revenues also are collected by counties, particularly when these revenues are generated by traditional industries, particularly manufacturing and agriculture. However, as land-related transactions have come to the forefront of public finance, local governments at the county, township, and village levels are increasingly competing for their share of revenues (Kennedy 2007; Hsing 2010).

38. Wong (2013).

39. Ang (2017).

40. The amount of land transfer fees collected by local governments in China was expected to surpass RMB 2 trillion by 2016, making such taxes a major source of revenue for municipalities. As land prices have increased over the last ten years, the amount collected by local governments on their percentage of land deals has risen accordingly. Government data show that from 2001 to 2003, land transfer fees totaled RMB 91 million, representing 35 percent of local government revenues, with an average value of just over RMB 30 million per year. In 2004, this figure rose to RMB 60 million (Rithmire 2013).

41. Li and Yang (2015).

42. Dai and Min (1999); cf. Lee (2007, 42).

43. O'Brien and Li (2006); Erie (2012).

44. Service/domestic work: Hanser (2008) and Otis (2008); factories and manufacturing: Lee (1998) and Pun (2005); construction: Swider (2015) and Pun and Lu (2010).

45. Burawoy (1982).

46. Migrant remittances: Murphy (2002) and Jacka (2012); peasant production: Shue (1988) and Oi (1999).

47. Polanyi ([1944] 2001, 64).

48. National Bureau of Statistics (2017).

49. National Bureau of Statistics of China (2009).

50. National Bureau of Statistics of China (2009).

51. Pun and Lu (2010).

52. Rural labor has always served the variable needs of construction; even during the socialist era, as early as 1953, construction enterprises were already hiring rural temporary workers via piece-rate wages on the side, to fill unanticipated demand. By 1953 these rural workers already constituted 44 percent of the national construction labor force (Swider 2015).

53. Shirk (1981).

54. Lu and Fox (2001).

55. State Council (1984).

56. Qian and Hui (2004).

57. Pun and Yi (2011).

58. Pun and Lu (2010).

59. Shen (2007).

60. Qi (2011).

61. Johnson (2015); Chen (2014).

62. Swider (2015).

63. Hsing (2010).

64. Polanyi ([1944] 2001).

65. Chen and Fan (2016).

CHAPTER 2. A TALE OF TWO VILLAGES

1. In 1989, 68 percent of collective output was rural, and 73 percent of rural output derived from collective enterprises (Walder 1996).

2. *Qianwei County Gazetteer* (1990–1994).

3. Arrighi (2007).

4. Whyte (2012).

5. Interview with Qianwei County government official, April 24, 2010.

6. Huang (2008).

7. Huang (2008).

8. Hung (2015); Zhu (2011).

9. Hung (2015).

10. Gallagher (2005).

11. Rozelle (1996).

12. One form of agribusiness reform is "dragonhead enterprises," large-scale agriprocessors that vertically integrate supply chains, with corporate food processors at the top and small household farms at the bottom (Yasuda 2017).

13. This survey recorded monthly income in intervals of 1,000 RMB.

14. Interview with Qianwei County official, March 2, 2010.

15. In any rural regions today, agnatic, exogamous kinship groups still tend to be localized within a restricted area. Maurice Freedman (1958) has shown of the presocialist era that a single village might consist nearly exclusively of a single lineage. Some studies of the postsocialist era find that socialist production preserved some of the geographical organization of lineage groups (Chan et al. 2009), but other studies also show the rising prevalence of rural-rural marriage migrations that have diversified lineage groups in villages (Fan and Huang 1998).

16. Debates over market transition theory have emerged over quantitative data showing a declining rate of economic returns to political offices throughout the 1980s (Nee 1989; Parish et al. 1995).

17. For reference, scholars have also indicated high levels of rural-urban integration in coastal counties like those in Zhejiang and Shandong Provinces, regions known for high levels of rural entrepreneurship (Nee and Opper 2012; Walder 1998).

18. Just as in Faming, where political elites such as Leader Cha concede status to labor brokers such as the Gao brothers, so too in Landing Village entrepreneurs inhabit the top rung of the local status hierarchy.

19. Rural-urban integration reform policies in Chengdu and Chongqing promulgated three priorities: (1) concentrating factories in industrial parks; (2) concentrating rural residents in dense, multistory, urban-like residential communities, which frees up new farmland, or relocating them to cities; and (3) concentrating farmland in the hands of large cultivators, including specialized households and agribusiness companies (Ong 2014).

20. Gomi (2013).

21. Gomi (2013).

22. Zhan (2017).

23. Zhan (2017); Fang (2011).

24. This was a practice counter to the norm in Faming, which dictated that married women typically relocate from their fathers' to their husbands' three-generational households, making it difficult for a daughter to promise a portion of remittance income to her natal parents (Freedman 1958).

CHAPTER 3. INTO THE WORLD OF CHINESE LABOR

1. Most rural migrants worked in the informal sector, where participation in pension insurance is extremely low. Therefore, by 2013 only 15 percent of rural migrants participated in pension insurance through their employers (Chen and Fan 2016).

2. Between 1995 and 2005, close to 100,000 firms with 11.4 trillion RMB worth of assets were privatized, comprising two-thirds of China's SOEs and state assets (Huang 2006).

3. (Huang 2006).

4. Chan and Zhang (1999).

5. Short-term changes in the *hukou* also allowed the state to make adjustments to this scheme according to labor needs. When urban heavy industries required a larger labor force in the 1960s, rural residents in selected regions were reassigned to nonagricultural work and transported to selected towns and cities, where they supplemented urban industrial labor. After they delivered the necessary production bump, however, these rural workers were returned to the communes (Cheng and Selden 1994; Wang 2005; Brown 2012).

6. Rural labor was only gradually incorporated into urban labor markets. The 1980s was a difficult time for migrants, who had to register for special *hukou* privileges (*zili kouliang*) in order to receive grain rations in cities. But by 1985 Beijing had created a "temporary residence permit," and in 1988 Tianjin, Shanghai, and Wuhan followed suit. By the 1990s temporary residence permits were issued freely in most Chinese cities. Finally, by the 2000s municipal officials had largely stopped monitoring the inflow of rural labor migrants through annual workforce inspections in factories and construction sites. Even without temporary residence permits, rural labor migrants were welcomed (Lee 1998; Guang 2001).

7. Kelliher (1992).

8. Smallholdings were allocated on the basis of their rural residence even to rural residents engaged in nonagricultural employment in state or collective enterprises located in rural regions. This was initially done during the early 1980s, when rural TVEs were emerging; some former farmers gained state employment, while other former rurally residing state workers lost their employment and returned to farming.

9. Kelliher (1992); Guang (2001); Cheng and Selden (1994).

10. Scholars note that the implementation of the household responsibility system was accompanied by a sudden growth in annual per capita grain production, from 661 pounds in 1978 to 881 pounds in 1984 (Lin 1988). Free to seek off-farm employment: Taylor (1988).

11. Rural banks and cooperatives make loans to rural *hukou* holders for housing purchases, but rural *hukou* holders generally qualify only for high-interest

loans due to their low income levels and temporary or contract employment arrangements.

12. Huang (2008).

13. Many scholars, including Arrighi and Yasheng Huang, have made note of the egalitarian quality of 1980s rural industrialization. Arrighi argued, for example, that the rural economy in the 1980s enjoyed the same wage subsidization mechanism that the urban economy did in the 1990s. Small landholdings allowed rural households to farm for subsistence while sending working-age members to TVE jobs. But Arrighi saw this wage subsidization mechanism as an egalitarian mechanism, since much of the surplus value captured by TVEs via wage suppression was reinvested back into the local welfare state via taxation and redistribution (Oi 1999; Arrighi 2009).

14. Rozelle et al. (1999); Scharping (1997).

15. *Qianwei County Gazetteer* (1990–1994, 2000–2001).

16. Jacka (2012, 2014); Judd (1994).

17. Pun and Yi (2011).

18. Qi (2011).

19. Murphy (1999, 2002).

20. Massey (1993).

CHAPTER 4. RURAL/URBAN DUALISM

1. Massey et al. (1998).

2. Graduates of vocational schools: Ling (2015); returning to farming: Han (2012).

3. Murphy (2002).

4. Murphy (2002, 125).

5. Bai and Hongyuan (2002); Wang and Fan (2006).

6. National enrollment rates for the rural pension scheme were low. By 2011 only 57.1 percent of all residents with rural *hukou* had begun paying into the social pension scheme, and 48.2 percent had begun receiving benefits. Rural benefits were also extremely low in comparison to urban pension benefits. In 2015 the national average monthly payout from the basic urban pension fund was 2,363 RMB, nearly twenty times greater than the rural average of 120 RMB per month. This differential reflects an underlying state rationale behind the different entitlements attached to rural and urban citizenship: Rural residents were expected to make up the gap between the 120 RMB monthly and actual living costs by continuing to farm village land (Qin et al. 2015; Shen and Williamson 2010).

7. Ling (2015).

8. Ling (2015).

9. Wu and Zhang (2015).

10. Chan (2014).

11. Chen and Fan (2016).

12. Silk (2014).

13. Urban health insurance is heavily subsidized by employers. In the city of Chongqing, employers paid 1,400 RMB per year for health insurance an urban worker, compared to 480 RMB for a worker with agricultural status (Huang 2010).

14. The pension system for urban employees was established in 1997 to extend pension coverage to the entire urban labor force, including the self-employed. Pension in-payments are provided by individual contributions, employer contributions, and provincial funds; contribution and benefit rates are uniform rates set at the provincial level. In 2010 an employer in Chongqing was required to pay 20 percent of an urban employee's monthly wage into a retirement pension fund, compared with just 12 percent for a formal rural-*hukou*-holding employee (Liu and Li 2015). Informal workers such as migrant construction workers receive no employer contributions.

15. Chan (2010).

16. Das and N'Diaye (2013).

17. Das and N'Diaye (2013).

CHAPTER 5. URBANIZATION AND THE NEW
RURAL ECONOMY

1. Polanyi ([1944] 2001).

2. Solinger (1999).

3. Marshall (1950).

4. Hsing (2010).

5. The particular state bodies responsible for household registration transfers and rural land expropriation, however, are different. While county-level public security bureaus typically handle household registration enforcement, municipal ministries of land management coordinate rural land-use contracts at the village level.

6. Rural-to-urban *hukou* transfers here typically refer to changes in the occupational registration of the household from agricultural to nonagricultural (*nongzhuanfei*).

7. The term "land transfers" refers obliquely to the transfer of land ownership rights from the village collectives to the state. As ownership rights are consolidated by the state, household land-use rights, granted by village collectives, are terminated.

8. Villagers were compensated 10,900 RMB ($1,816) per mu of land and an average payment of around 20,000 RMB for demolished housing (280 RMB per

square meter for houses made from stone, 180 RMB per square meter for houses made from mud and mortar).

9. Yeh (2005).

10. Huang (2010).

11. Solinger and Jiang (2016).

12. Lee and Zhang (2013); Su and He (2010).

13. Not all cases of rural-urban *hukou* transfer are compensated by one-time monetary payments for land. When the province or direct municipality directly expropriates household land for state infrastructural projects, such as highways or dams, villagers are re-registered under urban *hukou* status and compensated not through monetary payments but rather through social insurance plans, which guarantee 600 RMB per month after residents reach the age of sixty—the equivalent of a pension plan that would cost 20,500 RMB in premiums.

14. Lin and Song (2013).

15. Chen and Fan (2016).

16. The survey was administered by the Floating Population Dynamic Monitoring Surveys, conducted annually by the National Health and Family Planning Commission from 2010 to 2012 (Chen and Fan 2016).

17. Li (2011).

18. When rural land is confiscated for environmental preservation purposes, household land-use contracts are nullified for indefinite periods, and compensation payments are issued annually during these periods. Because the land is not used for market development, the market value of land is not a factor in setting compensation rates. Two policy programs, the Sloping Land Conversion Program (tuigeng huanlin huancao) and the National Forest Protection Program (tianranlin baohu gongcheng), authorize land-use rights to be nullified for purposes of environmental preservation (Yeh 2009).

19. Sublegal deviation from this division of revenues ran rampant. Lin and Ho (2005) found that in the Yangtze River region over 98 percent of conveyance fees collected between 1989 and 1997 were retained by the municipal government, and none were handed over to the central government.

20. Ang (2017).

21. According to the budget law before its revision in August 2014, local governments could not borrow to meet budgetary needs without central government approval.

22. In 2014 the central government established a municipal bond market in order to allow private investors to buy off this debt and encourage local governments to swap debt.

23. Cai (2003); Ho and Lin (2003); Ho (2001, 2005); Han (2009).

24. Yep (2015).

25. Hsing (2006).

26. Hsing (2010); Li (2004).

27. Jacobs, 2011); Buckley (2011).

28. Mattingly (2016).

29. Media reporting has framed *hukou* reforms as the lifting of an oppressive system of exclusion. A headline in a 2005 edition of the *South China Morning Post* reported: "Migrants win urban resident status" (Chan 2005). The *New York Times* declared: "China to drop urbanite–peasant legal differences" (Kahn 2005). *BBC News* declared: "China rethinks peasant 'apartheid'" (Luard 2005).

CHAPTER 6. PARADOXES OF URBANIZATION

1. Harvey (2003b, 2003c).

2. Cai (2017).

3. Nonlocal labor recruitment brought outside labor to many rural regions. In Yilong County, for example, the labor employed to build factories and highways was nonlocal, bused in from the Chengdu region, which was the domicile of the head contractor. In Faming Village I encountered a team of migrant laborers brought from northern Henan Province to work on a provincially funded highway development project.

4. These figures denote 2007 wage levels.

5. In Faming villagers were predominantly employed in the local and booming mining industry during the 1980s. Only after this mining industry crashed in the early 1990s did Faming laborers begin to seek work outside the village. This accounts for their consenting to accept low wages.

6. Pun (2005).

7. Zhang (2002).

8. It was rare for an older woman such as Zhou Zisu, age fifty-two, to continue to find factory jobs. But Zhou Zisu got her factory job through her daughter-in-law, whose wealthy uncle worked as a factory manager.

9. Polanyi ([1944] 2001).

10. Hsing (2010).

CHAPTER 7. THE FUTURE OF CHINESE DEVELOPMENT

1. Wen (2001); Wen et al. (2012).

2. Yasuda (2017).

3. Pei (2006).

4. Durkheim (1897).

5. France: Bourdieu (2008); Ireland: Scheper-Hughes ([1977] 2001).

6. Durkheim (1897).

7. Some women lived alone, but perhaps due to a widely cited gender imbalance wherein women outnumber men, and also due to norms of hypergamy that facilitate women's ability to marry out of unfortunate circumstances, bachelors and widowers outnumbered their female counterparts in both villages.

8. Levien (2012).

9. Levien (2013)

10. Rithmire (2013).

11. Such policy experiments are considered part of a unique "Chongqing model" of urbanization, referring to the city's more radical policies on rapid land expropriation and *hukou* reform in relation to other rapidly urbanizing cities such as Chengdu and Guangzhou.

12. Yep and Forrest (2016).

APPENDIX

1. Rabinow (1977).

2. Rabinow (1977).

References

Ahlers, Anna L., and Gunter Shubert. 2009. "Building a New Socialist Country-side: Only a Political Slogan?" *Journal of Current Chinese Affairs* 38(4):35–62.

———. 2013. "Strategic Modeling: 'Building a New Socialist Countryside' in Three Chinese Counties." *The China Quarterly* 216:831–849.

———. 2015. "Effective Policy Implementation in China's Local State." *Modern China* 41(4):372–405.

Andreas, Joel, and Shaohua Zhan. 2016. "Hukou and the Land: Market Reform and Rural Displacement in China." *Journal of Peasant Studies* 43(4):798–827.

Ang, Yuen Yuen. 2016. *How China Escaped the Poverty Trap*. Ithaca, NY: Cornell University Press.

———. 2017. "Beyond Weber: Conceptualizing an Alternative Ideal Type of Bureaucracy in Developing Contexts." *Regulation & Governance* 11(3):282–298.

Arrighi, Giovanni. 2007. *Adam Smith in Beijing*. London: Verso.

Arrighi, Giovanni, Nicole Aschoff, and Ben Scully. 2010. "Accumulation by Dispossession and Its Limits: The Southern Africa Paradigm Revisited." *Studies of Comparative International Development* 45(4):410–438.

Bai Nansheng and Song Hongyuan, eds. 2002. *Huixiang Haishi Jingcheng? Zhongguo Nongcun Waichu Laodongli huiliu yanjiu* [Out to the city or back to the village? The study of rural-urban return migration in China]. Beijing: Zhongguo Caizheng Jingji Chubanshe.

Bernstein, Thomas P., and Xiaobo Lu. 2003. *Taxation without Representation in Rural China*. Cambridge, UK: Cambridge University Press.

Bourdieu, Pierre. 2008. *The Bachelor's Ball: The Crisis of Peasant Society in Bearn*. Translated by Richard Nice. Chicago: University of Chicago Press.

Brandt, Loren, Hongbin Li, and Joanne Roberts. 2005. "Banks and Enterprise Privatization in China." *The Journal of Law, Economics, and Organization* 21(2):524–546.

Brenner, Robert. 2001. "The Low Countries in the Transition to Capitalism." *Journal of Agrarian Change* 1(2):169–241.

Brown, Jeremy. 2012. *City Versus Countryside in Mao's China: Negotiating the Divide*. New York: Cambridge University Press.

Buckley, Chris. 2011. "Chinese Official Says Wukan Protest Shows Rights Demands on Rise." *Reuters*, December 26.

Burawoy, Michael. 1976. "The Functions and Reproduction of Migrant Labor: Comparative Material from Southern African and the United States." *American Journal of Sociology* 81(5):1050–1087.

———. 1982. *Manufacturing Consent: Changes in the Labor Process under Monopoly Capitalism*. Chicago: University of Chicago Press.

Cai, Fang. 2011. "*Hukou* System Reform and Unification of Rural-urban Social Welfare." *China & World Economy* 19(3):33–48.

Cai, Fang, and Du Yang, eds. 2009. *The China Population and Labor Yearbook*. Vol. 1, *The Approaching Lewis Turning Point and Its Policy Implications*. Leiden, The Netherlands: Koninklijke Brill.

Cai, Meina. 2012. "Land-locked Development: The Local Political Economy of Institutional Change in China." PhD dissertation, Department of Sociology, University of Wisconsin, Madison.

———. 2014. "'Flying Land': Institutional Innovation in Land Management in Contemporary China." In *Local Governance Innovation in China: Experimentation, Diffusion, and Defiance*, edited by Jessica C. Teets and William Hurst, 60–83. New York: Routledge.

———. 2016. "Land for Welfare in China." *Land Use Policy* 55:1–12.

———. 2017. "Revenue, Time Horizon, and Land Allocation in China." *Land Use Policy* 62:101–112.

Cai, Yongshun. 2003. "Collective Ownership or Cadres' Ownership? The Non-agricultural Use of Farmland in China." *The China Quarterly* 175:662–680.

Chan, Anita, Richard Madsen, and Jonathan Unger. 2009. *Chen Village: Revolution to Globalization*. Stanford, CA: Stanford University Press.

Chan, Kam Wing. 2010. "A China Paradox: Migrant Labor Shortage amidst Rural Labor Supply Abundance." *Eurasian Geography and Economics* 51(4):513–530.

———. 2014. *Achieving Comprehensive Hukou Reform in China. Paulson Policy Memorandum.* Chicago: Paulson Institute.

Chan, Kam Wing, and Li Zhang. 1999. "The Hukou System and Rural-Urban Migration: Processes and Changes." *The China Quarterly* 160:818–855.

Chan, Minnie. 2005. "Migrants Win Urban Resident Status." *South China Morning Post*, October 27.

Chao, Kang. 1965. "Growth of the Construction Industry in Communist China." *The China Quarterly* 22:125–142.

Chen, Te-Ping. 2014. "Introducing China's Future Megalopolis: The Jing-Jin-Ji." *Wall Street Journal*, April 4.

Chen, Chuanbo, and C. Cindy Fan. 2016. "China's Hukou Puzzle: Why Don't Rural Migrants Want Urban Hukou?" *China Review* 16(3):9–39.

Cheng, Tiejun, and Mark Selden. 1994. "The Origins and Social Consequences of China's Hukou System." *The China Quarterly* 139:644–668.

Chun, Jennifer Jihye. 2011. *Organizing at the Margins: The Symbolic Politics of Labor in South Korea and the United States.* Ithaca, NY: Cornell University Press.

Dai Jianzhong and Zhu Min. "A Survey Report on Labor Relations in Private Enterprises and Women Workers' Problems." Unpublished manuscript, Beijing Academy of Social Science, 1999 [in Chinese].

Das, Mitali, and Papa N'Diaye. 2013. "Chronicle of a Decline Foretold: Has China Reached the Lewis Turning Point?" Working Paper 13/26. International Monetary Fund, Washington, DC.

Durkheim, Emile. 1897. *On Suicide.* Translated by Robin Buss. London: Penguin Books.

Erie, Matthew. 2012. "Property Rights, Legal Consciousness and the New Media in China: The Hard Case of the 'Toughest Nail-House in History.'" *China Information* 26(1):35–59.

Fan, C. Cindy. 2011. "Settlement Intention and Split Households: Findings from a Survey of Migrants in Beijing's Urban Villages." *The China Review* 11(2):11–42.

Fan, C. Cindy, and Youqin Huang. 1998. "Waves of Rural Brides: Female Marriage Migrations in China." *Annals of the Association of American Geographers* 88(2):227–251.

Fan, C. Cindy, Mingjie Sun, and Siqi Zheng. 2011. "Migration and Split Households: A Comparison of Sole, Couple, and Family Migrants in Beijing, China." *Environment and Planning A* 43(9):2164–2185.

Fang, Cai. 2011. "Hukou System Reform and Unification of Rural-Urban Social Welfare." *China & World Economy* 19(3):33–48.

Freedman, Maurice. 1958. *Lineage Organization in Southeastern China.* London: Athlone Press.

Friedman, Eli. 2014. *Insurgency Trap: Labor Politics in Post-Socialist China.* Ithaca, NY: Cornell University Press.

Gallagher, Mary Elizabeth. 2005. *Contagious Capitalism: Globalization and the Politics of Labor in China.* Princeton, NJ: Princeton University Press.

Garip, Filiz. 2008. "Social Capital and Migration: How Similar Resources Lead to Divergent Outcomes." *Demography* 45(3):591–617.

Garip, Filiz, and Sara Curran. 2010. "Increasing Migration, Divergent Communities: Changing Character of Migrant Streams." *Population Research and Policy Review* 29(5):659–685.

Gomi, Yuko. 2013. "Reform of Chongqing's Hukou System: Will It Help Stimulate Domestic Demand?" Newsletter 26. Institute for International Monetary Affairs.

Guang, Lei. 2001. "Reconstituting the Rural-Urban Divide: Peasant Migration and the Rise of 'Orderly Migration' in Contemporary China." *Journal of Contemporary China* 10(28):471–493.

Hagan, Jacqueline. 1998. "Social Networks, Gender and Immigrant Incorporation: Resources and Constraints." *American Sociological Review* 63(1):55–67.

Han, Jialing. 2012. "Rapid Urbanization and the Aspiration and Challenge of Second-Generation Urban-Rural Migrants." *Chinese Education and Society* 45(1):77–83.

Han, Jun. 2009. *Survey on China's Rural Land Issues* [Zhongguo nongcun tudi wenjuan diaocha]. Shanghai: Shanghai Far East Publisher.

Han, Libin, and Ming Lu. 2017. "Housing Prices and Investment: An Assessment of China's Inland-Favoring Land Supply Policies." *Journal of the Asia Pacific Economy* 22(1):106–121.

Hanser, Amy. 2008. *Service Encounters: Class, Gender, and the Market for Social Distinction in Urban China.* Stanford, CA: Stanford University Press.

Hart, Gillian. 2002. *Disabling Globalization: Places of Power in Post-Apartheid South Africa.* Berkeley: University of California Press.

———. 2007. "Changing Concepts of Articulation: Political Stakes in South Africa Today." *Review of African Political Economy* 34(111): 85–101.

Harvey, David. 2001. "Globalization and the 'Spatial Fix.'" *Geographische Revue* 3: 23–30.

———. 2003a. *The New Imperialism.* Oxford: Oxford University Press.

———. 2003b. *Paris, Capital of Modernity.* New York: Routledge.

———. 2003c. "The Right to the City." *New Left Review* 53:23–40.

———. 2005. *A Brief History of Neoliberalism.* Oxford: Oxford University Press.

He, Xuefeng. 2010. "Nongcun Tudi de Zhengzhixue" [The politics of rural land]. *Xuexi yu Tansuo* [Study and exploration] 2(187):70–75.

Heilmann, Sebastian. 2018. *Red Swan: How Unorthodox Policy-Making Facilitated China's Rise.* New York: Columbia University Press.

Heller, Patrick, K. N. Harilal, and Shubham Chaudhuri. 2007. "Building Local Democracy: Evaluating the Impact of Decentralization in Kerala, India." *World Development* 35(4):626–648.

Hess, Steve. 2010. "Nail-Houses, Land Rights, and Frames of Injustice on China's Protest Landscape." *Asian Survey* 50(5):908–926.

Ho, Peter. 2001. "Who Owns China's Land: Policies, Property Rights, and Deliberate Ambiguity." *The China Quarterly* 166:394–421.

———. 2005. *Institutions in Transition: Land Ownership, Property Rights, and Social Conflict in China.* New York: Oxford University Press.

Ho, Samuel P. S., and George C. S. Lin. 2003. "Emerging Land Markets in Rural and Urban China: Policies and Practices." *The China Quarterly* 175:681–707.

Hsing, You-tien. 2006. "Brokering Power and Property in China's Townships." *The Pacific Review* 19(1):103–124.

———. 2010. *The Great Urban Transformation: Politics of Land and Property in China.* Berkeley: University of California Press.

Huang, Qifan. 2006. "The Interaction Between Reform of SOEs and of Local Financial Institutions: The Case of Chongqing." [Guoqi Gaige yu Difang Jinrong Jigou Gaige de Huodong: Yi Dhongqing Wei Li] *Gaige* [Reform] 3(145):21–24.

———. 2010. "Chongqing Shi Hukou Zhidu Gaige de Zhengce Tixi, Zhenge Cuoshi Yiji san ge Yue de Shijing Qingkuang" [Chongqing's household registration reform policy system: Policy measures after three months of experience]. Press Conference, November 14. http://mcrp.macrochina.com.cn/u/60/archives/2010/2083.html.

Huang, Yasheng. 2008. *Capitalism with Chinese Characteristics: Entrepreneurship and the State.* Cambridge, UK: Cambridge University Press.

Hung, Ho-Fung. 2009. "America's Head Servant? The PRC's Dilemma in the Global Crisis." *New Left Review* 60:5–25.

———. 2015. *The China Boom: Why China Will Not Rule the World.* New York: Columbia University Press.

Hurst, William, and Kevin O'Brien. 2002. "China's Contentious Pensioners." *The China Quarterly* 170:345–360.

International Labor Organization. 2013. *Global Wage Report 2012/2013: Wages and Equitable Growth.* Geneva: International Labor Organization Publications.

Jacka, Tamara. 2012. "Migration, Householding and the Well-being of Left-behind Women in Rural Ningxia." *The China Journal* 1(67):1–21.

———. 2014. "Left-behind and Vulnerable? Conceptualising Development and Older Women's Agency in Rural China" *Asian Studies Review* 38(2):186–204.

Jacobs, Andrew. 2011. "Village Revolts Over Inequities of Chinese Life." *New York Times*, December 14.

Johnson, Ian. 2015. "As Beijing Becomes a Supercity, Rapid Growth Brings Pains." *New York Times*, July 19.

Judd, Ellen. 1994. *Gender and Power in Rural North China*. Stanford, CA: Stanford University Press.

Kahn, Joseph. 2005. "China to Drop Urbanite-Peasant Legal Differences." *New York Times*, November 3.

Kelliher, Daniel. 1992. *Peasant Power in China: The Era of Rural Reform, 1979-1989*. New Haven, CT: Yale University Press.

Kennedy, John James. 2007. "From the Tax-for-Fee Reform to the Abolition of Agricultural Taxes: The Impact of Township Governments in North-west China." *The China Quarterly* 189:43-59.

Kojima, Kiyoshi. 2000. "The 'Flying Geese' Model of Asian Economic Development: Origin, Theoretical Extensions, and Regional Policy Implications." *Journal of Asian Economics* 11(4):375-401.

Koo, Anita. 2012. "Is There Any Chance to Get Ahead? Educational Aspirations and Expectations of Migrant Families in China." *British Journal of Sociology of Education* 33(4):547-564.

Koo, Hagen. 2002. *The Culture and Politics of Class Formation*. Ithaca, NY: Cornell University Press.

Landry, Pierre. 2012. *Decentralized Authoritarianism in China: The Communist Party's Control of Local Elites in the Post-Mao Era*. Cambridge, UK: Cambridge University Press.

Lee, Ching Kwan. 1998. *Gender and the South China Miracle: Two Worlds of Factory Women*. Berkeley: University of California Press.

———. 2000. "The 'Revenge of History': Collective Memories and Labor Protests in Northeastern China." *Ethnography* 1(2):217-237.

———. 2007. *Against the Law: Labor Protests in China's Rustbelt and Sunbelt*. Berkeley: University of California Press.

Lee, Ching Kwan, and Yong Hong Zhang. 2013. "The Power of Instability: Unraveling the Microfoundations of Bargained Authoritarianism in China." *American Journal of Sociology* 118(6):1-34.

Legassick Martin. 1975. "South Africa: Forced Labor, Industrialization, and Racial Differentiation." In *The Political Economy of Africa*, edited by R. Harris, 247-251. New York: Wiley.

Lei, Yawen. 2017. *The Contentious Public Sphere: Law Media and Authoritarian Rule in China*. Princeton, NJ: Princeton University Press.

Levien, Michael. 2012. "The Land Question: Special Economic Zones and the Political Economy of Dispossession." *The Journal of Peasant Studies* 39(3-4):933-969.

———. 2013. "The Politics of Dispossession: Theorizing India's 'Land Wars.'" *Politics & Society* 41(3):351–394.

———. 2018. *Dispossession without Development: Land Grabs in Neoliberal India*. Oxford: Oxford University Press.

Li, Bingqin. 2007. "Pension Reform in China—Who Are Left Out?" In *New Perspectives on China and Aging*, edited by Ian G. Cook and Jason L. Powell, 29–48. London, Nova Science Publishers.

Li, Hongbin, and Scott Rozelle. 2003. "Privatizing Rural China: Insider Privatization, Innovative Contracts and the Performance of Township Enterprises." *China Quarterly* 176:981–1005.

Li, Huan, Xianjin Huang, Mei-Po Kwan, Helen X. H. Bao, and Steven Jefferson. 2014. "Changes in Farmers' Welfare from Land Requisition in the Process of Urbanization." *Land Use Policy* 42:635–641.

Li, Linda Chelan, and Zhenjie Yang. 2015. "What Causes the Local Fiscal Crisis: The Role of Intermediaries." *Journal of Contemporary China* 24(94):573–593.

Li, Peilin. 2004. *Cunluo de Zhongjie* [End of the village]. Beijing: Shangxu Chubanshe.

Li, Wei, ed. 2011. *Nongmingong Shiminhua: Zhidu Chuangxin yu Dingceng Zhidu Sheji* [Civilianizing the rural migrants: Institutional innovation and top-level design]. Beijing: China Development Press.

Lin, George C. S., and Samuel P. S. Ho. 2005. "The State, Land System, and Land Development Processes in Contemporary China." *Annals of the Association of American Geographers* 95(2):411–436.

Lin, Guanghua, and Xuefei Song. 2013. "'Sannong' Fazhan Xingshi, Wenti yu Zhidu Chuangxin—'Sannong Xinzheng Gaoceng Yantaohui' Guandian Zongshu" ["Three Rural" development, issues and institutional innovation: A summary of "The High-Level Seminar on New Policies on the rural issues"]. *Journal of Nanjing Agricultural University* (Social Science Edition) 13(6):119–128.

Lin, Justin Yifu. 1988. "The Household Responsibility System in China's Agricultural Reform: A Theoretical and Empirical Study." *Economic Development and Cultural Change* 36(3):199–224.

Ling, Minhua. 2015. "'Bad Students Go to Vocational Schools!': Education, Social Reproduction and Migrant Youth in Urban China." *The China Journal* 73:108–131.

Liu, Shouying, Michael Carter, and Yang Yao. 1998. "Dimensions and Diversity of Property Rights in Rural China: Dilemmas on the Road to Further Reform." *World Development* 26(10):1789–1806.

Liu, Tao, and Li Sun. 2015. "Pension Reform in China." *Journal of Aging and Social Policy* 28(1):15–28.

Lu, Yao, and Zhou Hao. 2013. "Academic Achievement and Loneliness of Migrant Children in China: School Segregation and Segmented Assimilation." *Comparative Education Review* 57(1):85–116.

Lu, Yinqiu, and Tao Sun. 2013. "Local Government Financing Platforms in China: A Fortune or Misfortune." IMF European Department and Monetary and Capital Markets Development. Working paper 13/243.

Lu, Youjie, and Paul W. Fox. 2001. "The Construction Industry in China: Its Image, Employment Prospects and Skill Requirements." Working Paper 180. International Labor Organization, Geneva.

Luard, Tim. 2005. "China Rethinks Peasant 'Apartheid'" *BBC News*, November 10.

Luxemburg, Rosa. 1951. *The Accumulation of Capital*. New York: Routledge.

Mao, Dan. 2000. *Yige Cunluo Gongtongtide Bianqian* [Transformation of a village collective]. Beijing: Xuelin Chubanshe.

Marshall, Thomas H. 1950. "Citizenship and Social Class." In *Citizenship and Social Class and Other Essays*, edited by Thomas H. Marshall, 1-85. Cambridge, UK: Cambridge University Press.

Massey, Doreen. 1993. "Power-Geometry and a Progressive Sense of Place." In *Mapping the Future: Local Cultures, Global Change*, edited by Barry Curtis and Lisa Tickner, 59–69. New York: Routledge.

Massey, Douglas S. 1990. "Social Structure, Household Strategies, and the Cumulative Causation of Migration." *Population Index* 56(1):3–26.

Massey, Douglas S., Joaquin Arango, Graeme Hugo, Ali Kouaouci, Adela Pellegrino, and J. Edward Taylor. 1998. *Worlds in Motion: Understanding International Migration at the End of the Millennium*. New York: Oxford University Press.

Mattingly, Daniel C. 2016. "Elite Capture: How Decentralization and Informal Institutions Weaken Property Rights in Rural China." *World Politics* 68(3):383–412.

Mertha, Andrew. 2005. "China's 'Soft' Centralization: Shifting Tiao/Kuai Authority Relations." *The China Quarterly* 184:791–810.

Meyer-Clement, Elena. 2016. "The Great Urban Leap? On the Local Political Economy of Rural Urbanisation in China." *Journal of Current Chinese Affairs* 45(1):109–139.

Miura, Yuji. 2012. "How Far as the Migration of Industry to Inland China Proceeded? Verifying the 'West High, East Low' Growth Pattern from Economic Census Data." *RIM: Pacific Business and Industries* 12(45):2–28.

Montinola, Gabriella, Yingyi Qian, and Barry R. Weingast. 1995. "Federalism, Chinese Style: The Political Basis for Economic Success in China." *World Politics* 48(1):50–81.

Murphy, Rachel. 1999. "Return Migrant Entrepreneurs and Economic Diversification in Two Counties in South Jiangxi, China." *Journal of International Development* 11(4):661–672.

———. 2002. *How Migrant Labor Is Changing Rural China.* Cambridge, UK: Cambridge University Press.

National Bureau of Statistics of China. 2004. *China Statistical Yearbook, 2003.* New York: Praeger.

———. 2009. *China Statistical Yearbook, 2008.* New York: Praeger.

———. 2017. *China Statistical Yearbook, 2016.* New York: Praeger.

Nee, Victor 1989. "A Theory of Market Transition: From Redistribution to Markets in State Socialism." *American Sociological Review* 54(5):663–681.

Nee, Victor, and Rebecca Matthews. 1996. "Market Transition and Societal Transformation in Reforming State Socialism." *Annual Review of Sociology* 22:401–435.

Nee, Victor, and Sonja Opper. 2012. *Capitalism From Below: Markets and Institutional Change in China.* Cambridge, MA: Harvard University Press.

O'Brien, Kevin, and Lianjiang Li. 2006. *Rightful Resistance in Rural China.* New York: Cambridge University Press.

Oi, Jean. 1999. *Rural China Takes Off: Institutional Foundations of Economic Reform.* Berkeley: University of California Press.

Ong, Lynette. 2006. "The Political Economy of Township Government Debt, Township Enterprises and Rural Financial Institutions in China." *The China Quarterly* 186:377–400.

———. 2012. *Prosper or Perish: Credit and Fiscal Systems in Rural China.* Ithaca, NY: Cornell University Press.

Ong, Lynette H. 2014. "State-Led Urbanization in China: Skyscrapers, Land Revenue and Concentrated Villages." *The China Quarterly* 217:162–179.

Otis, Eileen. 2008. "Beyond the Industrial Paradigm: Market-Embedded Labor and the Gender Organization of Global Service Work in China." *American Sociological Review* 73(1):15–36.

Parish, William, Xiaoye Zhe, and Fang Li. 1995. "Nonfarm Work and the Marketization of the Chinese Countryside." *The China Quarterly* 143:1–29.

Pei, Minxin. 2006. *China's Trapped Transition: The Limits of Developmental Autocracy.* Cambridge, MA: Harvard University Press.

Polanyi, Karl. 1944 [2001]. *The Great Transformation: The Political and Economic Origins of Our Time.* Boston: Beacon Press.

Post, Charles. 2009. "Agrarian Class Structure and Economic Development in Colonial British North America: The Place of the American Revolution in the Origins of U.S. Capitalism." *Journal of Agrarian Change* 9(4):453–483.

Pun, Ngai. 2005. *Made in China: Women Factory Workers in a Global Workplace.* Durham, NC: Duke University Press.

Pun, Ngai, and Lu Huilin. 2010. "A Culture of Violence: The Labor Subcontracting System and Collective Action by Construction Workers in Post-Socialist China." *The China Journal* 64:143–158.

Pun, Ngai, and Xu Yi. 2011. "Legal Activism or Class Action? The Political Economy of the 'No Boss' and 'No Labour Relationship' in China's Construction Industry." *China Perspectives* 2:9–17.

Qi, Xin. 2011. *Qianxin yu Taoxin: Gongdi Zhengzhi yu Laodong Guocheng de Shizheng Yanjiu* [Wage arrears: Worksite politics and labor relations in China's construction sector]. Beijing: Capital University of Economics and Trade Press.

Qian, Xiaoying, and Zhao Hui. 2004. "The Construction Sector in the People's Republic of China: Policy Analysis on Sectoral Development and Employment Changes." Socio-Economic Technical Paper 15. Geneva: International Labor Organization.

Qianwei Xian Zhi [Qianwei County gazetteer]. 1990–1994. Chengdu: People's Publisher of Sichuan.

Qianwei Xian Zhi [Qianwei County gazetteer]. 2000–2001. Chengdu: People's Publisher of Sichuan.

Qin, Min, Yaer Zhuang, and Hongyan Liu. 2015. "Old Age Insurance Participation Among Rural-Urban Migrants in China." *Demographic Research* 33(37):1047–1066.

Quan, Lu. 2012. *HelpAge Social Pension Database.* London: HelpAge International.

Rabinow, Paul. 1977. *Reflections on Fieldwork in Morocco.* Berkeley: University of California Press.

Rithmire, Meg. E. 2013. "Land Politics and Local State Capacities: The Political Economy of Urban Change in China." *The China Quarterly* 216:872–895.

———. 2015. *Land Bargains and Chinese Capitalism: The Politics of Property Rights under Reform.* Cambridge, UK: Cambridge University Press.

———. 2017. "Land Institutions and Chinese Political Economy: Institutional Complementarities and Macroeconomic Management." *Politics & Society* 45(1):123–153.

Rozelle, Scott. 1996. "Stagnation Without Equity: Patterns of Growth and Inequality in China's Rural Economy." *The China Journal* 35:63–92.

Rozelle, Scott, Li Guo, Minggao Shen, Ameila Hughart, and John Giles. 1999. "Leaving China's Farms: Survey Results of New Paths and Remaining Hurdles to Rural Migration." *The China Quarterly* 58:367–393.

Rozelle, Scott, Jikun Huang, and Honglin Wang. 2006. "Fostering or Stripping Rural China: Modernizing Agriculture and Rural to Urban Capital Flows." *The Developing Economies* 44(1):1–26.

Sargeson, Sally. 2012. "Villains, Victims and Aspiring Proprietors: Framing 'Land-losing Villagers' in China's Strategies of Accumulation." *Journal of Contemporary China* 21(77):757–777.

———. 2013. "Violence as Development: Land Expropriation and China's Urbanization." *Journal of Peasant Studies* 40(6):1063–1085.

Sassen, Saskia. 2014. *Expulsions: Brutality and Complexity in the Global Economy*. Cambridge, MA: Harvard University Press.

Scharping, Thomas. 1997. "Studying Migration in Contemporary China: Models and Methods, Issues and Evidence." In *Floating Population and Migration in China: The Impact of Economic Reforms*, edited by Thomas Scharping, 9–55. Hamburg: Institut fur Asienkunde.

Scheper-Hughes, Nancy. [1977] 2001. *Saints, Scholars, and Schizophrenics: Mental Illness in Rural Ireland*. Berkeley: University of California Press.

Shen, Ce, and John Williamson. 2010. "China's New Rural Pension Scheme: Can It Be Improved?" *International Journal of Sociology and Social Policy* 30(5/6):239–250.

Shen, Yuan. 2007. *Shichang, Jiejie yu Guojia* [Market, class and state]. Beijing: Social Sciences Literature Press.

Shirk, Susan. 1981. "Recent Chinese Labor Policies and the Transformation of Industrial Organization in China." *The China Quarterly* 88:575–593.

Shue, Vivienne. 1988. *The Reach of the State: Sketches of the Chinese Body Politic*. Stanford, CA: Stanford University Press.

Silk, Richard. 2014. "China's Hukou Reform Plan Starts to Take Shape." *Wall Street Journal*, August 4.

Silver, Beverly. 2003. *Forces of Labor: Workers' Movements and Globalization since 1870*. Baltimore, MD: Johns Hopkins University Press.

Solinger, Dorothy. 1999. *Contesting Citizenship in Urban China: Peasant Migrants, the State, and the Logic of the Market*. Berkeley: University of California Press.

———. 2002. "Labour Market Reform and the Plight of the Laid-Off Proletariat." *The China Quarterly* 170:304–326.

Solinger, Dorothy, and Ting Jiang. 2016. "When Chinese Central Orders and Promotion Criteria Conflict: Implementation Decisions on the Destitute in Poor versus Prosperous Cities." *Modern China* 42(6):571–606.

Somers, Margaret. 2008. *Genealogies of Citizenship: Markets, Statelessness and the Right to Have Rights*. Cambridge, UK: Cambridge University Press.

State Council. 1984. "Tentative Provisions for Construction Industry and Capital Investment Administration System Reform [1984] No. 123." September 18.

Su, Yang, and Xin He. 2010. "Street as Courtroom: State Accommodation of Labor Protest in South China." *Law and Society Review* 44(1):157–184.

Swanson, Ana. 2015. "How China Used More Cement in 3 Years Than the U.S. did in the Entire 20th Century." *Washington Post*, March 24.

Swider, Sarah. 2015. *Building China: Informal Work and the New Precariat*. Ithaca, NY: Cornell University Press.

Tan, Lin, and Susan E. Short. 2004. "Living as Double Outsiders: Migrant Women's Experiences of Marriage in a County-Level City." In *On the Move:*

Women and Rural-to-Urban Migration in Contemporary China, edited by Arianne M. Gaetano and Tamara Jacka, 151–176. New York: Columbia University Press.

Taylor, Jeffrey R. 1988. "Rural Employment Trends and the Legacy of Surplus Labour, 1978–1986." *The China Quarterly* 116:736–766.

Thireau, Isabelle, and Hua Linshan. 2003. "The Moral Universe of Aggrieved Chinese Workers: Workers' Appeals to Arbitration Committees and Letters and Visits Offices." *The China Journal* 50:83–103.

Thompson, E. P. 1963. *The Making of the English Working Class*. New York: Random House.

Tsai, Kellee. 2002. *Back-Alley Banking: Private Entrepreneurs in China*. Ithaca, NY: Cornell University Press.

Walder, Andrew. 1995. "Local Governments as Industrial Firms: An Organizational Analysis of China's Transitional Economy." *American Journal of Sociology* 101(2):263–301.

———. 1996. "Markets and Inequality in Transnational Economies: toward testable theories." *American Journal of Sociology* 101(4):1060–1073.

———, ed. 1998. *Zouping in Transition: The Process of Reform in Rural China*. Cambridge, MA: Harvard University Press.

Wang, Fei-Ling. 2005. *Organizing through Division and Exclusion: China's Hukou System*. Stanford, CA: Stanford University Press.

Wang, Wenfei Winnie, and C. Cindy Fan. 2006. "Success or Failure: Selectivity and Reasons for Return Migrations in Sichuan and Anhui, China." *Environment and Planning* 38(5):939–968.

Wen, Tiejun. 2001. "Centenary Reflections on the 'Three Dimensional Problem' in China." *Inter-Asia Cultural Studies* 2(2):287–295.

Wen, Tiejun, Kinchi Lau, Cunwang Cheng, Huili He, and Jiansheng Qiu. 2012. "Ecological Civilization, Indigenous Culture, and Rural Reconstruction in China." *Monthly Review*. Accessed January 17, 2018. http://monthlyreview.org/2012/02/01/ecological-civilization-indigenous-culture-andrural-reconstruction-in-china.

Whyte, Marty. 2012. "China's Post-Socialist Inequality." *Current History* (September): 229–-234.

Wong, Christine. 2013. "Paying for Urbanization: Challenges from China's Municipal Finance in the 21st Century." In *Metropolitan Government Finances in Developing Countries*, edited by Roy W. Bahl, Johannes F. Linn, and Deborah L. Wetzel, 273–308. Cambridge, MA: Lincoln Institute for Land Policy.

Wong, Christine, and Richard Bird. 2008. "China's Fiscal System: A Work in Progress." In *China's Great Transformation: Origins, Mechanism, and Consequences of the Post-Reform Economic Boom*, edited by Loren Brandt and Thomas Rawski, 429–466. New York: Cambridge University Press.

Wu, Xiaogang, and Zhuoni Zhang. 2015. "Population Migration and Children's School Enrollments in China, 1990–2005." *Social Science Research* 53:177–190.

Xu Min, Chunyang He, Zhifeng Liu, and Yinyin Dou. 2016. "How Did Urban Land Expand in China between 1992 and 2015? A Multi-Scale Landscape Analysis." *PLoS ONE* 11(5):e0154839.

Yan, Hairong. 2008. *New Masters: New Servants: Migration, Development, and Women Workers in China*. Durham, NC: Duke University Press.

Yan, Hairong, and Yiyuan Chen. 2015. "Agrarian Capitalization without Capitalism? Capitalist Dynamics from Above and Below in China." *Journal of Agrarian Change* 15(3): 366–391.

Yasuda, John K. 2017. *On Feeding the Masses: An Anatomy of Regulatory Failures in China*. Cambridge, UK: Cambridge University Press.

Yeh, Emily. 2005. "Green Governmentality and Pastoralism in Western China: Converting Pasturelands to Grasslands." *Nomadic Peoples* 9(1):9–30.

———. 2009. "From Wasteland to Wetland? Nature and Nation in China's Tibet." *Environmental History* 14(1):103–137.

Yep, Ray. 2015. "Filling the Institutional Void in Rural Land Markets in Southern China: Is there Room for Spontaneous Change from Below?" *Development and Change* 46(3):534–561.

Yep, Ray, and Ray Forrest. 2016. "Elevating the Peasants into High-rise Apartments: The Land Bill System in Chongqing as a Solution for Land Conflicts in China?" *Journal of Rural Studies* 47:474–484.

Yu, Jianrong. 2005. "Tudi Wenti yi Chengwei Nongmin Weiquan Kangzheng de Jiaodian" [Land disputes: The focus of rights-defending activities of peasants]. *Diaoyan Shijie* [The world of survey and research] 3:22–23.

Zhan, Shaohua. 2017. "Hukou Reform and Land Politics in China: Rise of a Tripartite Alliance." *The China Journal* 78:25–49.

Zhang, Li. 2002. *Strangers in the City: Reconfigurations of Space, Power, and Social Networks within China's Floating Population*. Stanford, CA: Stanford University Press.

Zhang, Qian Forrest. 2012. "The Political Economy of Contract Farming in China's Agrarian Transition." *Journal of Agrarian Change* 12(4):460–483.

Zhou, Feizhou. 2007. "Shengcai Youdao: Tudi Kaizhan Zhong de Zhongfu yu Nongmin." [Creating wealth: Governments and villagers in the development and transfer of land]. *Shehuixue Yanjiu* [Sociological research] 1:49–82.

———. 2009. "Creating Wealth: Land Seizure, Local Government, and Farmers." In *Creating Wealth and Poverty in Post-Socialist China*, edited by Deborah Davis and Feng Wang, 112–125. Stanford, CA: Stanford University Press.

Zhou, Jing. 2018. "The New Urbanisation Plan and Permanent Urban Settlement of Migrants in Chongqing, China." *Population, Space and Place* 24(6):1–13.

Zhou, Minhui, Rachel Murphy, and Ran Tao. 2014. "Effects of Parents' Migration on the Education of Children Left Behind in Rural China." *Population
and Development Review* 40(2):273–292.

Zhou, Xueguang. 2011. "The Road to Collective Debt in Rural China: Bureau-
cracies, Social Institutions, and Public Goods Provision." *Modern China*
38(3):271–307.

Zhu, Rongji. 2011. *Zhu Rongji Jianghua Shilu* [A veritable record of speeches of
Zhu Rongji]. Vol. 1. Beijing: Renmin Chubanshe.

Index

agrarian transition, 174–76

agribusiness, government appointed, 145

agricultural modernization, 175

Arrighi, Giovanni, 14–16, 38, 64

Auntie Luo: and behavior expectations for rural women, 66; and feminized agriculture, 59–61; on Old Luo, 178–79; and recruitment politics, 76–77; rural pension scheme, 93–95; and Shu Li, 97; on village life expectations, 87

authoritarian state, character of, 9–10

bamboo production, 39–40, 47–48

Beijing Ministry of Land Management, 19

Big Gao: on Chen Zhong, 107–8; and gendered division of labor, 65; as local entrepreneur, 55; as multi-sited broker, 77–78; and recruitment politics, 75–76; and single-village business model (labor brokerage), 78–79; village economy and labor brokerage, 70–73

BNSC. *See* Build a New Socialist Countryside campaign, 2006

Boss Bo: and brokerage economy, 40–43, 68–70; and construction labor brokerage network, 29; and disruption of rural life, 112–13; finances and *hukou* registration, 100–101; and fracture of kin networks,

162; as labor broker, 46–47; as long-distance broker, 186; modernization and changes in recruitment channels, 148–53; and New Land Township jobs, 141–42, 146; and New Land Township reforms, 147; recruitment and contract sites, 149*map*; recruits in Faming Village, 40–42, 57, 59; and rumors of expropriation, 111; two village labor network, 77–79; in 2014 (after modernization), 178. *See also* New Land Township

Boss Gao, 178–79

Boss Liu, 148

Boss Zeng: and construction labor brokerage network, 29; earnings as labor broker, 67; as labor broker, 46–47; modernization and changes in recruitment channels, 158; as multi-sited broker, 77–78

Boss Zhou, 147

Bourdieu, Pierre, 179–80

brokerage economy, entrepreneurial, 66–70

brokerage networks/recruitment networks, 28, 32, 54–56, 82–83, 109, 169, 186, 196

Build a New Socialist Countryside (BNSC) campaign, 2006, 3–4, 7–8, 18–19, 115, 118, 121, 132–33

Burawoy, Michael, 14, 87

of labor brokerage, 79–82; 1980s: flourishing Faming Village, 36–39; 1990s labor diversification, 47–48; 1990s: rural decline, 39–40; overview, 35–36; revisit, 177; subsistence farming economy, 79–82; as supplier of migrant laborers, 109; and urbanization, 4
Fan Bing, 81
feminized agriculture economy, 64–66, 81
fictitious commodities, labor and land as, 16, 26
fiscal inequality, rural-urban, 63–64
Five Guarantees Scheme, 93
Five-Year Plan, eleventh, 3, 7
"free to work or free to starve," 171

Gao brothers, 43
Gao family, 55
global financial crisis, 2010, 2
global free trade, rise of, 5
Great Leap Forward (1958-1962), 39
gross domestic product (GDP): of cities, effect on rural economies, 2–3; growth construction sector, 22; rapid growth of, 4–8

Hart, Gilliam, 15
Harvey, David, 11–13, 142–43
He Taikun, 182
Heilmann, Sebastian, 9
Ho-Fung Hung, 40
Household Responsibility System, 1981, 40–41
Huang Rong, 65, 90–92, 147, 165, 182
hukou: industrialization and, 6–8; and local political economies, 52; politics as growth system, 114–17; problems with rural-to-urban transfers, 85; redrawing the divide, 103–4; reforms: and social mobility, 86; reforms and urbanization, 29; reforms: coastal migrants pulled inland, 108–9; reforms: headlines on, 209n29; register: as contingent on property ownership, 100; register: as records of Chinese population, 61–63; register: state bodies responsible for, 207n5; restrictions, lifting of, 96–97; rural land rights guarantees, 112; rural-to-urban transfer, 103–4, 116–17, 124–33, 159–61, 207n6, 208n13; short-term changes, 205n5; special *hukou* privileges (*zili kouliang*), 205n6; system as growth engine, 113–17; urban status and education, 99, 102; urban status and

land-use rights, 131; urban status and New Land Township, 28; urban status and relocation of rural residents, 138–40; urban status and rights, 86; urban status and urban welfare state, 20–21; urban status and village land ownership, 105; urban status as upgrade, 33, 50, 112–13; urban status, prerequisites for, 103–5, 114, 127; urban status: residence requirements, 8; urban status through marriage, 100; voluntary *hukou* transfer programs, 116–17; wage suppression, 16–21; and welfare restrictions, 168

"ideological re-education" meetings, 131–32
informal lending network, 55–56, 71–72

Jiang Zemin, 1994 reforms, 202n34
Jiangsu Province study, TVE decline, 40
Jinshu Mine, 56–57
jobs creation, and urbanization, 142–43

kin networks, 204n15; fractured, 48, 160–63

labor: as act of barter, 22; brokerage and migration economy, 40–43, 66–70; brokerage and village economy, 70–75; brokerage as village entrepreneurship, 22–24; brokerage in Faming Village, 59; commodification of, 16, 19, 111–12; discipline, 70–75; economy of migration, 40–43; Gao family as labor brokers, 54–55; iworld of: n Faming Village, overview of, 55–56; labor reproduction versus social mobility, 86–87; labor service markets (laowu shichang), 23; labor-intensive export production, developmental strategy of, 1–2; market transition theory, 21–22; migration and disruption of rural life, 29–30; migration and land dispossession, 19*fig.*, 163–66; migration as primary source of livelihood, 47–49, 54; recruitment, 148–53; reproduction of, 15, 56, 67*fig.*, 88–92, 103, 109; supply of, 5–6; world of: conclusion, 82–83; world of: entrepreneurial brokerage economy, 66–70; world of: feminized agriculture economy, 64–66; world of: historical evolution of migration, 60–64; world of: laborers and brokers: two separate classes, 79–82; world of: new economy of migration, 56–60; world of: recruitment politics,

Founded in 1893,
UNIVERSITY OF CALIFORNIA PRESS
publishes bold, progressive books and journals
on topics in the arts, humanities, social sciences,
and natural sciences—with a focus on social
justice issues—that inspire thought and action
among readers worldwide.

The UC PRESS FOUNDATION
raises funds to uphold the press's vital role
as an independent, nonprofit publisher, and
receives philanthropic support from a wide
range of individuals and institutions—and from
committed readers like you. To learn more, visit
ucpress.edu/supportus.